Out of the Classroom and into the World

Out of the Classroom and into the World

Learning from Field Trips, Educating from Experience, and
Unlocking the Potential of Our Students and Teachers

Salvatore Vascellaro

THE NEW PRESS

NEW YORK
LONDON

Requests for permission to reproduce selections from this book should be mailed to:
Permissions Department, The New Press, 38 Greene Street, New York, NY 10013.

Published in the United States by The New Press, New York, 2011
Distributed by Perseus Distribution

LIBRARY OF CONGRESS CATALOGING-IN-PUBLICATION DATA

Vascellaro, Salvatore.
Out of the classroom and into the world : learning from field trips,
educating from experience, and unlocking the potential of our students and teachers /
Salvatore Vascellaro.
p. cm.
Includes bibliographical references and index.
ISBN 978-1-59558-682-7 (pbk.)
1. School field trips—United States.   2. Active learning—United States.
3. School improvement programs—United States.   I. Title.
LB1047.V37 2011
371.3'84—dc23   2011016423

The New Press was established in 1990 as a not-for-profit alternative to
the large, commercial publishing houses currently dominating the book
publishing industry. The New Press operates in the public interest rather
than for private gain, and is committed to publishing, in innovative ways,
works of educational, cultural, and community value that are often
deemed insufficiently profitable.

www.thenewpress.com

Composition by dix!

Printed in the United States of America

2 4 6 8 10 9 7 5 3 1

For my daughter Anne
and in memory of her grandmother Anna,
with love and gratitude

There is the understanding that comes from knowledge of facts and the intellectual process of working out relationships among facts, which constitutes thinking. . . . And there is also the learning that comes from a living, gripping experience where a feeling tone is added to thought. This second kind of learning often stimulates the desire for the first.

—*Lucy Sprague Mitchell*
Founder of Bank Street College

You have to be passionate about what you are doing and have to believe in it for it to take shape. You get that from experience. And you need the passion to be a teacher.

—*Karen Kriesberg*
Third-Grade Teacher
Locust Valley, NY

CONTENTS

ACKNOWLEDGMENTS

I have many people to thank. First, I thank the stars of this book, the many teachers of children and adults who have given heart and mind to teaching and whose work forms the substance of *Out of the Classroom and into the World*. I am deeply grateful to Laura Gerrity, who did what she thought she could not and went beyond any expectations; Trish Lent, who brings an artist's sensibility to everything she does and astounds everyone; and Karen Kriesberg, whose exploration of the Nissequogue River and visit to the Shinnecock Reservation have inspired countless teachers. Their energy, vision, struggles, and achievements spark our imaginations, and inspire, encourage, and challenge us. They honor children, children's families—and honor what it means to be a teacher.

I also thank Roberta Altman, for illustrating the power of learning through movement; Pat Arpino, who every day models what it means to be a teacher; Leslie Day, whose energy and passion have inspired the many groups of students she has led through the 79th Street Boat Basin; Elizabeth Mann, whose books have set a new standard for nonfiction; Michelle Shemin, an ever-questioning young teacher whose recycling curriculum has already influenced the work of her peers; Lois Wolf, for reviving in the 1970s Lucy Sprague Mitchell's environment course; Grace Cohen, for illustrating for me and countless teachers how to challenge children's thinking, while inspiring them to meet the challenge; and Michael Scimeca, for being a steady influence throughout.

The students and colleagues of Lucy Sprague Mitchell and Eleanor Hogan generously shared their experiences and brought them to life for me through their passionate accounts. I am grateful to Herb Barnes, Jean Ewing, Sally Kerlin, Vecelia McGhie, Allen Ohta, Tirzah

Schutzengel, Jean Todd Welch, Joie Willimetz, Janet Wilson, and Marguerite Hurrey Wolf. I am especially grateful to Ruth Bigel, Courtney Cazden, Elisabeth Olesen Garvais, Ellen Hausknecht, Elizabeth Helfman, Willie Kraber, Florence Krahn, Claudia Lewis, Wilbur Rippy, Sheila Sadler, Norma Simon, and Olga Smyth. I also thank the many graduates who responded to the questionnaires I sent them. Elisabeth Olesen Garvais, whose photographs documented the 1941 long trip, and Emil Willimetz, who photographed the 1948 trip, graciously sent me copies of their photos, explained them, and granted permission to use them. Their penetrating photos evoke the power of their trips onto the streets of New York City and of the "long trips" to other parts of the country. The account by Mary Ellen Gilder, Eleanor Hogan's daughter, of her mother's role at Bank Street was invaluable. I also acknowledge with gratitude the many people who supported my work investigating the long trips, especially Leah Levinger, Edna Shapiro, Leslie Williams, and Celia Genishi.

The book could not have evolved as it did without the immeasurable help of two colleagues and friends: Harriet Cuffaro and Karen Weiss. I could not begin to catalog the influence Harriet Cuffaro has had on my thinking as an educator, and in a sense this book grows from so much that I have learned from her. For over thirty years she has been mentor, colleague, and friend. She has deepened this book by her probing questions, her invariably generative comments, and by ever challenging my thinking on education as force for social justice. Karen Weiss was my partner in researching, planning, and teaching the "environment" course reminiscent of Lucy Sprague Mitchell's. Working with Karen on that course will forever be a high point for me. When I was a graduate student at Bank Street, I searched for the perfect teacher. Karen was that teacher. She lived the process of learning and teaching promoted in this book and exemplifies its values. Her critical reading of drafts was invaluable. The unfailing support of Harriet and Karen made a potentially lonely process a joy.

I thank Fern Khan and Carol Hillman for reviving the long trips, inviting me to join them, and for being who they are. Ever steady, caring, and capable, their leadership has been an inspiration and a joy. The trips they have planned and led to areas of the country and world demonstrate the enduring power of educators moving outward as a way of vitalizing learning and teaching.

I also acknowledge the students who participated in the curriculum course Karen Weiss and I developed. Getting in touch with them after seven years was a pleasure. I thank them for giving the time and thought to writing about their experience of the course and its impact. Special thanks to my colleagues and students at Bank Street College for the many conversations we have had during my years of working there. Their influence is everywhere present in the book. For their passion as educators I am ever grateful. The ultimate form of this book was influenced by the inspiring work of Dorothy Carter, Miriam Cohen, and Nina Jaffe, whose fiction and folklore embody the power of story.

Marc Favreau, my editor at The New Press, encouraged me from the time when the book was an idea right through its completion. I am grateful for how he so patiently, and subtly, guided my work. His sensitive reading and ever-generative recommendations were invaluable.

My wife, Nancy, has encouraged me throughout and has helped me maintain a sense of humor, especially about myself. My father's stories of growing up during the Depression made the 1930s real and vivid for me.

And finally, I am grateful to Mr. Albok the tailor, who taught a group of six- and seven-year-olds how to sew a button and so much more.

PREFACE:
"EVERYONE SHOULD KNOW HOW TO SEW A BUTTON"

We began with walks in our Manhattan neighborhood: on the school block, around the block, to the avenue filled with small stores, over to the East River, into Central Park. All the while I saw the neighborhood through the eyes of my first and second graders. While investigating the types of stores around the block, I noticed that the children were particularly interested in the tailor shop, the shoe repair, and the florist. Perhaps it was the cat in the window or all the plants or all the black-and-white photos on display that attracted the children to the tailor. For many of the children the draw to the shoe repair was the window display model of an impossibly large shoe. Almost in unison they asked if it was real. I think it was the florist's massive arrangements of fall flowers and autumn leaves and multicolored corn stalks that captured their interest.

I thought this would be a good opportunity to visit work sites in the neighborhood, so I visited the shops myself, explaining that we were learning about the work done in the neighborhood, and arranged three simultaneous trips. Before I left the tailor shop, the tailor said he wanted to teach the children how to sew a button.

I would take a third of the class to the tailor, my assistant would bring a group to the florist, and, because the shoemaker was more fluent in Greek than English, a good friend who spoke Greek and was also a teacher would bring the third group to the shoe repair. Before going, each of the groups met to plan the trip. In each group, children discussed what they thought they would see and developed a small list of questions for the shopkeeper; even though we worked in separate groups and hadn't done this before, the questions of each group were surprisingly similar. I wrote each question on a small strip of paper and handed it to the child who asked the question. Though some children couldn't read yet, they were able to read their question. These were their questions for the tailor: How big is your washing machine? Why do we need a tailor? How did you learn how to do your job? Do you like your job? Do you have any children?

Equipped with clipboards and pencils for sketching, we set off. When we arrived at the shop, the tailor greeted us at the door, asked us to please take off our coats and rest them on the chairs, locked the door, turned his door sign around to display the word "Closed," and pulled the shade down. Though it was only late November, it was especially cold that year, and, as we watched him pull the door shade, through the large window we saw the first snow of the season blanket the street we had just been on.

Mr. Albok went to stand behind his counter and we gathered around him. As I looked at the children and Mr. Albok, I was struck by how small and young these children were. Mr. Albok was over six feet tall and in his eighties. It was at this moment that one child looked up at him and asked, "How large is your washing machine?"

Mr. Albok responded, "I don't have a washing machine! If you want your clothes washed, go to a laundry. If you want your clothes made, come to me, a tailor."

Another child asked, "Why do we need a tailor?"

Mr. Albok responded, "What were you wearing when you were born?"

They all responded, "Nothing," and to this he said, "That is why we need a tailor."

A child asked, "How did you learn how to do your job?"

Mr. Albok thought for a minute and said, "I come from a country far away from here, Hungary. When I was a boy, in that country, the son learned his father's work. My father was a tailor, a master tailor, and I learned this work from him."

"Do you like your job?"

When asked this question, Mr. Albok looked intensely at each of the children and said, "I *love* my job, and I want to tell you something very important. Make sure that you too love what you choose to do."

"Do you have any children?"

Upon hearing this question, Mr. Albok reached under his counter and showed us a large black-and-white photo of a young woman, his daughter. The children responded, "She's very beautiful." And he added, "Yes, she is very beautiful."

At that moment, he held a piece of black cloth in his hand and said, "Before you leave, I want to teach you something very important: how to sew a button. Everyone should know how to sew a button. Too many people walk around with missing buttons or buttons hanging off."

Holding a pair of large scissors the way only a skilled craftsperson does, he quickly cut the cloth into the shape of a small coat about nine inches long and, as though magically, threaded a needle and began to sew a button. With the tips of his fingers, he made a small space between the button and the cloth, "so that it won't snap off or loosen," sewed it to the cloth allowing for the space, and then wound the thread many times around the connecting threads so that "it's strong and won't pop off." He handed the coat with its well-secured button to me.

Following the three simultaneous trips, children discussed, drew, and wrote about their experiences. The six-year-old who drew this picture wrote: "I liked the man in the tailor shop. He sewed a button on a piece of pattern."

With Mr. Albok's permission, children began to sketch things they found interesting: his tools, the cat, all the plants, the many photographs, and the mannequin dressed in a silk tuxedo. When Mr. Albok saw a small group gather around the mannequin, he wheeled it forward, rubbed his hand across the rich fabric, and said, "This is a tailor's Mona Lisa. I did this when I was much younger." He then followed the children as they sketched and said to them, "It is very important what you are doing. Too many people stop drawing as they grow up. If you would give me your drawings when you are done, I will send them to my relatives in Hungary so they will know what my shop looks like." The children were ready to tear the sheets off their boards on the spot. I explained to Mr. Albok that these would be used to share with other classmates and as material for more finished drawings in the classroom. At that point, if the children wished—which they all did—we would gladly give the sketches to him.

We thanked Mr. Albok, put on our coats, made our way through what looked like seven inches of snow, and returned to school with our sketches and the little coat with the button. The other groups carried scraps of stitched and nailed leather and a beautiful flower arrangement. In the classroom, all the children, red faced from the snow, excitedly shared their "gifts" and stories.

Out of the Classroom
and into the World

Introduction

Mr. Albok and those first and second graders have come back to me again and again throughout my career in education and, in a sense, inspired this book. That trip symbolized what I wanted for children, their teachers, and myself. Before this trip, I had taken children on walking trips in the neighborhood. We walked the school block and on another day walked around the block, discovering so much that we had never noticed before, including a veterinarian's office and two other schools, all on our school block, which many of us, including myself, had never noticed before. We walked to the street island in the middle of Park Avenue and 116th Street that overlooks the spot where the Metro North speeds into and exits the tunnel. Each time a train approached the tunnel and was virtually directly below the children, the children waved to the conductor. He waved back and tooted his whistle, while the children screamed with excitement. On a crisp, clear fall day we walked to the East River, observed the boats on the river, crossed the pedestrian bridge at 96th Street, and picnicked on Wards Island. It all went perfectly until we took out our lunch. We were vividly reminded of the science teacher's lesson on the signs of fall when a swarm of yellow jackets descended on the children's food. I couldn't believe that I was picking them off the children's sandwiches and drinks with my fingers and didn't get stung; but one child was stung—and for the rest of the day proudly showed everyone the red mark.

We examined the stores around the school block, which led to the simultaneous trips to meet the tailor, the shoemaker, and the florist. At the shoe repair, the shoemaker let each of the children operate the various machines, stitching and nailing the leather. They especially loved

ejecting nails of different lengths simply by turning the dial to the desired length. The florist told the children that the shop had been in the
family from the time of his grandfather. He slowly and carefully made
an arrangement for the class, explaining why specific flowers are selected and how they are trimmed and assembled into an arrangement.
As with the tailor's little coat, the other groups returned to school with
gifts—pieces of thick, hard leather they had stitched and nailed, and a
fall flower arrangement, filled with bright yellow mums and autumn
leaves. Little wonder they were so excited to share their experiences.
The next day the children drew pictures of what they found most interesting and wrote about it, and each group wrote a thank-you letter.
The pictures and writing were assembled into books. Two children from
each group brought its book to share with the shopkeeper, delivered the
letter, and, for Mr. Albok, delivered the trip sketches for his relatives in
Hungary.

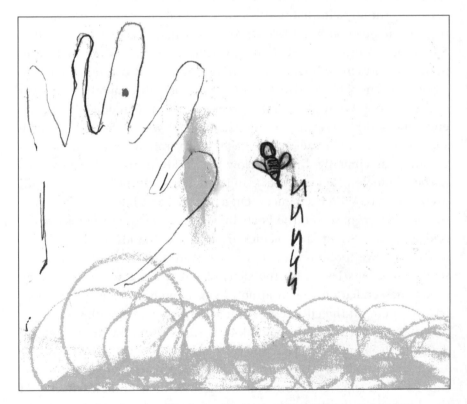

The six-year-old who proudly showed everyone the sting mark drew his stung
hand and the culprit yellow jacket. He wrote: "The bee stung me on the finger!"

The children who went to the shoe repair shop were excited to tell their class-mates that they had operated the nail machine. The seven-year-old who drew this worked hard to make the machine "look real." She wrote: "This is me working the nail machine."

This seven-year-old carefully rendered each detail of the florist shop. He wrote: "The florist gave us a bouquet of flowers free! He was very nice."

All of the neighborhood trips that preceded these three were engaging and important but were different in tone and depth of encounter. This was the first time for me as a teacher and the first time for the class that year that we traveled to meet people and learn from them about their work. When I reflected on the experience, I realized that the three simultaneous trips furthered our study of the neighborhood and the city in ways I had hoped for and in ways I had never anticipated. As I had hoped, the children had used reading, writing, and drawing to record their impressions and extend their understanding of the experience. They had learned that their questions were important and that they themselves could obtain answers. The class became a forum for sharing individual experiences of a trip, thereby enlarging everyone's experience. They saw how work done by people in the neighborhood was connected to them and their families. What I discovered from these three trips, and from so many that followed, was that the people we interviewed embodied the ethic of their work and so generously offered to the children models of competence, which I believe sparked their imaginations, and may have influenced their lives. Also at a time when New York City was not as safe as it is today, when the news was full of violent drug-related crimes and street muggings, children were learning that there were aspects of their world that they could trust and build on.

My Background:
The Sources of This Book

Taking trips grew directly from my course work and fieldwork experiences as a master's degree student at Bank Street College in the early 1970s. I now realize how fortunate I was to enter education at that time. In *How Teachers Taught: Constancy and Change in American Classrooms*, Larry Cuban called the mid-1960s to mid-'70s the second wave of progressivism in American education, the first being the 1920s–'30s.[1] With the excitement over Head Start, the British Infant Schools, and the open classroom movement, it was a period of ferment, promise, and experimentation, especially for teachers interested in the early childhood and early primary years. And I felt a part of the ferment and promise. Instead of the current mantra, "How can we raise children's test scores?" people were asking, "What is important for children to learn and how should they learn it?"

The Environment Class

My imagination was fueled by the pervasive sense of possibility. For me, the possibility was made concrete by the belief, which permeated my graduate experience, that education should move the learner outward physically and socially, as well as intellectually. It was specifically in the class Environment: Core of the Early Childhood and Elementary Curriculum that the belief crystallized for me. Lucy Sprague Mitchell, who founded Bank Street, created the original course in 1930. After years of neglect, the course was revived amid the excitement over the British Infant Schools and the open classroom movement. I enrolled in the first rerun of the course, which spanned June and July 1973. Together, the instructor and students ventured outside to explore the neighborhood and followed a chain of food from local stores backward to large wholesale markets and farms. We walked to the Hudson River, which was just down the block, across Riverside Park, and by train followed the river north—throughout connecting what we experienced to the geography of an island city. And we also ventured "behind the scenes" into the workings of the college building itself, getting to know about the work that sustained our experience there from the people who did that work. In the classroom at the college, we discussed what we had experienced and lost adult inhibitions as we expressed our experience in writing, painting, block building, map and model making, music, and drama. I experienced the intensity and pleasure of being fully engaged in what I was doing. On the trips and in the classroom, we formed a bond that was different from anything I had experienced in classrooms. I knew I wanted to offer children the opportunity to learn in these ways. And we developed curricula to make this possible.

The Old Photo in the College Lobby

I remember being puzzled that summer by an old photograph displayed in the college lobby. It showed Lucy Sprague Mitchell, faculty colleague Eleanor Hogan, a group of young graduate students—all female except for one male—and their bus driver, all posing together in front of a Howard Johnson's convenience stop along the Pennsylvania Turnpike. The accompanying caption stated "1941 Long Trip to Pittsburgh Coal Mining and Steel Areas," and further described how these week to ten-day trips were taken throughout the Depression and into the early post-WWII years. Students traveled together in buses with wooden seats over a thousand miles to the mining areas of West Virginia, Tennessee, and Pennsylvania; the Tennessee Valley Authority (TVA); the Highlander Folk School; and an all–African American agricultural community. All the trips we had taken in the environment class modeled what a teacher might do with children. This was different. I remember wondering, *What did these trips have to do with educating children?*

When visiting the college in subsequent years, I went back to this photo, still asking myself the same question. I would have never imagined that one day I would contact and speak with almost everyone in that photo. But that was after years of leading many groups of children on trips; after continually reexperiencing the kind of person-to-person intimacy that made the trip to the tailor so powerful; after being continually humbled by how freely and deeply the people we met gave of themselves to the children—and how much the children gave to them.

The Long Trips

When the long trip resurfaced for me in 1995, I was a relatively new faculty member at Bank Street. Now my focus was on the education of teachers as well as children. I was reading Joyce Antler's biography of Lucy Sprague Mitchell, in which Antler gave a vivid portrait of the experience.[2] I read through Mitchell's autobiography looking for what she herself said about the trips.[3] I saw that she viewed the trip as a "climax" to all of their explorations of the physical and social world in New York City and surrounding areas. She said that "staff and students felt that life would never be quite the same again."[4] Determined to learn what this had to do with teaching children, I began an investigation that led me into the starkness of the Depression years, government's "New Deal" for people, the burgeoning labor movement, and the beginning of the post-WWII era, characterized by a sense of hope, a burgeoning economy, and the beginnings of a struggle for civil rights that would change the nation, yet shadowed by the atomic bomb and McCarthyism. I read the meager information on the trips in the college archives. The archives also had a series of powerful photos from the 1941 and 1948 trips. But I needed the explanations to bring those photos to life.

Realizing that the meaning of the experience resided essentially in the memories of the participants, I began a trip of my own into the long trips. I interviewed and sent questionnaires to the now elderly participants of these trips and was transported by their forceful and passionate

stories of their experience and of the teacher education program that led
to the trip. While listening to the participants' accounts, I found myself
captivated by the drive, conviction, knowledge, and seemingly tireless
work of the trip leaders, Lucy Sprague Mitchell and Eleanor Hogan, who
so meticulously planned and so passionately led the trips.

I didn't expect that my investigation would also lead me into the
roots of my own practice as an educator, what has made teaching vital
and important to me. I learned how the process and content of the curricula I had worked so hard to offer children were originally conceived
as part of a continuum of experience all leading to a thinking, feeling
citizen committed to democratic values.

I saw how the concept of the trips offered an expansive way of thinking about educating teachers and children: a pedagogy spearheaded by
democratic purpose; a view of education that contributes to our understanding of relevance, personal engagement, and participation; and a
vision of academic excellence based on learning from experience. My
investigation crystallized the aims and process of educating teachers to
challenge their complacency as citizens; to care deeply about the lives
of children and about the world in which children live; to connect with
people person-to-person across distance and culture and expand their
circle of understanding, caring, and commitment; and to expand that
circle to the physical world and realize the intimate connection between
the use and abuse of natural resources to the pressing social issues of
our time.

Ultimately, the trip leaders believed and hoped that the knowing,
the feeling, and the experiencing of the trips would *change the person*,
which would influence all of his or her work with children. Unlike so
much of the current fixation with test scores and standards as ultimate
educational goals, the trip leaders seemed to be asking, "What are the
standards of a human being?"

Teaching and Researching

Out of the Classroom and into the World grows from and reflects my own
"long trip" in education across time and place. It draws from years of
teaching children in day care, Head Start, and elementary schools, and
from the planning and leading of many trips with children into their
world in the present and past, into the "here and now" New York, the
immigrant New York, the Dutch New York, and the Native American
New York. It grows from the *experts* we consulted—the Iroquois mother

who grew up on a reservation in Canada; the children's parents and grandparents who immigrated to this country from all over the world; the African American grandmother who risked her life during the civil rights movement; the parent bus driver who, to the consternation of other passengers, departed from his bus route and dropped the class off at the school; and from so many others.

The book draws from years of teaching graduate students pursuing degrees in early childhood and elementary education at Bank Street College—from the many trips with them modeling what they might do with children. It also draws from my work with these adult students as a curriculum course instructor and thesis mentor, and from their curriculum studies that cover most neighborhoods of Manhattan and surrounding areas: such as the Long Island Native American study, for which the student contacted a tribal historian at the Shinnecock Reservation to learn what members of the Shinnecock believe to be important for Long Island children to know, and for which she explored forest and seashore areas, and followed the Nissequogue River to the bay to understand why Indians settled in certain places; the Brooklyn Bridge study by a teacher who thought she'd never understand how the bridge worked; and the Brownsville, Brooklyn, study, which the student's school colleagues tried to discourage her from doing, saying there was too much neighborhood violence and disintegration—and so many others that, unfortunately, I am unable to discuss in one book.

The book draws from my experience visiting hundreds of classrooms across New York City to observe fieldwork advisees; doing presentations and workshops for teachers, administrators, and families; and working with teachers in their classrooms on their curricula. It also reflects my experience as an elementary school principal working with teachers and children and their families.

And, finally, the book draws from my investigation of the long trips into the Depression and postwar years, and how the soul-searching, penetrating stories of the participants' experience of the trip changed me as an educator. It reflects the resulting clearer sense of purpose and driving need to experiment—the modest ways I tried to incorporate principles of the long trip into the curriculum classes I teach; the designing and teaching with a colleague an environment course that was reminiscent of Lucy Sprague Mitchell's original course; and finally the excitement—and anxiety—of co-planning and co-leading long trips to places in the country and world "where things were happening."

Ideas That Underlie *Out of the Classroom and into the World*

Out of the Classroom and into the World focuses on the importance in the education of teachers and children of moving beyond the school building and beyond the book. It illustrates how venturing into the world out there:

- enables learners to experience the deep connections that exist between the physical and social worlds around them and understand how these connections affect their lives; how human existence is dependent on a complex weave of people's work, people whose lives and work too often remain invisible; how daunting social issues of our time are illuminated by examining how humans use and abuse the natural world to satisfy basic human needs, such as energy and food;
- builds on learners' natural desire to make sense of and be competent in their environment and sparks their imagination and stimulates questioning and the search for explanations;
- uses what are commonly called "the skills"—reading, writing, and math—and "the arts"—painting, drawing, music, and movement—in service of learners' investigations and in representing and deepening their experiences;
- fosters a community in the classroom that includes the people and places learners have encountered; this process of going out into the world together and the discussions and shared work that follow all offer the learning opportunities essential to community;
- enlarges a learner's circle of understanding, caring, and commitment through the encountering of the realities of others; in this way are cultivated socially conscious individuals who are committed to the well-being of each other and the world out there, which is critical to a society that calls itself democratic.

A Brief Overview

The story will move back and forth in time, featuring long and short trips with adults and with children to places as different as the coal-mining regions of West Virginia, a barbershop in Brownsville, Brooklyn, flood-torn areas of New Orleans, the 79th Street Boat Basin in Manhattan, the first school for slaves just freed by the Union Army, the boiler room in the school building, a major New York City Transit Authority bus depot, and Mr. Albok's tailor shop.

Part 1, "Teachers 'Experimenting with the World,'" illustrates how a teacher's active learning process can profoundly influence a child's. The section follows three public school teachers at different points in their careers, working in different settings and teaching different topics to different grades, as they research and teach a social studies curriculum based on the children's social and physical environment. Though they experience the vulnerability of not knowing, they forge ahead and engage the world around them. With their own experience as a base, they plan for and guide children as they in turn explore and discover. This part of the book ends with an analysis of what surfaces as salient and important across differences in setting, teacher experience, topics, and grades taught.

Part 2, "'An Education in What America Is, What It Could Be,'" moves into the past to trace the sources of the process of learning and of teaching children featured in part 1. This section examines the student teachers' experience of a process of educating teachers that paralleled, on an adult level, what they were being asked to do with children. It explicitly connects that process to a way of thinking, learning, and living together that promotes and sustains a democratic society. To illustrate the students' experience, Lucy Sprague Mitchell and Eleanor Hogan are followed (from 1935 to '51) as they lead student teachers on many local trips to explore the social and physical world around them, so that they would resonate with the environment and be alive to its potential with children. The section then follows them as they venture beyond their everyday worlds and travel to regions of the country where "things were happening," and confront the daunting social issues of the time. This part of the book ends by examining the profound impact these experiences had on their lives as teachers and citizens.

The section moves from the starkness of the Depression and the complex political world of the post-WWII years to the present, and compares the experiences of the students of the past to those of present-day long trip participants who also travel to distant areas of the country.

Part 3, "Staying Vulnerable," examines the modest ways in which I experimented with offering adult students opportunities to experience the world around them as an important part of their becoming teachers: the trip I incorporated into the curriculum class I teach and the environment course a colleague and I created and taught that was inspired by Lucy Sprague Mitchell's original course.

The concluding chapter, "'This Going Off Together, There's Something to It,'" attempts to penetrate what that "something" might be. In essence, the chapter examines what *we* might take away and use as educators and citizens from their ventures beyond the school building. Ultimately, the conclusion asks that we consider questions of why we educate, to what ends; what knowledge is most worth knowing, how do we decide what to teach; how do we educate, what will our process be; and what is the relationship between the *why*, *how*, and *what* of what we do. How we answer these questions can have profound implications for this society, the society in which the children and adults we teach attempt to build a future.

PART ONE

———

Teachers "Experimenting with the World"[1]

A student in my curriculum class called me at home in the evening. I could hear the distress in her voice as she told me that she couldn't do the final assignment. The assignment asked students to develop a social studies curriculum using the children's own environment as the primary source material, which in most cases meant trips and interviews. Students designing curricula for kindergarteners might choose to study families or the school, using the actual families of children they were teaching or the people and facilities of a specific school. Teachers of first and second graders often planned studies of the school's neighborhood and of the city. These topics roughly paralleled New York City's designated curricula for the early grades. The student having difficulty with the assignment, Laura Gerrity, was teaching third grade, and the mandated curriculum was Communities of the World—a topic she felt was far removed from the children's experience and their world, which was Brownsville, Brooklyn. But it was more than this; she had twenty-nine students, no paraprofessional to assist in the class, and limited materials. Most important, her school was under fire for low test scores, which forced teachers to focus intensely on skill development.

She wondered at the sense of studying "communities of the world" when so many of her children were unfamiliar with important aspects of their own neighborhood. Brownsville had been a bustling neighborhood full of stores and factories and rich street life, with old-fashioned street pushcarts right into the early 1960s. But by the end of the '60s most of the factories had moved out of the city or closed down altogether, leaving many people from Brownsville and elsewhere jobless, and one by one the stores that drew people to the neighborhood closed.

People were left with no jobs and little hope for similar jobs, buildings stayed deserted, basements flooded, and crime proliferated. Little wonder that so many of the children's parents, to protect their children from street violence, had them spend most after-school time at home. The children knew about the danger and the crime but seemed unaware of other aspects that were important and sustaining. When she mentioned using the neighborhood as source material for curriculum, colleagues advised against it, and she wondered if parents would respond similarly.

I was about to ask her to think about alternatives to the assignment that would make sense to her. But somehow I held back discussing other options, and instead asked her what she would like to teach if she had the support she felt she needed. She said she wanted them to study Brownsville, to begin the study personally by tracing children's family history in the neighborhood and then venture into the neighborhood. From across her own elementary school experience, she especially remembered studying family history in the fifth grade. She interviewed her parents, both immigrants, and remembers how interested she was in their stories of coming to the United States and how proud of them she felt. She wanted to do something similar with her children. By the conviction in her voice, I could tell that she wasn't ready to give up on this idea. As though hoping to hear "yes" from me, she asked if I thought she could do it—even with all the constraints. I told her that I did think she could do it and also not compromise the children's skill development. I said that for the first half of the study, instead of going out into the neighborhood, she could bring the neighborhood into the classroom. She—or I—could never have imagined what grew from that conversation.

Part 1 of this book features Laura's struggles and successes, and the work of two other public school teachers. They are very different individuals at different stages in their careers, working on different topics for different settings—Laura Gerrity's family history and neighborhood study for third graders at her school in Brownsville; Trish Lent's study of the Brooklyn Bridge for an interaged class of second and third graders at a school in the Tribeca area of Manhattan; and Karen Kriesberg's study of Long Island Native Americans for fourth graders for a school in Suffolk County, Long Island.

Through the courses I have taught, the theses mentored, and the classrooms visited, I have had the privilege of working with hundreds of teachers, many of whom approach their work with sensitivity, thoughtfulness, and passion. But I chose to focus on these three teachers because I had the opportunity to work closely with them on the studies featured in this part of the book. I witnessed the evolution of each study, as thesis mentor to Laura and Karen and as fieldwork advisor to student teachers in Trish's class. As thesis advisor, I met with Laura and Karen regularly and became a participant observer in their process and planning. As fieldwork advisor to student teachers in Trish's class, I visited the class regularly and, through regular discussions with the student teachers, came also to understand the study through their eyes. The differences in school settings, ages of children, and topics pursued were also reasons to feature the work of these three teachers. And each of these teachers created a curriculum that honored the children's environment as an essential aspect of their education. It must also be said that they exemplify a process of learning about teaching and children.

Chapter 1

"Slavery Was a Business!"

Laura began with a simple homework assignment that asked the children to find out where their family had come from before living in New York and why they had chosen to come here.[1] She thought that when they shared what they had learned, children would be interested in each other's findings and discover similarities as well as differences in their backgrounds. But during the sharing, the children seemed interested only in their own answers. Showing complete disinterest, one child said, "My family just came from New York"; similarly, another said, "We always lived here"—even though their homework sheets indicated that their families came from Virginia and South Carolina.[2]

Upon reflection, she realized that she was asking twenty-nine nine-year-olds to listen patiently to each other's story at one sitting. It was too much information at once, especially for a group that seemed uninterested in what each other had to say. As she did throughout the study, she restructured the experience for them. She studied the family background information on the children's homework sheets and, based on the findings, divided the class into three groups: families that came from the Caribbean, from states other than New York, and from outside North America. Each group would present its family history on a separate day. In this way, each child would have more time. This would not only make the sharing of their findings more manageable, but also help them structure their thinking.

She also posted three maps, of the United States, of North America, and of the world. So that each child could have his or her place of family origin represented, she drew in Caribbean Islands not shown on the map. On their designated day, one at a time the children found the place of family origin and traced a line to New York City and wrote their names on the line. When drawing the line from Guyana, a child started talking about the beaches and small towns in Guyana. Children responded about the beaches and storms in Grenada, about the heat of Panama, about how people built their own homes, each engaging the other. That was the beginning, and the stage was set for bringing the major sources of the curriculum into the classroom—the children's parents and teachers.

The Visitors

Although Laura eventually did what she thought she could not do— venture out into the community with her children—she began the study by bringing the community to the children. The rich sources she drew from are available to every teacher and school, regardless of economic status of the student body or of the limited resources of the school: the children's parents and other teachers.

The children seemed interested when they heard that their first visitor would be Ms. Hale,[3] an African American teacher who had taught many of them in kindergarten. She would be talking with them about growing up in North Carolina and then moving north to Brooklyn. The children and Laura prepared questions for her. They wanted to know why she came to New York, what it was like in North Carolina, how she traveled to New York, if she liked North Carolina, and what the weather was like there. This last question would come up throughout the study. Laura felt the questions were focused and generative. She asked the children to wait until Ms. Hale was finished with her presentation before asking their questions. She wanted Ms. Hale to have the opportunity to tell her story in her own way, without questions intruding on the presentation or leading it into a direction Ms. Hale hadn't intended. Laura followed this procedure with all subsequent visitors.

Before the visit, Laura and Ms. Hale discussed the purpose of the visit, the kinds of information that would interest the children, and the children's prepared questions. Laura also asked Ms. Hale if she would share a skill she had learned as a child that was important to her, something the children could also learn. The previsit discussion seemed so important that Laura had similar discussions with most of the subsequent visitors, and they appreciated it—especially the parents and community people, who, unlike the teacher guests, were not used to speaking with groups of children.

When Ms. Hale entered the classroom, it was as though a "wonderful aura" descended upon the class. And they sat in "rapt attention" as Ms. Hale described what it was like growing up in North Carolina. She told them about how she had worked hard on a farm, cared for the animals, grown vegetables, and picked cotton. She told them how skilled her father was at farming, and though he never learned to read or write, "He was a smart man." She showed the children a cotton stalk, and they were amazed. She passed it around and the children handled it with care. When it came time to tell the story about her father's land, she faltered, the words wouldn't come. It was so painful to her that she asked Laura if she would tell the story. Laura told the class that Ms. Hale's father was born just after slavery was abolished, had not been allowed to learn to read, and had been cheated out of most of his land. Laura looked at her silent group of children and saw the deep concern on their faces. She knew the children could not possibly understand the full complexity of the story but seemed to realize that they were being trusted with and asked to think about something important. And the topic that would resurface throughout the study was introduced—slavery and its legacy. Children who had lived in the South or visited relatives shared their own experiences. They asked their planned questions and others. Then Ms. Hale taught the children to sew, a valued skill she learned growing up and used to earn extra money. They made pouches, something she made as a child. For this activity, as she would do for all of the visit activities, Laura made sure she had assembled everything that was needed. Laura had collected pieces of fabric, scissors, thread, and needles with large eyes. She also asked another parent to come in and help, which ended up being critical. The adults seemed to be in constant motion, threading needles, attending to the shock of needle punctures, and simply having the patience and giving the time to teach the skill itself. But she saw, once the children got going, how calming and satisfying it seemed.

A few days after Ms. Hale's visit, the two children who essentially didn't participate in the original family history activity approached her. One child said, "Ms. Gerrity, we aren't from New York. We're from Virginia." The other said, "Remember when you asked where my family was from? We came from North Carolina. Can I put that on the map?"[4] Another child came in brimming with excitement, announcing that a relative had just emigrated from Africa.

The warmth and intimacy of Ms. Hale's visit is conveyed in this child's writing.

As it turned out, because of the next guest's schedule, her visit had to occur the day after Ms. Hale's. Laura was sorry that she didn't have time to fully discuss the visit with the children and have them formulate questions ahead of time. Most of all she regretted what it did to both visits, intruding on the time needed to follow up the first visit and not giving the time interval between visits that would help children look forward to it and see it as special. Laura also wanted the visitors to come away from the visit feeling good about it and sense how special it was to the children. The visits weren't simply for the children to amass information, but to connect them in new and deeper ways to the people and places in their world—which required the time needed for thoughtful preparation. The importance of the timing of the visits was reinforced dramatically on December 21. Laura said that next year she would place a sign on her desk warning, "Never schedule a visit two days before the winter holiday!"

The second visitor was Ms. Farrell, a parent who, as part of her college work, had traced generations of her family's background. Ms. Farrell's college work paralleled what the children were doing, which in itself made a strong impression. She told them that she learned that on her mother's side she was a descendant of the longest living slave that we know of. He had been born in Africa, brought to America as a slave, and had lived long enough to be freed from slavery. His descendant, her great-great-grandfather, an African American, married a Crow Indian woman from Montana, her great-great-grandmother. Like the first visitor, her father's side of the family came from North Carolina. Ms. Farrell learned that her grandmother moved to New York for a better life, and settled in Brooklyn, where she met the man who would become Ms. Farrell's grandfather. To end her talk, she showed photos she had collected of Crow Indians and read parts of her college papers. Laura noticed how the class was leaning forward, fully absorbed in what she was showing and saying. Interestingly, one child's spontaneous question was, "How did you find out about your family?"[5] Her response made a strong impression on them. Most of what she learned she found out by asking family members—just as they were doing. Laura regretted that the second visit wasn't followed up by an activity. The arrangements were made much too late for that. Somehow the format they followed for the first visit—a brief presentation, children's questions and comments, and the activity—worked well for the children. They engaged readily with the activity, but more than that, it offered a different kind of insight into a valued aspect of the visitor's background. They also came together as a group in a different way. Children adept at threading needles or even making stitches had helped their struggling classmates.

Their next and third guest, Ms. Barton, was a second-grade teacher who had taught many of the children the year before. Laura asked her to talk about her recent visit to Africa. However, when Laura described the focus of the visit to the children, most of their questions were about slavery and racism, such as: "Is it true that black people hate white people and call them devil?" "Who was the first person who decided they should take slaves?" "Were there white slaves?"[6] The children also wanted to know what made Ms. Barton go to Africa, where she went in Africa, and if there were other tourists. Laura was unsettled by the first set of questions. During her first year of teaching at the school, she asked the class paraprofessional, who was African American, to discuss issues of race when they surfaced in the class. Concerned about the subtle message being given to the children, her colleagues, mostly African American, felt that she, *their teacher*, should be having these discussions with the children—regardless of her race. With trepidation, she began to lead discussions on racism. As it became apparent that the children were eager to have these discussions, her comfort grew. But this curriculum demanded more of her; it placed race in the forefront. And it was as though this study were forcing her to confront her position as a white teacher of primarily African American children.

Based on what Laura told Ms. Barton about the recent visits and what children most wanted to know about, she focused her talk on slavery. Ms. Barton began by posting two large maps on the board, one a world map and another entitled "African Americans—Unwilling Immigrants," showing routes of the slave trade that branched across the world from Africa. She paused, giving children time to think about that title, while she looked directly into the eyes of each child, then stated with the force of authority, "Slavery was a business!"[7] Then she answered some of the children's questions that had so unsettled Laura. She told them that slavery went back to the beginnings of human history, and that "there were white slaves, Asian slaves, Native American slaves—all different kinds of people were slaves"[8]—a fact that seemed to be tremendously important to the children. It was as though Ms. Barton were demanding they realize that their ancestors and they had not been marked by fate. It was cold-blooded business ventures that uprooted many of their people, as it had other peoples throughout history. Laura felt that something important was happening for her third graders, though they probably could not put it into words. She also realized that had she steered the visit into more personally comfortable territory, she'd have robbed the children of pursuing what seemed vitally important *to them*.

Ms. Barton ended her talk by showing them a picture of the "door of no return," a stone doorway on the coast of West Africa through which African men, women, and children were led in chains to the slave ships. She described how the teenagers on her tour—who throughout the trip had acted as though they were uninterested—were crying just like the adults. Laura realized that this last detail left them with a "powerful impression." The children had so many questions and comments that grew from the presentation that their guest promised to come back.

> MS. Barton Said when She went to Africa she saw a cave Where they put the slaves Chained up. When MS. Barton went to Africa She was no Slave. MS. Barton Saw the place Where the Slaves had to sit in the hall. When MS. Barton went to Africa she the door of no return.
>
> The door of no Return

The stark simplicity of this child's writing and drawing reflects the power and importance of Ms. Barton's presentation. Laura realized that had she steered the visit into a more personally comfortable direction, she would have robbed the children of pursuing what was important to them—the issue of slavery.

More parent visitors followed, such as the mother from Trinidad and the mother of the only Thai child in the class. The visitors brought distant places to life, creating portraits with distinct climate, foods, and types of homes. On maps they traced the route from their country of origin to New York, and their children wrote their names on the route. As with past visitors, Laura's discussing the visit beforehand with the guest was critical and greatly appreciated.

Following the visits, children discussed what they found interesting, what they had never known before, and what surprised them; they wrote and drew about the visitor's story; they also wrote thank-you letters, which they mailed. They asked so many new questions. They created a temperature graph, in which once each month they charted the temperature of the places that surfaced in their study. They examined the results and were struck by the differences but also by the similarities in climate in the southern United States, Thailand, and Trinidad. Each child contributed to a book that featured the visits. They and Laura proofread their work and produced a carefully written finished work. Finally, to include families who didn't visit the class, each child was asked to interview an older adult in his or her family and write a report, which each child presented to the class.

"You Should Be Happy with the Color You Are"

Laura began to notice how these students, who started the year showing little interest in what their peers had to say, "were much more responsive to the people [each other, teachers, and visitors] around them than . . . students from years past." She realized that they were engaged *emotionally* as well as intellectually. "They paid attention, they asked meaningful questions, they were respectful, and most importantly, they seemed to enjoy listening"—all very different from the ways in which previous groups responded to their work.[9] Laura also found herself engaged emotionally and seemed to have a heightened sensitivity to the children's comments and questions. She brought a different kind of investment to her work and felt energized by the visitors and children's reactions to them. Personally convinced of its importance, she had conceived the study and planned its broad strokes, yet saw it grow as an interaction between herself, the children, the parents, and other teachers.

Laura realized the impact of the study when, right before the winter holiday break, the children—like so many school children—seemed unable to focus on anything except the holiday. Just to keep them busy for a while, she asked them to write in their journals, which they hadn't done in a while. What they chose to write about surprised her. One child wrote of her sadness at not being able to see her family at Christmas. To this, another child said she knew how she felt—her parents had died. Another said she wished she could see her mother for the holiday. A child responded that his mother had forbade him to see his father. From hurt feelings, the children's conversation shifted spontaneously to experiences of name-calling. One child spoke about how his brother's friend was teased and ostracized because he was light skinned. Another talked about a Jewish friend who wanted to be black and to whom she said, "You shouldn't want to be black, you should be happy with the color you are." Others spoke of situations where people were treated badly because they were different and emphasized that this was not right.[10]

Laura realized that, unlike the classes she had taught previously, these children had gotten the message that in school they could speak about what was important to them. This kind of discussion showed that the children had come to know and trust each other. She had never said that they were learning to understand and respect differences among people—it was the curriculum that demonstrated these values.

Into the Neighborhood

When this phase of the study ended, parents eagerly volunteered to accompany the children on trips into the neighborhood. Before arranging any trips, Laura struggled with the focus. She wondered whether she should feature only "success stories," but was concerned that this was sanitizing harsher aspects of the neighborhood. She decided this wasn't the case. Children, in fact, were so aware of the street violence, the drug addiction, and the deserted houses that other aspects paled. She decided to focus on what was affirming and signified hope. And as she explored the neighborhood herself to plan the study, Laura found that she too was seeing the neighborhood differently. She was no longer merely noticing what was *not* there.

And together the children, Laura, and parent escorts ventured out into the neighborhood. They brought with them and built upon all that they had learned from their hard work in the classroom. They met a construction supervisor who told them about the newly constructed block of two-family homes just three blocks from the school; a restaurant owner of a Brooklyn landmark just ten blocks from the school that was famous for its southern cooking; the barber, whose shop, like other barbershops in the neighborhood, was a social gathering place; and others who also gave of themselves so generously.

Through their own backgrounds and the backgrounds of the people they met, which spread from Africa, the Caribbean, Asia, and the southern United States, places that would have seemed foreign to the children had become real, with distinct cultures. In exploring their own school and neighborhood, the class had come away with a deeper understanding of Communities of the World—the mandated curriculum.

Chapter 2

"Could We Build a Poem Like a Bridge?"

There they were on the pedestrian walkway with the Manhattan tower of the Brooklyn Bridge smack in front of them.[1] It was as though there was nothing else, no rest of the bridge, no river—the tower consumed the entire field of vision of Trish Lent's class of second and third graders. All of them had seen photographs of the Brooklyn Bridge, some had seen it from a distance, and many had driven over it, yet they hadn't expected this. The wooden pedestrian walkway they were standing on vibrated, and the sound of car engines, vibrations, and wind seemed overwhelming. They were surprised and somewhat dismayed that through the spaces between walkway boards they could see that the bridge roadway was directly below them, filled with cars ceaselessly speeding by. The wind was fierce and the pages of their sketchbooks were hard to hold down while they sketched details that were interesting to them, such as the cable patterns, the stonework, and the contours of the towers. Trish, their teacher, could tell that some of the children were uneasy and seemed relieved when the time came to turn around to head back to school.

They could not imagine then that the time would come in the not-distant future when they would walk the bridge as though it were theirs, feel proud that it stands so close to their homes, and consider themselves Brooklyn Bridge experts. The chapter traces an evolution from Trish's initial reluctance to accept her grade-level team's decision to study the Brooklyn Bridge, through her ceaseless efforts to understand the engineering, up to the point where the study was as thrilling for her as it was for the children.

Though the historical, geographic, and engineering strands were each central aspects of the study, this chapter will focus primarily on the engineering. The process of coming to understand the engineering posed the greatest challenge for Trish and the children and ultimately offered the greatest rewards. Their imaginations soared as they visited the bridge, became the bridge, and built the bridge with words as well as cardboard. The engineering also integrated the history and geography and practically every other aspect of the curriculum.[2]

The 1996 publication of Elizabeth Mann's nonfiction children's book *The Brooklyn Bridge* inspired bridge studies in a number of Brooklyn and Manhattan public schools.[3] So in 2006 the Brooklyn Bridge was "in the air" when Trish and the three other teachers on the grade level were deciding on a topic for a half-year study. One of the teachers wanted to incorporate architecture into the study, and another who had formerly been a science teacher thought the science of suspension bridge construction could play an important part in the study. Her colleagues also pointed out that the bridge was a major transportation hub that played a crucial role in the historical growth of New York as well as in the present life of the city. And it was just a short walk across town from the school. In spite of her colleagues' excitement over the topic, Trish felt at a complete loss. She "didn't even know what a suspension bridge was."

Researching the Topic

Even though she felt "naturally drawn" to the historical aspects of the study, she began her own research with the engineering because it was a "complete mystery" to her. David McCullough's epic *The Great Bridge*[4] and Mann's *The Brooklyn Bridge* introduced her to the drama of the bridge construction, and specifically to the engineering. (As part of this chapter, I include for the reader bridge construction information that was important to Trish's growing understanding of the engineering and formed the basis for the activities she planned for children.) She was fascinated to learn that a suspension bridge is in fact suspended, held up by suspender cables that hang from the two main cables. The main cables are "anchored" firmly on each end of the bridge and stretch over each of the towers, which hold the cables up.

Though Trish was getting a general idea of how a suspension bridge worked, aspects of its construction were confusing. She just couldn't understand what was happening with the caissons or how the main cables were spun right on the bridge.

In describing the caissons, Mann asked her readers to "imagine a building three stories tall and big enough to cover much of a city block. Imagine the top two stories were made of solid wood, and the building had no floor."[5] These would be constructed on land, floated by tugboats over to the exact locations for the two bridge towers, and sunk. The air pressure in the box would keep the river water from entering. As the caisson workers dug mud and rocks out of the riverbed, the caisson would sink deeper. At the same time, stone workers were constructing the towers right over the caissons, and the weight of the stone would sink the caissons farther down. When bedrock was reached, the caissons were filled with concrete and became the foundation for the towers.[6]

Trish knew the children would wonder how a box with its bottom side open (a caisson) could be submerged without water filling it up. She had to find a simple way to demonstrate what was happening. So she and her husband got some simple equipment and "acted out" the process. They used a small watertight wooden box that was open on one side. They held it with the open side facing a tub of water and forced it to the bottom. When they removed it, Trish felt the satisfaction of seeing that it was completely dry, just as it was supposed to be. Trish mentioned that, when doing this with children, one of her colleagues first placed a paper towel on the bottom of the box. When the box was removed from the water, the dry paper towel "proved" that no water entered the box. To demonstrate first to herself and eventually to the children the process of how the caissons would sink because of the stone being laid on top of them, she and her husband created a two-dimensional "moving cardboard version" of the process.[7]

Spinning the cables was a harder process to simulate.

To simulate this process, Trish and her husband, David,

The cables were not hung fully assembled. The total weight and half mile span of each cable made this impossible. The cables were literally spun right in place on the bridge. Each cable would be made from 5,282 pencil-thick steel wires, of which each set of 278 wires was bound into a strand. The completed cable had 19 strands. With a complex pulley system, each individual wire traveled the half mile from the Brooklyn anchorage, over each tower, to the Manhattan anchorage.[8]

first purchased from a hardware store clothesline rope, two old-fashioned clothesline pulleys, and string. She described what they did:

> We set up at home with each of us being an anchorage, and two chairs being the towers. We followed McCullough's narrative to get the first "traveling wire" up and over the towers from a "boat" on our carpet. We used a clothesline for the traveling wire.
>
> Once it was up and over the tower we threaded it onto the clothesline wheels and taped the ends together. Now we had a continuous loop that went from one anchorage, up and over both towers (chairs) and to the second anchorage. I sat on the Brooklyn side holding one wheel, and David sat on the Manhattan side holding another wheel, ready to "receive" wires (all the wires for the bridge were strung from Brooklyn to Manhattan, none from Manhattan to Brooklyn). We used string for the cable wires, attaching a piece of string from a spool to the clothesline using a pulled apart paper clip as a hook.
>
> We then moved the clothesline loop across (just like you would if you were putting clothes out to dry) until the string got to David. He held on to that end, I cut the string at my side and held on to it; then we sent the clothesline loop back and attached a new piece of string and sent that over to David. We kept doing it until we had about a dozen pieces of string strung together, and then taped them into the first "bundle."

The process was thrilling to Trish—the challenge of doing it, turning her living room into a workshop, working with her husband as a bridge construction team, the string making its way from one anchorage to the other, and, most important, coming to understand a process she thought she'd never understand. Now she felt confident that she could demonstrate it with children and was excited at the prospect.

These efforts to understand how a suspension bridge worked preceded any bridge study work with the children. This was her learning process, which didn't end here but continued throughout the study and enabled her to ask the kinds of questions that sparked children's curiosity, encouraged them to think deeply, and stimulated children's own questions. She had experienced the excitement of discovery and was then able to plan learning opportunities that would fully engage children—physically and emotionally as well as intellectually.

Needless to say, when the time came in the course of the study to do these demonstrations with the children, they were "a big hit." They set up their meeting area as Brooklyn, the East River, and Manhattan, and used chairs as the towers. One child was stationed at the Manhattan anchorage to hold the clothesline wheel, with two children at the Brooklyn anchorage, one to hold the wheel and one to hold the cut strings. To make it even more real for the children, she copied a picture of the engineer who rode along the traveling wires across the span of the bridge. She attached him to the string as it was about to make its journey, and they were all excited to see him travel the distance with the "wire." When they had strung a number of them, they bundled them into a strand, just as it was done on the Brooklyn Bridge. During a scheduled choice time, groups of children worked hard at spinning and bundling strands that they tied together to make a cable.

Beginning the Study

The classroom study didn't begin with these complex demonstrations. It began with a simple assignment, to draw a picture of a bridge. Interestingly, many of the finished drawings showed bridges freestanding, not bridging one space to another. The children who drew suspension bridges showed main cables but no suspender cables.

Trish followed this activity by asking them, "What is a bridge?" They seemed to agree that a bridge "helps you get someplace" and that a bridge "connects." Trish didn't press them further because she knew that throughout the study their concept of a bridge would evolve and deepen through their own experiences. This discussion would stimulate over the next week a wave of comments and new questions. All of the children had grown up on an island in a city of islands where bridges served as major transportation routes for traveling from one city borough to another and for entering and leaving the city. With a heightened awareness, they would enter the class excitedly proclaiming that over the weekend they crossed three bridges, five bridges, and even fifteen bridges. Children described situations where roads connected and asked if these were bridges. Trish felt they were trying to figure out how far their class definition of a bridge could be stretched.

At a morning meeting, the class sat huddled around a blank, plastic outline map on which they could write and erase. Most of them knew what they were examining—the outlines of New York City's boroughs and surrounding water and other areas, such as New Jersey and Westchester and Nassau counties. She asked them to think about why bridges might be important to this city, and then asked them to think about where *they* might build bridges. This type of activity was characteristic of class discussions throughout the study—they were given *time to think together*. Then children drew in bridges and explained why they chose the specific locations. This is just the kind of experience Mitchell had wanted for children. Using this "tool map," they are placed in a position to see relationships between their immediate physical environment and how humans interact with that environment to satisfy basic human needs.

Once the bridges were drawn in, Trish posted next to the outline map a map that identified the area names and showed the bridges. They were surprised and delighted to see that all the drawn-in bridges except for one were in their actual locations. That one exception went from Staten Island over New York Bay to lower Manhattan. The child chose that location so that people in Staten Island could get to work in the city. Other children said the distance was too long for a bridge. Then one child shouted out, "But there's a ferry there!" They were noticing that there was order and logic in their environment, that important decisions were not made arbitrarily, that "Things didn't just happen."[9] Mitchell had hoped that once children and their teachers realized this, they would look for the logic and order in important aspects of their environment, aspects they had previously given little thought to. They might ask themselves, "What makes that bridge stand?" or "Why was that bridge built in that location?"

Their next step was to visit a bridge. Fortuitously, close to the school there was a pedestrian bridge across the Westside Highway. They sketched the bridge, capturing the impressive steel arch that extends over the bridge and the pattern of the metal rods that connect the arch to the roadway. As they walked across it, they measured the length of the roadway. When discussing the trip back in the classroom, a number of children felt there was no need for the bridge. Trish asked them to think about why the bridge might be there. Children who crossed the highway every day said the traffic lights change so quickly that they have to run across. Another said that there were three schools nearby with a lot of children crossing the highway, so it was needed for safety.

The bridge they crossed was one example of an arch bridge. Trish had learned from her research that there are three main types of bridges: beam, arch, and suspension. To see different examples of beam and arch bridges, the class traveled to Central Park. Though they passed and even walked across and under many of the park's picturesque stone bridges, they focused specifically on three. For each they noticed whether it was an arch bridge or a beam bridge, sketched it, felt the cold roughness of its stone, and measured the bridge using arm spans or their feet as a unit of measure. Then they had the fun of playing in a large field of grass.

Once the children studied each of the three major bridge types, they drew, painted, and constructed each type. This is a third grader's rendition of the three types. The middle drawing depicts an arch bridge the children examined in Central Park.

The Experiments: "I Can't Believe This!"

Back in the classroom they deepened their understanding of how these bridges worked. Trish selected a series of simple experiments that she found in a book for children on how bridges work. She'd never done formal experiments with children before this and had no idea how to go about it, but with the help of her colleague who'd been a science teacher she structured the experiments. She could not have imagined that from these simple experiments, she and the children would be "hooked into the engineering."

The children would work on these experiments in teams of three. While researching the engineering of bridges, Trish had read that the parts of a bridge are called *members* because they all have to work together to make a bridge function. Over time she began to think about this fact as a metaphor for the class. Though working in a team hadn't come naturally to Trish, she learned from this class of children and this curriculum the power of working in teams.

Each member of the group of three would have a distinct job, either to set up the experiment, to record results visually, or to record in writing. All of the experiments used the same materials: two unit blocks from a set of children's wooden building blocks; sheets of construction paper; and unifix cubes, which are plastic math manipulative materials that stack one on top of another to form ever longer rods of the cubes. The experiments focused on beam and arch bridges and demonstrated physical concepts of stress and load. They used sheets of paper as a bridge roadway and two unit blocks placed six inches apart as the supports. Unifix cubes served as the load. Fortunately, I saw these experiments firsthand because I was observing a graduate student who was student teaching in the class.[10]

To test the simplest type of beam bridge, they folded the paper lengthwise and placed it over the block supports. Then they carefully stacked individual cubes on the paper roadway. It sagged at two cubes and caved in at four. While they were performing these experiments, Trish circulated from one group to another, asking questions to fine tune their observations, such as, "Where were the blocks placed when the road gave way?" or "How did it give way?"—trying to "pull" and introduce more precise descriptive language.

Then they tested what would happen when another folded sheet

When the children tested the simplest type of beam bridge, the paper roadway sagged at two cubes and caved in at four. (Photograph by author)

With the added support of an arch, the paper roadway held twenty-three to forty-five cubes before sagging. When children saw this, their interest mounted, and they were eager to try the next experiment. (Photograph by author)

of paper was curved upward and inserted under the beam roadway with its two ends wedged against the block supports. With the added support of the arch, their bridges held twenty-three to forty-five cubes. The excitement started to mount.

Then they tested two versions of beam bridges in which the roadway material was folded differently. This would show how the same materials used in different ways could make the roadway stronger. First, they folded the two lengthwise sides of the paper roadway upward about three-eighths of an inch on each side to form a gutter. Their bridges drooped at three to six cubes and collapsed at twelve to fourteen. The children's interest was sparked, and they began looking excitedly at what was happening with each of the other groups.

For the final experiment, they folded the paper lengthwise to make accordion folds—mimicking the metal supports right under or just above the roadway. Then they started placing cubes on the roadway. As the roadway kept holding more and more cubes, a child shouted, "I can't believe this!" It kept holding so many loose cubes they began to fall off, so they made stacks of unifix cubes to load onto the paper. They experimented with how many should go in a stack and how they should be placed on the roadway. As they kept loading stack after stack, the children were

When children folded the long ends of the paper roadways to form a gutter, it sagged when the seventh cube was added and collapsed at thirteen. (Photograph by author)

The children screamed with excitement when they saw that the accordion-folded paper roadway held over 200 cubes. This example held 250 cubes without sagging. (Photograph by author)

screaming with excitement. The accordion-folded roadway held over 200 cubes!

I wanted the graduate students in my curriculum class to experience the same excitement, so I held a class session in Trish's classroom. First, Trish presented the broad strokes of the study and set the context for the experiments. These were set up for the graduate students at the children's tables, with the same worksheets to guide them. As they progressed through each experiment their voices grew louder, they jumped up from their tables to see what was happening at the other tables, and, as their own stack grew to what seemed like an impossible height, they laughed out loud. Their obvious pleasure and intense engagement confirmed for me that teachers need to experience this type of learning to truly understand its importance.

To the Brooklyn Bridge

Once the children completed the experiments and discussed the findings, it was time for the study to move on to suspension bridges, to the Brooklyn Bridge. The trip to the small, picturesque stone bridges of Central Park, surrounded by lush green grass, certainly hadn't prepared them for their first trip to the Brooklyn Bridge

As described in more detail at the beginning of this chapter, every-thing was different—the wind, the noise, the vibrations, the speeding cars, the wooden walkway through which they could see the roadway below them, and the sheer size of it. The massive Manhattan tower dominated their view. When it was time to head back to school, their relief was palpable. Trish had planned the trip as an impressionistic in-troduction to the bridge, never imagining the sensory overload.

Their second trip was different. It was to an area of the South Street Seaport where the entire bridge is fully visible. Children saw the stark bridge contours set against a clear blue sky, with sunlight sparkling through the cables. On their trip worksheets they sketched what they found interesting: the bridge projecting from Manhattan across the East River to Brooklyn, the Brooklyn skyline, the endless stream of cars traveling along the bridge roadway, the "tiny" people on the pedestrian walkway where they had been on the last trip, and the river life of boats and barges sailing under the bridge. On an unlabeled diagram they drew lines from the list of bridge member names to the actual members in the diagram.[11]

The shore at South Street Seaport offered the perfect vantage point from which to study the bridge and identify the major bridge members. (Photograph by and courtesy of Trish Lent)

On the next, third trip to the bridge, they walked the half mile across from Manhattan to Brooklyn. Along the way they stopped at three key points to photograph. The computer teacher was teaching the class how to use the school's new digital cameras. They were divided into small groups, each sharing one camera. At the key points they each used the "zoom in" and "zoom out" features to photograph a long shot and a detail. Trish noticed that the children walked leisurely, talking and laughing so comfortably, pointing out to each other aspects of the bridge that interested them. Back in the classroom they would learn how the bridge worked.

Trish struggled to find a way for them to understand what she had learned from her research and "experiments": how the different members of a suspension bridge worked in concert. She didn't want them to simply amass facts; she wanted them to *experience* how the bridge worked. Knowing that children's most intense learning is sensorial, she had them become the bridge. An open area in front of the classroom became Manhattan on one side, Brooklyn on the other, and the East River in between. Two children became each of the towers and took their position and faced each other so that a cable could hang from each of their shoulders. A number of children became the anchorages for each cable on both sides. Using clothesline rope a cable was held tightly, "anchored" by a number of children on one side, hung over one child's shoulder, hung loosely to the next child's shoulder, then anchored by children on the other side. The parallel cable was anchored by other children and hung from the tower children's other shoulder. With a foam-core board as the roadway, suspender cables were tied on to one of the main cables, swung downward under the board and then upward to be tied to the other main cable. With all the suspender cables in place the roadway was suspended securely.

However, with such a light roadway, they had little sense of the dynamic interaction among the bridge members.

> Mann compares how the different bridge members work together as a "a tug of war [that] is constantly happening. The heavy roadway pulls down on the main cables, but the anchorages hold them firmly and keep them from sagging."[12]

So they removed the board, and a child positioned lengthwise with arms stretched overhead acted as the roadway. The anchor children had to hold on to the cables with all their might, and the tower children struggled to hold up the weight being supported by their shoulders. When the tower children were bending under the weight, their road-way classmate was suspended crooked almost touching the floor. Chil-dren shouted, "Stand tall. Don't bend." They stood tall with all their strength and the road straightened. The onlookers cheered. Then other children wanted to be the bridge members, so they repeated this a num-ber of times, and each time, the children were glued to the drama. Now they knew the process in their muscles[13] as Trish had wanted and would never forget it. And during free time and at home, children fashioned suspension bridges using chairs, books, cereal boxes, cans, and all kinds of found objects that became the towers, roadways, cables, and anchor-ages. By the time they created their large, working suspension bridge, they were ready for the challenge.

Before they started constructing the suspension bridge, the class visited the bridge one last time, this time to interview the people walk-ing across the bridge. Trish said that "they loved interviewing; they felt like experts." She said it was as though the children owned the bridge and the walkers were their guests. It was cold, noisy, the bridge vibrated, but the children didn't seem to notice. Their poise, comfort, and obvious pleasure stood in stark contrast to their first visit to the bridge.

Children created suspension bridges using all kinds of materials. This child fash-ioned a suspension bridge out of cereal boxes, cardboard, rope, string, tape, and wooden building blocks. (Photograph by and courtesy of Trish Lent)

This eager interviewer learned about what the bridge engineer was doing on top of the bridge tower. (Photograph by and courtesy of Trish Lent)

One exciting aspect of taking trips is that neither the teacher nor the children can predict all the particulars of their experience—there are surprises. While interviewing the pedestrians, the children noticed a worker way up on top of the Manhattan tower. They all, including the pedestrians, stopped what they were doing, stood silently, eyes glued to the worker as he—like a tightrope walker—slowly climbed down the long and steep main cable, making his way onto the walkway where they were standing. Apparently there are handrails, not visible from a distance, running the length of all the main cables. A child ran up to the worker and excitedly asked if he'd like to be interviewed. He agreed, and the eager interviewer found out that he was a bridge engineer and learned about the work he was doing on top of the tower. Trish felt that of all the trips, this would be the one they'd remember. It was the thrill of asking adults questions and feeling so proud of all that they knew.

Ending the Study

The class concluded their half-year study with two culminating activities: a large model of the Brooklyn Bridge and a "poetry bridge." To build the large model, for which they'd be following the construction sequence of the Brooklyn Bridge, they would need to know the story of its construction. In preparation for the study, Trish had immersed herself in the dramatic story. In essence, the story of the Brooklyn Bridge dramatically illustrates the interaction between a human society and the physical world, which Mitchell believed was so important for children to understand.[14] Trish didn't expect children to learn all the social and historical subtleties, but her own deep knowledge of the subject—gained from all of her research—would enable her to ask thoughtful questions, be responsive to what the children bring to the study, and plan opportunities for experiences that would enable children to come to their own understandings.

The children's imaginations were captured by the dramatic story of the Roebling family, who conceived, designed, and oversaw the construction of the Brooklyn Bridge. And they learned about workers who risked their lives every day in the caissons, constructing the towers, and working on the cables—and were in awe of the workers' bravery. As they learned about the construction process they did the caissons demonstrations and the cable-spinning activity that are described early in the chapter.

The children were so engaged with the bridge story that by the time Elizabeth Mann was invited to the class to read and discuss her book, they felt like experts and spoke with her as though to a peer. At this point, as they were approaching the last phase of the study, the children had more knowledge about the bridge than anyone they knew.

When I visited the class, I saw how proud the children were of the model they had built together, how each detail of its construction was important to them. The care with which they walked around this twenty-one-foot model that occupied one-quarter of the room was striking. (Photograph by and courtesy of Trish Lent)

Bridge Members Have to Work Together to Make the Bridge Stand

They spent two weeks working on the model. Each bridge team worked on the member it had researched earlier in the study, and they followed the construction sequence of the Brooklyn Bridge. Trish found it "spectacular" that something so "wonderful" could be created from such ordinary materials—cardboard boxes, paper, rope, tape, and paint. It stood twenty-one feet long; the roadway was suspended from the cables, which were chained to the anchorages. They had a ribbon cutting to announce its opening, and to simulate the fireworks set off at the opening of the Brooklyn Bridge the children excitedly shot party poppers into the air.

When I made a special visit to the class to see the bridge, I noticed how carefully the children walked around this structure that covered one-quarter of the room. A child saw me looking at the bridge and proceeded to tell me the entire story of the Roeblings and how the Brooklyn Bridge was constructed, and then the story of their own suspension bridge. Other children joined us and added to her story. I was struck by how important each detail was to these children and how proud they were of what they had created. And the bridge was indeed as Trish described it, wonderful. When they painted it, they departed from the grays of the Brooklyn Bridge and covered the sections in lush, deep color. Its bright greens, purples, and yellows sparkled as the sun poured in through the classroom windows.

Building a Poem Like a Bridge

The study ended with the poetry bridge. This bridge seemed to grow naturally from the shared experience of the study, specifically from the bridge trip to Central Park; the children's enjoyment of "concrete" poems, which are written in the shape of the topic; and their special love of one particular poem. On the park trip Trish had asked the children to take their time, look carefully at each of the three bridges they were focusing on, observe them from different angles, walk across them, touch the stone, think hard to find the words that expressed their experience of the bridge, then record the words on their trip sheets. Back in the classroom Trish listed all of their words on a chart paper. They read the words together and then wrote bridge poems using these evocative words and others. From the weekly reading and sharing of many different kinds of poems they, like most children, found concrete poetry fun and enjoyed creating their own.

These were the influences, but the idea to do the poetry bridge came from a child's simple question, "Could we build a poem like a bridge?" The idea of creating a concrete poem in the shape of a bridge seemed to capture the children's imaginations, and throughout the project the child's original wording stuck—they were *building* the poem. But they just couldn't figure out how to do it. Trish suggested they write separate poems for each of the main bridge members. Each bridge team could focus on the bridge member it had researched earlier in the study. Then they'd write their poem into the shape of the towers, the roadway, the cables, the caissons, or the anchorages.

The children were thrilled when Trish suggested they use their favorite poem, "Things to Do If You Are a Subway" by Bobbi Katz, as a model for their writing:

Pretend you are a dragon.
Live in underground caves.
Roar about underneath the city.
Swallow piles of people.
Spit them out at the next station.
Zoom through the darkness.
Be an express.
Go fast.
Make as much noise as you please.[15]

They spent time looking at the poem together and discussing what they noticed. They saw that the reader was asked to be the subway, but also that it was more complicated than that—they were being asked to pretend to be an animal that is like the subway, that becomes the subway. They also noticed that every line began with an action word and learned that these were verbs.

So their task was to think of an animal that was like the bridge member and then find the action words that fit the animal being the bridge part. Trish knew this would be difficult, so she spent time working with each group. Essentially, they were being asked to stretch their knowledge of the bridge member to the point where they bring it to life and give it character. They were also stretching their ability to use language in evocative ways. And they spent a lot of time thinking of just the right animal and then the right verbs. The roadway team was stumped, until one child compared the roadway stretching from one side to the other to a gazelle leaping across space. They had it—"Pretend you are a gazelle." The towers became giraffes, the caissons giant turtles, the main cables pythons, the suspender cables monkeys, and the anchorages elephants. They worked hard on each of these poems and seemed to love them.

This "Brooklyn half" of the nine-foot poetry bridge is practically a mirror image to the "Manhattan half." Notice the anchorage (box to the left that reads, "Pretend you are an elephant . . .") and the caisson (box below the tower that reads, "Pretend you are a turtle . . ."). (Photograph by and courtesy of Trish Lent)

Now they needed the actual bridge form to make this a concrete poem—or "cement" poem as the children kept calling it. For this, Trish selected a clear, simple diagram of a suspension bridge taken from Mann's book. She photocopied it, and they learned how to enlarge the diagram using the grid method. On brown paper they enlarged it to approximately nine feet in length. Then, as carefully as they could, each group wrote its poem within or on the bridge member.

Their plan was to present it to their parents. So each group rehearsed its poem. Trish said they always emphasized the first word, "pretend." On the big day, Trish arranged it so that the parents sat in the middle in a circle and the children stretched around the perimeter, so that their voices would surround the parents. Then, each group performed its poem. After they were through, Trish said that these bridge members didn't work one at a time but worked together to make the bridge stand. So then they began again, and after the first group said its first two lines, the second group joined in with its poem, emphasizing "Pretend you are . . ." Each group joined in after two lines of the previous group. All their voices filled the room and the din was reminiscent of the bridge itself, until all you heard was the last lines from the tower group: "Stand tall. Don't lean. Be proud."

Chapter 3

"I Didn't Even Know There Was a River"

Unlike many of her peers who also relocated to New York City to attend Bank Street, Karen Kriesberg had no thought of remaining in the city once she completed her master's degree.[1] Up until that year, she had spent her entire life on Long Island, and it was her home. Her goal had always been to teach in a Long Island public school. So when she decided on a topic for her thesis, she chose to expand the study she had developed in the fall 1990 semester for the curriculum class I taught. It was a curriculum on Native Americans of Long Island for fourth graders—the grade she most wanted to teach and the mandated social studies topic for fourth graders for many of Long Island's school systems. I agreed to be her thesis advisor and throughout the spring 1991 semester saw how intensively she worked on the project. What distinguished her study from most of the standard curricula on Native Americans was that it focused not on some generalized group of Eastern Woodland Indians or the Plains Indians during some idyllic past, but specifically on the Native Americans of Long Island, in the present as well as the past.

This section follows Karen as she explores forest and sea shore areas, follows a river to the bay, climbs to Long Island's highest point, visits the Shinnecock Reservation, and gets to know the tribal historian and his family. Though the finished study reflected extensive research using secondary sources, it was what she learned through these firsthand experiences that enabled her to craft opportunities for children to explore and experience the excitement of making their own discoveries.

Ironically, throughout Karen's nineteen years of teaching on Long Island, though she has taught almost every elementary school grade, she has never taught fourth grade or the study of Native Americans. Yet the process of developing that study has served as a model for the many social studies curricula she has developed.

It was as though all the aspects of her degree came together in this thesis study. She said that the study "was all about making connections"—between geography and culture, between ignorance and stereotyping, and also between what she experienced and what she planned for children. While working on her thesis, she was student teaching with a teacher who made an indelible impression. What and how this teacher taught was a serious pursuit. The class was studying the early Dutch settlement of Manhattan, which Karen had known little about. During weekends the teacher worked in a colonial village in New Jersey and was skillful at and demonstrated many essential crafts, such as carding of wool, spinning, and weaving. Karen visited her there and realized how much of herself this teacher brought to her work in the classroom and how much she brought that couldn't be obtained solely from books. Also this teacher modeled what Karen was learning in her graduate geography and curriculum classes. With this mentor teacher and the children she was student teaching, she explored downtown Manhattan and retraced the steps of the early settlers. Throughout the study, the class used a large relief map they had created using sawdust and wheat paste as the modeling mixture. This "working" map showed the land contours on lower Manhattan and of surrounding areas and showed the waterways. Each time they made new geographic discoveries or learned about such topics as housing or travel routes, they represented what they had learned on the map. In this way the blank geographic map grew into a model of a functioning colony, with houses, boats, roads, fields, and the wall for which Wall Street would be named. The map also served as a focal point for thinking together and drawing relationships between the geography and the kind of settlement that emerged.

Karen and her mentor teacher had both been inspired by Lucy Sprague Mitchell's vision of teachers who actively engage with the physical and social world themselves. Mitchell believed that the environment, the physical-social world teachers and children inhabit, offers the raw material for discovering human-geographic relationships—the ways in which the natural world is used to meet human needs and the ways in which the earth "conditions" the lives of humans. She believed that firsthand investigation of the environment would offer generative source material for curricula—for her graduate students as well as for children.[2] In *Young Geographers*, a classic work on geography education for children, Mitchell wrote, "[Teachers] must . . . be experimenters; they must hunt for sources and study the relationships; they must explore the environment; they must analyze the culture of which they are a part, see what part of it is geographic, what part historic; they must think; they must play."[3] So in developing her own curriculum, Karen immersed herself in the environment she thought she knew so well, and could never have anticipated where this exploration would lead her.

Exploring the Forest and the River

She began her thesis research with the geography. In doing this Karen built upon Mitchell's belief that human beings, like all other living

As Karen followed the stream, she learned from a map that the stream extended underground to Long Island's drinking water. (Photograph by author)

species, are essentially geographic entities. They live *on* the earth and sustain themselves through "earth forces"—air, water, soil, what we call natural resources. For Mitchell and others who espoused the new "human geography," specific cultures could not be understood without fully knowing about the dynamic interaction between people and the natural world they inhabit. So Karen set about "living" Long Island's seashores, rivers, and forests.

On a bitter cold day in early February, Karen and her mother set out by car for the Caleb Smith State Park. It is a 543-acre wildlife preserve with 145 species of birds and 20 species of mammals using the park. There were freshwater wetlands, streams, upland woods, and the freshwater part of Nissequogue River flowing through it. Karen left the warmth of the car to follow the river on foot south to where it washes into the Long Island Sound. As she did this she remembered her Bank Street geography professor exclaiming, "You have to follow a river to the bay to understand its importance." (Using Karen's account as a guide, on a cold February day I retraced her steps with a camera. Although it was nineteen years later, it was as though I were walking alongside her, seeing the river and bay through her eyes. The photographs try to capture some of the detail of what she discovered.)

The stream flowed gently into this pond. (Photograph by author)

As she walked, she noticed the variety of trees and the "gently flowing" stream that led into a pond. She found these on the map she carried and learned that the stream water flowed from underground layers of porous rock and sand, and that these extended from the water table that supplies Long Island's drinking water. She realized that up to that point, she had not thought much about the source of her drinking water. She wondered if many Long Island children would have a sense of where their water came from. She remembers feeling "embarrassed." She had grown up nearby and gone to school nearby but "didn't even know that there was a river." It is unlikely that she had never seen the river, but it was background, essentially a word, an idea. She had never gone to the river or looked at it as a source of life that sustained plants, animals, and people. She had never felt the cold freshness of river water or noticed its beauty. She realized the profound difference between the knowing of something casually and *experiencing* it. And the words she wrote in a paper on John Dewey's *Experience and Education* were vividly illustrated for her—that for an experience to be educative, there had to be an interaction between the person and the environment in which the person is fully present.[4] And as Dewey might have predicted, both she and the river would never be the same—*and neither would her teaching.*

Karen had never before felt the cold freshness of the river water or noticed its beauty. (Photograph by author)

When Karen saw the massive root structures of many of the overturned trees, she realized that some of them were extremely old. (Photograph by author)

She placed her hand in the ice-cold river feeling its current and re-alized that the river was flowing north. She thought about how many children, once they acquire a sense of direction, tend to believe that rivers must flow from north to south. Throughout her exploration, she was experiencing the river as an adult and at the same trying to capture a child's-eye view, what the experience might be for a fourth grader. She saw all the uprooted trees in the wetlands and just how massive the roots were and realized that these trees were probably very old. At one point she saw a dam and noticed how rapidly the water flowed to the dam. She saw a marker on the side of the river that gauged the depth of the river. She read on the map that the Nissequogue was known as a "meandering river." She knew that had she merely read this, she could never have imagined the beauty of its graceful "meandering."

Karen returned to the warmth of the car, and she and her mother followed the river north to its mouth at Short Beach in Smithtown Bay. She saw how the river widens as it approaches the bay. She saw the bluffs and necks of the north shoreline. When they arrived at the estuary, she left the car again and explored the beach area. The beach erosion was noticeable. She stood on the end of the Short Beach peninsula and watched the fresh river water flow into the salt water of the bay. She saw a "vast quantity" of clam and mussel shells on the bay's shoreline and imagined how the river and bay teemed with life when Native Americans inhabited this area. On one of the maps she was using, it stated that this area was the site of a major settlement of the Nesaquake Indians—and all of a sudden, it "all made sense." "All the elements of culture were there." There was the freshwater from the river for drinking, bathing, and fishing; the salt water of the bay as a rich source of shell fish; the silt that washed onto the banks leaving fertilized soil, ideal for planting; the forests for hunting and for many of the raw materials for housing and tools; and the waterways for travel. Now she felt she could plan opportunities for children to explore and discover, to see for themselves that "it all makes sense," and experience the thrill of it as she had.

As Karen approached the beach environment of the bay, the river widened, and freshwater from the river flowed into the salt water of the bay. It was at that moment that it all "made sense" to her. She understood why Native Americans made this area the site of a major settlement. (Photograph by author)

When Karen saw all the clam and mussel shells, she imagined how the river and bay teemed with life when Native Americans lived in the area. (Photograph by author)

As part of the geography phase of the study, Karen knew she wanted children to climb all the way to the top of Jane's Hill, the highest point of Long Island. She wanted the children to look out over a vast panorama, just as she had done as a child. In retracing her steps as an adult, she saw how what had seemed like a mountain was really a hill, and the climb was not steep or long, which gave her insight into a young child's experience of the place. Once she reached the highest point, she was stunned by what she saw. During the seventeen-year interim between her visit as a child and the visit for the thesis, the young trees that had covered the hillside had grown so tall and full that there was no view at all. Though it was a disappointment, she realized just how important it is for teachers to go on the trip beforehand, even if they think they know the place.

A Visit to the Shinnecock Reservation

In mid-February, while still working on the geographic phase of the study, Karen read an article in the Sunday magazine section of a prominent Long Island newspaper on how Native Americans are portrayed in

Long Island school curricula. The article sparked a series of events that had a profound impact on Karen as a person as well as a teacher, and altered the meaning of the curriculum for her. The article described how Long Island Native Americans, if mentioned at all, play a minor role in school curricula on Long Island history. The article quoted the tribal historian, Eugene Cuffee, of the Shinnecock people who maintained that populations of Indians who continue to live on Long Island are not mentioned in the schools. He decried how children are exposed regularly to many demeaning and "inauthentic" images of Native Americans: on greeting cards, children's play costumes, wrapping paper, sports' teams logos, costume and play jewelry, songs, cartoons, movies, and, perhaps most egregious, in school textbooks. He wanted Long Island Indian history and culture to be given its long overdue place in the curriculum, and wanted children to learn about the lives and culture of Long Island Native Americans today, which would help counteract the impact of the demeaning images.

Through contacting the newspaper, Karen was given Cuffee's phone number. When she called to ask if she could interview him about his comments in the article, he said he gave interviews infrequently. When she explained what she was working on, without hesitation he set a meeting for early March. They would meet at his home on the Shinnecock Reservation.

The 750-acre Shinnecock Reservation is three miles west of Southampton, which, since the 1920s, has been one of the wealthiest resort towns on the East Coast. The reservation now has approximately 500 residents, 180 households. The median income is $14,000 a year. Relatively recent archaeological discoveries show that the Shinnecock have lived in this area of Long Island for over a thousand years. The Shinnecock are considered one of the oldest self-governing Native American tribes in the country. Since 1979 they have been fighting for federal recognition as an Indian nation, which would entitle the Shinnecock to a full range of federal benefits.

Though Karen had done research on the Shinnecock and specifically on the history of the illustrious Cuffee family, she was intensely aware of what she didn't know and approached the visit with trepidation. She knew that if she hoped to design a curriculum entitled "Native Americans of Long Island," she had to understand this community herself before she could even begin to think about what she would plan for children.

When Cuffee greeted her warmly, she started to calm down. He walked her through the grounds. She was struck by just how run-down the houses were and learned that because the land was being held in trust for them by the government, they could not receive mortgages. And given the low income levels, much of the housing was substandard and even dangerous. She noticed that there were "no plantings of any kind" and no fences. The roads were dirt. The bitter cold and threatening gray overcast added to the depressed quality of the community. As they approached her host's home, she noticed a dog tied to a post. Cuffee said the dog's name was Wolf, because he was part wolf. At that moment she realized just how unaware she had been. It was as though, just a few miles from where she had grown up, she had entered an "alternate universe." And the contrast to nearby Southampton seemed "insane."

Cuffee's home was more substantial than many of the others. She was invited in and welcomed by his wife and daughter. She remembers the relief she felt by the warmth from the fireplace and her gratitude for the hot tea they served her. They showed her tribal artifacts, some of which had been skillfully crafted by Cuffee and his family. When he proudly showed a decoy, she shared what she had learned about Cuffee's ancestor, who is famous for his carved decoys—and they felt honored that she had taken the time to learn about the family. He described the dream he had of a Shinnecock museum that would make public their history, culture, and artifacts and crafts. Karen saw just how important this dream was to them and found that she shared their hope but was saddened by the thought that they might never have enough money to make this a reality.

They looked at archival and family photographs and told her the stories the photos evoked. They discussed issues of tribal governance, the struggle to receive federal recognition, their endless legal battles with Southampton to regain lands they believed had been illegally taken from them, and their efforts to revive the oyster farming, which had been an important source of income until it was killed by the pollution of the waters. She shared their excitement when they showed her the fledgling oyster beds. They said that most residents work as groundskeepers at the nearby wealthy estates and at the famous golf course or as domestic servants.

Then they talked about the schools. Cuffee mentioned that his and other residents' children went to the Southampton public schools, and if they studied Native Americans, it was frequently the Plains Indians—and there was never any mention that Native Americans lived nearby and not only attended their school but were members of the class. He talked about the damage that continues to be done by the stereotypes that are perpetuated in schools.

Karen asked him what he thought was important for school children to know about Native Americans. He was clear about this. There were three understandings he wanted children to come away with:

He wanted children to know how, since the War of 1812, Native Americans came to the defense of this country. This was even before 1924, when Congress finally considered them worthy of citizenship. Right up to World War II, their participation was voluntary, and a large majority of the 25,000 Native American men and women who fought in WWII volunteered. . . .[5]

The Long Island whaling industry owed its success to Native Americans. Seldom would a whaling ship leave Sag Harbor without Native American crew members, especially the harpooners. The Shinnecock were most important because of their "uncommon skill" and experience, which dated to long before Europeans arrived on Long Island. Though school textbooks speak of the importance of whaling to the Northeast and the bravery of the captains and crews, little if anything is mentioned of the central role of Native Americans. . . .[6]

Most important, Native Americans exist today. They are not some artifact of history. And Native Americans live on Long Island, they are their neighbors, hold jobs on Long Island, and attend the public schools. Not only are they real and part of the community, they are endlessly "fighting to hold on to their heritage."[7]

Her visit lasted most of the day. Though she knew she would need time to think about all that she had experienced that day, she left feeling a greater sense of purpose. Meeting Eugene Cuffee, spending the day with his family, and seeing and learning about the reservation seemed to transform the project. She felt a sense of responsibility she hadn't before. The study now represented the people she met that day and the others she hadn't met. It was now more important for Karen to create the study and bring it to life with children. Karen said, "It was no longer just a thesis. . . . You have to be passionate about what you are doing and have to believe in it for it to take shape. You get that from experience. And you need the passion to be a teacher."

The Thesis and Beyond

The finished study began with the geography. Maps, which Karen considered "a piece of the puzzle," became a focal point for thinking together about the relationship between the physical and the social world, a tool for understanding the kind of culture that evolved. On large teacher-made maps the children would chart their own travels and, through the place labeling, learn the reasons for the names given to locations. A large relief map made of plasticine, a water-resistant oil-based clay, would be placed in a watertight rectangular plastic tub. The map would be "flooded" with water. The resulting land and water masses would illustrate that islands are part of the surrounding land and don't float, as so many children imagine, and that rivers flow from high to low ground. They would also illustrate other land and water formations found on Long Island.

In 2001, against overwhelming odds, the Shinnecock realized their dream of opening a museum dedicated to their people's history, culture, and lives today. This visitors' sign can be seen from the Montauk Highway, one-quarter mile east of Southampton College. (Photograph by author)

With geography as a base, the thesis study investigates "strands of culture," such as food, housing, social organization, modes of travel, religion, folklore, crafts, and the current Native Americans of Long Island. Though she never had the opportunity to teach this study, the principal who hired her asked her to share the study with the teachers of fourth grade, and they used it for years. It was also used in other schools. At Bank Street College, throughout the nineteen years since it was created, it may be the most read and used thesis ever. Last year the library had to bind another circulating copy.

Visitors are taken with the raw power of the wooden relief sculpted onto the entrance doorway. (Photograph by author)

Over the next nineteen years, Karen developed studies of Ancient Egypt; the Inca; the Aztecs; the Middle Ages; the school neighborhood; and, for this school year, a study of Japan. She said she has never felt at a loss, that she always "goes back to her roots." She finds a way into the culture through geography and works to clarify for herself what she thinks is important for children to learn about the people they would be studying. As she did for the Native American study, she seeks to experience and "live" the topic so that it "makes sense" to her. She believes that only then is she able to shape a learning process that would also "make sense" to children.

For years Karen kept in touch with Eugene Cuffee. When the thesis was completed, she presented a copy to him to be used as a resource on the reservation. When she married, she brought her husband to the reservation to introduce him to Cuffee. And for years they were invited to and attended the Shinnecock powwows. In 2001, the Shinnecock National Cultural Center and Museum opened, the first and only Indian-owned museum on Long Island, and the only museum completely constructed by Native Americans. They have also revived the oyster farming and in June 2010 received the federal recognition they had sought for so many years. Even against overwhelming odds, the Shinnecock have made some of their dreams real—such an important and hopeful message for children.

Chapter 4

Three Teachers Honoring Children's Environment

Across the three studies, portraits emerge of three distinct teachers, each approaching the process of learning and teaching as an individual. Yet their stories share common concerns, questions, and directions as they make decisions about what they consider most important for their students to learn and decide how they should learn it. This chapter examines the common paths taken across the dramatic differences in the topics pursued and in the children's worlds:

- the physical setting of the study, the *where*, profoundly influenced the *what* of curriculum, the substance of what they learned
- teachers ventured into uncomfortable terrain
- teachers came to know a topic more deeply through interactions with colleagues, children's parents, experts, and family members and friends
- teachers' own process of coming to know vitalized what they did with children
- a study evolved through a dynamic interaction among the children, their teacher, and the substance of the curriculum
- children were introduced to impressive role models
- children engaged with a rich body of content, and used academic skills to deepen their understanding of that content
- ultimately, through the process of working and learning together, classes became communities.

The *Where* Influenced the *What* of Curriculum

Each teacher made the decision that in-depth knowledge of the children's environment was important. Laura Gerrity wanted her children to penetrate the world around them before they move beyond it. She believed that before her children could venture into "communities of the world," they needed to broaden their understanding of their own community and discover that it *was* a community, that the violence and abandoned buildings were by no means the total picture. She wanted them to have the experience so important to all children's development—to explore their environment physically and socially as well as intellectually and build a base upon which to understand the concept of community. In doing so, the children not only deepened their understanding of their own background, they learned about the backgrounds of their classmates and of their teachers—and school became relevant *to them*. It was as though they woke up. Listening was not just something they should do because the teacher said so. The class discussions were interesting and seemed important to them; they weren't just about giving right answers, and they learned that they had something to say.

Trish Lent and her grade-level colleagues focused on the Brooklyn Bridge because it is a major transportation hub located just a short walk from the school. The focus built on young children's love of roadways and conveyances, which is endlessly displayed in the children's play. It also built on the six-, seven-, and eight-year-olds' drive to understand how things work. Investigating the story of the Brooklyn Bridge offered a unique entry into the city's history and geography. As the study unfolded, Trish and the children saw how the Brooklyn Bridge could be a symbol for a city of islands, and the concept of a bridge was forever changed for all of them.

Karen Kriesberg, in developing her study for Long Island children, focused on the relationship between the way of life Native Americans developed and the specific physical environment they inhabited. In visiting the Shinnecock Reservation, Karen discovered for herself that Native Americans were and always had been her neighbors. They may have even been classmates of hers or would be of the students she would teach. As she explored that environment, the study grew in importance and complexity for her, and one could easily imagine that it would be important for the children she would teach. No longer was it solely a study of a people living in some timeless past. Following her visit to the

Shinnecock, she shared her experience with the New York City children she student taught. Though all of them had studied Eastern Woodland Indians the year before, they were stunned that Native Americans lived on Long Island and asked if they lived in teepees.

Each of the three teachers drew from Lucy Sprague Mitchell's belief that children have a driving need to know and be competent in their own environment, that it is inherently interesting to them—in fact Mitchell believed, and teachers have repeatedly confirmed, that children have a romance with the world around them—the roadways, trains, bridges, boats and rivers, tall buildings, construction sites, parks and trees, and workers who keep their world functioning. For Mitchell, in-depth exploration of the "here and now" world offers the generative content that children could build on as they grow and examine how their world connects in time and place to ever larger spheres—the state, region, nation, and world.

Perhaps most important, each of these studies would link children to their immediate environment. They would be sensitive to and care about aspects of their world that previously were background or virtually nonexistent. Their neighbors, the river, and the land were no longer background.

Each Teacher Ventured into Uncomfortable Terrain

To develop the studies, each teacher ventured into the unknown. Laura knew this study would be different from anything she had done before. Gradually she integrated activities in which the children were more actively engaged. Deep down she felt that the engaging activities were pleasurable but unsystematic, and she questioned whether the activities were serving her sense of being a "progressive" teacher more than serving the children. Dewey's comments in *Experience and Education* resonated when he spoke of learning experiences that were "agreeable" but "not linked cumulatively to one another."[1] She understood that the continuity of learning opportunities would enable children to draw from and build on what they had already learned from their own experience as they encounter a new idea, a problem, a new experience—and deepen what they know and understand. For Dewey, the continuity is essential to learning from experience.[2] She would work to resolve this through the study.

By embarking on the curriculum, she departed from ways of teaching that had grown comfortable. She was putting herself on the line by teaching in a way she believed would meet the needs of her children. As a result she ventured into the complex, emotionally charged topic of race. Through her years of teaching she had grown gradually from relying on other teachers to discuss issues of race with her class to leading these conversations herself. These discussions of race would arise around Martin Luther King Day or when children brought a related news item into the class. Her present curriculum would demand much more of her emotionally as well as intellectually. She knew the topic of race could pervade the neighborhood study, and she would continually have to examine who she was as a white teacher in the lives of predominately African American children.

Though Trish had traveled over the Brooklyn Bridge an untold number of times, she had never given any thought to how the bridge worked. She said she "knew nothing about the bridge or bridges in general," and feared she might never understand how they work.

Karen felt unsettled when she realized that she knew so much less about her physical and social environment than she had thought, and as she investigated the topic, she realized how much she needed to know. Though she had done research on the Shinnecock Reservation and the Cuffee family, she asked herself, "Who am I to be interviewing a tribal historian when I know so little about the lives of Long Island Native Americans?" She "felt too young [twenty-three at the time], uninformed, and inadequate." But, like Laura and Trish, she had a purpose and driving need to know.

Each teacher placed herself in the uncomfortable position of *not knowing*, a state children live in throughout their schooling. Most teachers have taught children who feel they should know, they must know, and expend tremendous energy on appearing to know, which makes it so much harder for them to learn. It is not so different for teachers—whom many view simply as the possessors and dispensers of knowledge. And yet, to learn, by definition, one has to not know. By tolerating the vulnerability of not knowing, these three teachers opened themselves to possibilities they could never have predicted. They invested themselves, became more sensitive to the experience of their students as they themselves faced the self-doubt, struggles, and frustrations of learning, and also experienced the resulting satisfaction, joys, and excitement. As Laura, Trish, and Karen embarked on their curricula, they approached the teaching-learning process with humility and modeled what they were asking of the children as they continued learning along with them. Consequently, their teaching remained fresh and vital.

The Teachers' Own Process of Coming to Know Vitalized What They Did with Children

Each study was transformed through the teacher's learning from experience. Though it may sound simplistic, what each teacher achieved grew from her personal efforts to understand the topic. Unfortunately, it is significant to state that they researched the topic at all. Too often, the content of a social studies curriculum grows primarily from chapters in a textbook—the reading of the chapter and the answering of the questions at the end. Or teachers simply follow a script in a teacher's guide or the instructions of "the consultants." Frequently, when teachers do research a topic, they first search the wealth of possibilities offered by the Internet. The problem is that the research too often ends there—without penetrating the wealth of resources in the world around them.

Even more important than these considerations, through their own research they questioned themselves, explored different ways of knowing, and experimented. In the process they discovered the power of discovery and the excitement of learning from experience. They grew to know the topics in their hearts and bodies as well as their minds. And they grew in their ability to offer learning through which their students would also discover and experience the power of learning. In becoming learners they made the study their own; each became more of a teacher and more of a person. Throughout her nineteen years of teaching, Karen has continually gone back to the same method of research, which has kept her teaching alive. There seems always to be talk about how to keep teachers from leaving the profession. Perhaps we should be asking how teachers could remain alive to the rewards of learning.

Trish never could have predicted that her homemade efforts to understand the complex process of building the Brooklyn Bridge would spark her imagination and fuel a drive to know more. Her own explorations of neighborhood bridges and the Central Park bridges broadened her perspective as she built for herself a concept of *bridge*. Her exploring the Brooklyn Bridge and the geography it spans and connects stimulated some of the major learning opportunities she offered to children.

When Laura explored the neighborhood herself, it was as though she were seeing it for the first time and was surprised at the richness she discovered, which was what she wanted for the children in the first place. Her teacher colleagues, the children's parents, and community people became major sources of the curriculum, made it relevant to the children's lives and concerns, and ultimately brought the study to life.

When Karen explored the Nissequogue River and followed it to the bay, the relationship between geography and human society was no longer an abstraction. And when she climbed Jane's Hill, she discovered that it no longer offered the panoramic view of the surrounding land, making it unsuitable for a class trip. Her visit to Shinnecock Reservation and speaking with Cuffee and his family transformed the study for her. It was "no longer simply a thesis." Consulting solely the Shinnecock Reservation website could not have produced this result.

In addition to the generative primary sources, each teacher searched for and amassed a range of secondary sources. They selected a rich collection of children's books to read aloud, use for class research assignments, and place on the library shelves. The selection included fiction and folklore that added valuable material for discussion and nonfiction that read with the elegance of the best fiction. They also amassed maps, illustrations, and photographs. But none of these resources was or could be a substitute for their own firsthand experience.

The Teacher Came to Know the Topic More Deeply Through Interactions with Others

In the process of researching and developing the studies, each teacher worked with others. What may have begun with individual questions moved to conversations with others—colleagues, children's parents, community people, family members, and college professors. Through these exchanges the teachers developed stronger working relationships, experienced the benefits of working as a team, grew to understand the complexity of the topic and think deeply about it, explored the topic in ways they would never have anticipated, and received the encouragement and support to forge ahead.

When Laura's colleagues said that she, *their teacher*, should be leading the discussions on race, their obvious trust and faith in her enabled her to move forward as a teacher and ultimately become "more of [herself]." Before she began the study, she hoped it would be important to the children. Yet she never imagined the depth of meaning that would unfold through her discussions with the parents and teachers who visited the class and the community people the class visited. She never expected the power of the presentations and the intensity with which the children responded. And it was fun for the visitors, as well as for Laura and the children, to work together sewing, cooking, and creating toys and games. Little wonder that when the class started taking trips into the neighborhood, there were many parent volunteers. Her relationships with her colleagues and the children's families had grown stronger. And working together was modeled during the classroom visits when the children saw their teacher work as a team with their parents and other teachers—which was asked of them and of so many school children throughout the country. Trust and caring were illustrated dramatically to the children when their first classroom visitor, Ms. Hale, who had been many of the children's kindergarten teacher, asked Laura to tell the story of how her father was cheated out of his land, because it was too painful for her to tell.

In her exchanges with the people they visited in the neighborhood, Laura realized that it was not just she and the children who benefited, but also those they visited, who were given an opportunity they may seldom, if ever, get to discuss their background and the importance of their work with a large group of admirers.

Throughout the Brooklyn Bridge study, Trish worked with her three grade-level colleagues. They pressed her to do the study in the first place, which ended up being a high point of her nine years of teaching. From the colleague who had taught science, she learned how to do experiments with the class, which she had never attempted before, and the experiments fueled an excitement in the children and in her that she had never expected. Also, with her husband as partner, she tackled aspects of the construction she found the most confusing, the cable spinning and the complex process of the work in and above the caissons. Doing the homemade experiments with her husband gave Trish the confidence to try working out the dynamic interaction of the separate members of a suspension bridge by using the children as the members—which enabled them to experience and understand the interaction through their bodies. What she had feared the most, the engineering, became her greatest source of satisfaction.

Through Karen's interactions with Eugene Cuffee, the thesis study changed dramatically. Information she had acquired as a child about Native Americans—such as their fighting in the nation's wars, even when they were denied citizenship—was suddenly no longer simply facts she learned in school; they applied to people—people she now knew and cared about. Learning about how the Shinnecock oyster business collapsed because of water pollution made her more conscious of the relationship between the natural world and people's ways of life—which was an idea that stimulated much of what she created in the thesis. Throughout her process of creating the study, she consulted her mentor teacher with whom she was student teaching, who had deep knowledge of Eastern Woodland Indians and of teaching children. Her ongoing discussions with her Bank Street geography professor influenced how she did her research and the ways in which she gave geography a central role in the study.

The experiences of Laura, Trish, and Karen illustrate just how important it is for teachers to discuss their work with colleagues, mentors, and friends. Through such exchange with others, each grew as a teacher and as a person. I am reminded of what I learned early in my career, that "teaching is too hard to do alone."

The Study Evolved Through Dynamic Interaction Among the Children, their Teacher, and the Substance of the Curriculum

Teaching and Learning as an Interaction

For Laura, Trish, and Karen, the stimulus to learn came from the children's world and the children themselves. The studies that evolved were not geared to an abstract notion of "the child" or a grade-level norm, but to the actual individuals—who have their own histories, interests, aptitudes, and struggles.

In a real sense each curriculum grew from an interaction among these individuals, their teacher, and the content, which personalized what they were learning and made it relevant to their lives. For Laura, the children's questions and comments helped shape the learning opportunities that ended up being so important to the children and their families.

Throughout the Brooklyn Bridge study, the children's contributions fueled their investment. The most dramatic example of their influence on the study is how one child's suggestion led to what Trish described as the "most magical moment in any classroom"—the creation and dramatization of the poetry bridge.

Though Karen never taught the Native American study, she designed it as an interaction, an organic process, and not as a blueprint. The

children's immediate environment would offer the content, not necessarily the places and people featured in the study. All the trips, discussions, and activities are designed as "possible" learning opportunities,
modeling what can be done.

In each study children's desire to learn grows from having an impact
on their environment, realizing that who they are and what they think
are important. And in each study, teachers are making curriculum
decisions based on their deep knowledge of the content and on where
their children take that content.

Following Scripts

The results Laura and Trish achieved would have been impossible had
each teacher followed a predetermined script and a predetermined
timeline. Teachers reading this might rightfully say that their principals would not let them teach in these ways—which is just what
Laura thought before she even attempted the study. Both Laura and
Trish were respected and trusted by their principals. More important
than this, they presented their principals with detailed, coherent plans,
showing the substance of their studies and how skill development was
integrated throughout. I encourage students in the curriculum class
I teach to present to their supervisors the strenuously researched and
thoughtfully detailed studies they create for the course. When they do,
many are surprised at the administrator's interest in their work and
even more surprised that they are given the opportunity to depart from
the script and teach the studies they developed specifically for their
children.

I remember when I was required to use a script with children. I had
to go out to schools and demonstrate learning materials for an educational resource center. I especially remember my first day "in the field."
I sat with a group of six-year-olds, their teacher, and the principal. The
materials had a series of activities. I followed my script through the first
activity, and the children responded just the way the script said they
would. They felt smart and were beaming—and I thought this job was
going to be fun. We moved to the second activity, but this time the children's responses were completely different from the script. I gave the
recommended prompts to help them, but to no avail. The recommended
comments did not please them. I particularly remember one little girl's
scowl. The third activity was just as bad—none of the answers, prompts,
or comments made a difference. It was years later, when I was pursuing

a degree in education, that I realized that the children's responses were in fact logical, which I was unable to see because I was looking for the answer they were *supposed to give.*

I observed a similar, though more serious, experience when visiting the classrooms of two student teachers, each working in a second grade in different public schools in different parts of the city. Both schools hired the same consultants, and in both classes the children had to do the same activity. They were asked to use their favorite stuffed animal, doll, or toy and describe in writing a memory the object evokes for them. On the day they were to read these, they brought in their treasured objects—stuffed animals that had been so loved they were about to disintegrate; dolls; and toy trucks and cars and planes, all full of dents and scratches. As they unpacked their objects their spontaneous discussion could have gone on all morning. It was touching to see a big seven-year-old holding a panda bear as though it were a newborn chick. Then they read their writing. Each child, instead of writing about a specific memory, wrote about what the objects meant to them—how they felt when they received them as a gift, how they played with them, and how they still go to sleep with them. The sense of well-being in that class was palpable, until the teacher said, "All of you did it all wrong. You were supposed to do . . ." I remember seeing their smiles drop. What drove the teacher's response was not that she was uncaring or unkind, but that she was looking for the prescribed response to the assignment and was blinded to what they did and what it meant to them. The children in the other class responded to the assignment in the same way and, most telling, so did the teacher.

The consultants are part of a trend in which teachers are being given scripts, precise vocabulary, and rigid sequences, regardless of who the children are and what their experience has been. Quite literally, the children are bypassed. It is important to realize that the teacher also is bypassed. New teachers tend to need guidance, but does telling them exactly what to do promote their growth as professionals? The learning process is reduced to technique and the teacher reduced to a technician. Perhaps most harmful is how easy it is for teachers to rely on the directions and not see themselves as capable decision makers.

The Children Were Introduced to Impressive Role Models

It is almost a cliché to say that as children's teachers, we want to form partnerships with families. The parents of Laura's students *functioned* as partners in their children's education, and the children experienced them as such. They were major sources of the curriculum. One can imagine what this meant to the families.

I witnessed a similar experience when I was working with teachers on their social studies curricula in a bilingual middle school in a predominantly Dominican area of the city. The students were mostly children of immigrants or immigrants themselves and had a history of repeated school failure. An eighth-grade teacher noticed that the children, when speaking with each other, would ridicule their parents for not speaking English fluently, their accent, the way they dressed—for not being "American." Her family had emigrated from Mexico, and she understood how these adolescents wanted to fit into the prevailing popular culture, yet saw them as "stuck" and believed that they needed to embrace their backgrounds if they were to move forward as students and people.

Her plan was to invite one family member for each child to come to class and describe what his or her life was like in their previous country, why they came to this country, and what they wanted for their children. She called every family herself and insisted that they participate. She set up a flexible visit schedule to accommodate their needs. The children were asked to write about what they thought of the family member. Over a period of three months each guest told his or her stories, many of which the children had never heard before. A father, in Spanish, told the class about how he and his two brothers had only one outfit suitable for wearing to school, and so each brother would go to school every third day. And he told them, like most of the other parents, that he came to this country for a better life for his own children. The room was silent; it was as though he were speaking to each child individually. At a certain point, his daughter put her head on the table and cried. When he was finished speaking and answering students' questions, his daughter walked up to him and read what she had written. She thanked him for how hard he had to work, for all the things he'd done for her. She told him how much she respected, loved, and admired him. Tears streamed from her father's eyes; he pulled her to him and hugged her. Through these visits, as in Laura's class, the children saw their parents differently and learned that in spite of the many differences among their classmates' backgrounds, there were striking similarities. After years of teaching, teachers come to realize that there are no panaceas in education. Yet for these children, school became a different place. They made academic and social strides their teacher could only have hoped for. And for many of the parents, the experience in their child's school remained significant.

When Laura's class began exploring the neighborhood, the people they visited, like the parent and teacher visitors, gave of themselves as they spoke about their backgrounds and their work. They were caring, knowledgeable individuals who modeled competence—and more than that, a love for their work. The founder of a landmark restaurant spoke of how she learned the business, how she learned to cook, and how her restaurant served the freshest and the "best" vegetables, all from her father's farm in Georgia, which he trucked up himself. And the children were treated to the restaurant's famous homemade pie and a drink. They visited a local barber, learned of his background in the South, and asked about how he had learned to do his work. He demonstrated his craft by cutting a classmate's hair, which had been arranged beforehand—with the child's parents as well as the barber. As he cut the boy's hair, he explained how each tool is used. At the time, African American boys were having razor-cut designs sculpted into the hair on both sides of their head. As he began doing this, the children screamed with laughter, shouting, "Cool!" When it was done, the children complimented the boy and the barber—and many kids said they were going back there to get their own hair cut.

In Trish's class, it was the Roeblings and the bridge workers who offered powerful models of tenacity and competence: John Roebling, the famous engineer who started the project; Washington Roebling, John's son, who took over the project after his father's untimely death; and Emily, Washington's wife, who, after Washington developed the mysterious "caissons disease," managed the project under Washington's direction. It is staggering to think of this woman in the late 1800s, who was not an engineer, managing and obtaining the respect of a huge male workforce for the largest construction project in the world—quite an impressive role model. The class discussed the kind of people they were and who *they* would want to work for. The stories of the courageous workers fascinated the children, especially of the workers who spent their days digging in the caissons at river bottom while massive towers were being constructed above them.

3/21/97

Dear Ms Lara,

        I loved your apple
Pie it was so good. Anyway I thank
you for the soda and the pies
That you gave the class. and I like
the model that you did for
Carolina Country kitchen. I took
the orange soda to match with my
pie. Did you always since you started
this store have a special room
for you geust:

As Laura and her children ventured into the neighborhood, they were continually struck by how specially they were treated. This thank-you letter conveys that specialness and the child's appreciation.

Karen designed the study so that portraits of Long Island Native Americans emerge as models of skill and competence—in using the raw materials of their physical environment to make tools, to get food, to make their clothing and dwellings. Also modeled is a way of thinking about the physical world that resonates with current human ecological concerns. The portraits emerge through the explorations of the forests, rivers, and seashore; the museum exhibitions they would visit; the experts they would consult; and the stories she would read to the children. And of the Native Americans today, the children would learn of their ceaseless efforts to redress wrongs, their pride in their heritage, and the successes achieved in spite of overwhelming odds.

Throughout the three studies, each teacher modeled thinking, being a learner, working with others, caring about the children and the world they live in, and being knowledgeable. Each teacher made *stories of people* an essential part of the study. Each placed children in a position to see that people acting together or alone can make a difference.

The Children Engaged with a Rich Body of Content and Used Academic Skills to Deepen Their Understanding

Offering Multiple Ways of Knowing

Through the integration of different disciplines, the arts, crafts, and "skills," children deepened and demonstrated their understanding. The expansiveness of each topic enabled the teachers to integrate into the study the disciplines of mathematics, science, literature, history, and geography, and the skills of reading, writing, and research. Painting, drawing, writing, drama, and crafts became integral to each study. Each discipline offers a unique perspective, a different way of seeing and understanding the world. The arts, like the academic disciplines, also offer different ways of seeing and knowing, and just as important, they offer dynamic ways to *represent* understandings, to externalize them and make them public, and raise them to a different level of consciousness. Reading, writing, and research offer *means* to pursue knowledge. What is significant about this kind of integration of disciplines is that through it children are offered multiple vantage points and means from which to explore, understand, and represent their experience and understandings. Also, in a sense, the complexity of *social* studies, of people's relations to each other and to their environment, *requires* a variety of ways of knowing and of expressing learning.

The different modalities also accommodate different learning styles, different strengths, interests, and aptitudes. It is not uncommon for teachers to be surprised when they discover that the child they thought had little understanding of a topic brings it to life with subtlety and complexity through drama or painting or poetry. The many modes offer ways for children who might struggle with reading or writing to excel and to show their classmates, themselves, and us what they are capable of. They also enable us to know our children more fully and resist defining them.

Too frequently, social studies topics are chosen and studied to reinforce or even teach reading and writing—as though the topics were solely vehicles without deep intrinsic worth. In the three studies, the content was viewed as essential and gave children *a reason* to read, write, use mathematics, and do scientific experiments. These academic subjects, like listening, are often categorized by children as "things we have to do in school," appearing to have little, if any, relevance to their lives or the world.

When there is integration of disciplines through social studies, typically it is on a superficial level. Karen Kriesberg's study of Long Island Native Americans is dramatically different from the familiar formulaic study in which children learn a song, a dance, read about the housing and food, do a report, make a craft, perhaps create a diorama—all without connection to themselves, or, in reality, any deep connection to Native Americans. Songs, dances, and crafts are not merely fun or "enrichment" activities; they can offer insight into a way of life. But to arrive at that level of insight, children have to move beyond superficial understanding of the topic.[3]

In each of the three studies, integration of disciplines, the arts, crafts, and skills was used *in service to* fuller and deeper understanding of the

The simple craft projects that were part of classroom visitors' presentations personalized the visit. Each detail of the project was important to this child.

topic. Laura's children came to understand geography through tracing their families' origins and discovered commonalities across the backgrounds of their peers. Regions discussed became less abstract as they used math to graph the temperatures of these regions, and again saw commonalities. The stories visitors told were extended and became more personal through the crafts and cooking they did with the children. The children wrote thank-you letters to the visitors, wrote about their trips, read about the places discussed, and read African folktales. They interviewed class guests and the people they visited and recorded what they learned. They gained deeper insight into their own background when they used the interviewing skills to do a report on a relative. Throughout, they did drawings reflecting their experiences. After visiting the barber, instead of sending the usual thank-you letters, they made business cards for him, which he loved.

The barber loved the business cards. Every time he saw Laura walking past his shop, he'd ask, "When are all of you coming back?"

This child struggled to get the tape measure around the huge cable. He calmly persevered, succeeded, and got an accurate measurement. (Photograph by and courtesy of Trish Lent)

The children in Trish's class used reading and writing throughout the study. They sketched during each of their trips and recorded words that would evoke what they saw. From their sketches of architectural details of the Brooklyn Bridge, they created colorful paintings illustrating the intricacies they discovered. They also photographed the details using digital cameras. They used nonstandard measure, which they were learning about in math, to measure the neighborhood bridge, the Central Park bridges, and eventually aspects of the Brooklyn Bridge. And in the process, they realized quickly that, though their own foot size offered a suitable measure for the length of the Central Park bridges, it was definitely not suitable for the Brooklyn Bridge roadway. To measure the circumference of a main cable they found a tape measure more useful than nonstandard measure. Through the science experiments they learned how the strength of a material changed when the material was folded. To count the number of unifix cubes the different roadways could hold, they had to use high numbers, which was a goal for them in math that year. They used so many cubes that some groups ran out. They were so engaged with the experiments they worked on a solution to the problem. They figured out that they could substitute a butter-stick-shaped wooden block from their class block set. They used balance scales to see how many cubes the block balanced. The sophisticated mathematical solution grew not from an academic exercise but from the children's desire to see just how many cubes the accordion-folded roadway could hold.

They came to understand the physics of what makes a suspension bridge stand, the "tug of war" among its members, learning dramatically through their bodies and through their building a model of a functioning suspension bridge. In teams they researched bridge members, constructed members for the model, and evoked the members through their poetry. They studied the geography of the city and its history to fully understand why and how the bridge was built.

Interviewing became a way for the children to find answers to their own questions. They wanted to know who walked across the bridge, why, and where they lived. To do this the class developed a simple interview sheet. Based on a classmate's idea, they made posters with a bold "STOP" sign on the top and then the question, "Would you like to be interviewed?" The child who interviewed more people than anyone else had emigrated from China, struggled with English, and rarely spoke. When children's minds and imaginations are engaged, they can surprise us, which can shake up our preconceived notions of who they are and of what they are capable.

Though Karen did not teach the thesis study she created, she made map study and map making critical to learning about the relationships between people and their environment. As with the two other studies, experiential writing and drawing are used throughout. Reading to the children and their reading on their own offered a route into the past. Scientific methods were used to understand the properties of water and to understand that an island is an extension of the land under the water that surrounds it and doesn't float above the water, which many children think. Replicating crafts and work processes, such as the grinding of corn, were used throughout to give insight into people's daily experience, as another way to "feel into another's life."[4]

I realized just how important this type of activity could be when I was a teacher of third grade and the class was studying how Eastern Woodland Indians got their food. I brought in ears of dried corn to be ground down with a mortar and pestle so that we could make corn pudding using a Native American recipe. I wanted children to gain insight into one small aspect of getting food, to see how strenuous and time consuming the work was. First the children worked to remove the kernels from the husks, and a few children volunteered to grind the corn. It didn't take long for the children's arms to tire and for them to ask to stop, even though, for all their labor, they had produced a tiny amount of ground corn. We discussed what we should do, and one child suggested that everyone in the class have a turn. I created a week's schedule, and each day, from arrival to 3:00 PM, they took turns grinding corn. By the end of the week we had a bowl of ground corn. Not only was it not enough for the recipe, it was so hard and gritty I was concerned that if we made it into the pudding, someone might crack a tooth. One child, expressing a shining moment of insight gained from the ceaseless corn grinding, concluded, "We do *nothing* from scratch." She said to the class that even when we say we bake a cake from scratch, someone had to grow the wheat and grind it into flour, someone had to milk the cow and get the eggs. She said with authority, "The Native Americans did *everything* from scratch."

Each of the three studies cultivated children's ability to acquire information from their own experience. They learned to interview, to observe with focus, and to record their observations. They experienced the vibrancy of learning through their senses. Ultimately, they learned to trust their ability to discover and to see themselves as a source of knowledge.

The Central Role of Discussion

Discussion was essential to all three studies. Discussion offered the forum in which listening to others became more than just something you were supposed to do in school. Listening became an important way of finding out. And they listened with an intensity that surprised their teachers. When a visitor to Laura's class struggled to find the right word to capture how she felt in the city after moving from the South, the room was silent, children bent forward out of their seats, their eyes directly on her, and a child whispered, "In a cage."

Trish, Laura, and Karen planned discussions carefully. Children wanted to participate because the discussions were built on their experiences, and they each would have something to say, which for some children was in itself a revelation. Too frequently, when classes have discussions, information is drawn solely from text. Instead of organizing discussions around a question, which might imply a right and wrong answer, Karen would begin discussions with an invitation to participate, using the words, "Let's talk about . . ."

Through discussion children's curiosity was sparked, they clarified their ideas to express them to others, became open to others' comments, reformulated their own thoughts, drew inferences, and asked relevant questions. They saw ideas bound and rebound and came to know each other and themselves differently—through language.

What we often call "critical thinking" was cultivated through discussion. It is common practice in schools for critical thinking "skills" to be "learned" through workbook exercises, abstracted from the living situations that demand reasoned judgments—as though thinking were merely technique. As the children moved beyond superficial knowledge of the content and the topics became more important to them, they were better able to reflect on and weigh the comments of others based on what they themselves had experienced and learned. With a body of knowledge to work from, they could compare and contrast, analyze, and synthesize information. They were becoming thinkers.

Through the Process of Working and Learning Together, the Classes Became Communities

The word *community* has been so overused, it is unclear what's meant by it. *Community* is invoked to justify political positions on the right as well as the left. I have even heard teachers, when their students are careless in fulfilling classroom responsibilities, shouting, "This should not happen because *we are a community*!" It is as though shouting the words make it a reality or that communities are created through fiat. In spite of the varied interpretations and haphazard use of the term, the three teachers appear clear in their plans and actions that they are striving to create a particular type of community, a *democratic* community. Probably every social studies text states that the ultimate goal of social studies in general is to cultivate citizens for a democratic society. It is equally probable that most public school mission statements proclaim the same aim. Yet how many settings intentionally strive to meet this aim as a major thrust of their work?

Each teacher was influenced by John Dewey's belief that "democracy is more than a form of government; it is primarily a form of associated living."[5] This form of living together requires that individuals see their interests as tied to those of the larger community, feel responsibility toward that community, and act on that sense of responsibility. It requires that they express their opinions and ideas and, just as important, listen to and entertain opinions of others. And it requires that they exercise reasoned judgment when considering issues affecting the community as a whole and its individuals.

Embedded in the three studies is a *process* for creating a democratic community in a classroom with children, and in each the curriculum offers the raw material. Through the shared experience of the study a sense of *we* was formed. And like the bridge members, each class member was critical to the functioning of the totality. Through a curriculum that spoke directly to the children and that *they* believed was important, they grew to share a common purpose and a sense of responsibility for that purpose. They grew to care about what they had experienced and created together. In each study, a community was cultivated and kept alive through the children's sharing of ideas and questions; participating in joint problem solving: and seeing that their decisions are acted upon, that they can have an impact on their environment.

In Laura's class the curriculum sparked the children's interest in what each other had to say and placed them in a position in which they indeed had important things to say. Through the process of the study, this group that started out showing little patience for each other grew to trust each other to share their feelings about name-calling, scapegoating, their families, and racism. Through the curriculum, they experienced the visitors' respect for them as thinkers and trust in them as sensitive people. And they became worthy of that respect and showed it in return. They also shared the fun of watching as their classmate received the cool haircut, the fun of visiting the Carolina Country Kitchen and being served pie and a drink in a room reserved for special occasions, and of helping each other do the craft projects. Ultimately, through the shared process of the study they grew to feel special.

Trish's class experienced together the transformation from that first frightening trip to the Brooklyn Bridge to the time they felt as though the bridge were theirs. Through repeated trips to the bridge, they shared the fun of interviewing pedestrians, the sketching, photographing, and measuring. Through these trips and the class activities they became Brooklyn Bridge experts. They shared the experience of hearing the heroic stories of the Roeblings and the brave bridge workers and saw how people working together can make a difference. They shared the excitement of getting the child roadway to stand, of spinning cables, of doing the experiments, of building the model they were so proud of, and finally their creating and performing the poetry bridge.

Karen viewed "a community of learners and explorers" as "a requirement and a goal" of the study, and built in "children's common endeavor of exploring, discussing, problem solving, planning and working together," all of which she believed would "support, develop, and maintain the community within the classroom." [6]

The connections forged in the school and neighborhood made the studies alive and important to the children, their teachers, and members of a community they helped create. In each study, education was viewed as more than simply knowing; otherwise, texts, demographic facts, and "how-to" manuals might have been the major sources of knowledge. The studies were built on relationships, which engaged the learners emotionally and physically. The children's parents, teachers, and neighborhood people were respected as the experts. They were given opportunities to talk about things that were most important to them, and in the process they had their lives and work affirmed. It is not surprising that the children's related academic work was of a high quality; the children and their teachers were fully present in the learning process.

Each study placed the learners in a position to challenge assumptions—about their family history, country, neighborhood, parents, teachers, and each other. What they learned was not separate from how they learned. They learned about community by entering the community and, in the process, became a community that extended beyond the classroom.

All of this demanded time, time for children and teachers to explore, discover, try out, make mistakes, even fail—and reflect and try again; time for teachers to plan carefully; time for guest presenters; time for trips into the community; time to extend and represent understandings through many discussions, research, writing, model making, painting, crafts, and drama; time for children to build complex concepts of *river, neighborhood, diversity, family background,* and *bridge*—and time for children to think and to wonder.

PART TWO

"An Education in What America Is, What It Could Be"

Finally, the war that consumed the entire nation had ended. Though the period was shadowed by the atomic bombs dropped on Hiroshima and Nagasaki, Americans were infused with a sense of optimism. It was a time of new beginnings. Wartime rationing of fuel had been lifted, and trains and buses that traveled the nation were no longer filled with troops and soldiers' families. And in 1948, Bank Street resumed its long trips, which had been suspended during the war.

On the April morning of departure, the sun was shining, and the street and sidewalk around 69 Bank Street were filled with students' families and faculty seeing them off. For many, it was the first time they traveled apart from their families. And students were thrilled to leave the city and go anywhere. They were young and felt the anticipation of an adventure about to happen. It was as though their lives were just beginning. One student described herself as "a very new person." She was nearly twenty, yet had "rarely been over the Brooklyn Bridge."[1]

One of their destinations was the Tennessee Valley Authority (TVA), the massive regional project to control and harness the power of the Tennessee River. It was a major effort of the Roosevelt administration to bring electrification to the rural South, alleviate poverty, and stop the floods that eroded hillsides and washed away plowed land. For many progressive-minded Americans, the TVA was "the proving ground of a dynamic democracy."[2] The TVA cut across state boundaries to harness the "earth forces" that consumed people's lives. It seemed to epitomize what government could do for people.

In preparing for the trip, the students had read about the TVA, but nobody imagined the grand scale of the great dams—"Tons and tons of concrete holding back tons and tons of water . . . creating power which pulses over the whole valley, tremendous power and simple beautiful lines."[3] They saw what government could do to improve people's lives and entered the Norris Dam building feeling that the future held great promise. The art deco structure mirrored the grandeur of the Norris Dam itself. While walking through the building, students stopped and were still. They were staring at Allen Ohta, a Japanese American student, who was standing in front of the drinking fountain. His gaze was fixed on the stainless-steel, stylized word over the stylized granite fountain—"COLORED." The students knew the South was segregated and had cringed each time they saw the often sloppily-made signs indicating where "colored" were to eat, drink, shop, or use a bathroom. Here the sign was artistically built into an imposing federal government building.

It's likely that most of the students had read Richard Wright's *Native Son*. Yet for those who remember Allen standing in front of that fountain, it was "one of first times where it *really* hit what segregation was really all about."[4] Almost everyone imagined Allen wondering whether "colored" applied to him or not. For his classmates, whether it is from the memory of the experience or what the photograph of Allen by that fountain evoked, segregation became real and shocking, and seemed to define that trip. Although the word "colored" above that fountain was relatively small and made of metal, students remember it as bold and large, "carved . . . into the stone." Students who had recently emigrated from Europe and Israel were disillusioned. They wondered how this could be when it was the United States that saved them from racism. Their eyes were opened to the contradictions, the hypocrisy, and complexity of the country. Like the children in Laura Gerrity's class, they woke up—this had to do with them. One of the students thought, "Maybe we're not such a great country after all."[5] And many realized how sheltered they had been and how they lived in a white world and took it for granted.

In our interview I asked Allen what he was thinking when he saw the fountain. He said he was stunned, like his peers, to see "something like this in such a monstrous big building . . . so elaborate . . . built by the government." He thought about how he, unlike his father, had escaped the racism leveled against Japanese Americans. He recalled when his father was thrown off a Virginia beach: "They looked at me, then a child, and said, 'You can stay.' And they looked at my father and said, 'You're too dark. You have to go.' "[6] For the rest of the trip issues of racism and civil rights dominated. It was for this kind of experience that Lucy Sprague Mitchell and Eleanor Hogan planned the long trips.

When students on the 1948 long trip saw Allen Ohta standing in front of the "colored" drinking fountain, "it really hit what segregation was all about." (Photograph by and courtesy of Emil Willimetz)

• • •

The actions of the three teachers featured in part 1 are based on their commitment to what they believe is important for children to know and to a way of learning. Their venturing outward on their own and with their students illustrates how learning is personalized, intensified, and deepened. The *how*, *what*, and *why* of their work grew from a rich history of progressive education theory and practice. As a teacher of children and teachers who was influenced profoundly by this history, I embarked on a process of researching and uncovering a unique chapter in progressive teacher education.

Part 2 attempts to penetrate this history, make it accessible to educators, and explore its relevance for today. It follows the process of Mitchell and Hogan's environment classes that led to the Norris Dam drinking fountain. It follows Mitchell and Hogan and the student teachers venturing out together onto the street corner; into the neighborhood, the city, and surrounding areas; and one thousand miles from their homes to encounter places and situations they had only read about. Throughout, they forge connections "more real than can be made with words"[7] with each other, the natural world, and the people they meet. The story will move back and forward in time to compare the experiences of student teachers in the past to those of educators today who also venture into seemingly familiar worlds and beyond. And I answer the question I came back to each time I looked at the photograph in the college lobby: What do these trips have to do with teaching?

Chapter 5

"We Went on Trips Morning, Noon, and Night"

Lucy Sprague Mitchell's Environment Class

The "Kick-Start" Assignments

"It was startling to be standing there with your eyes shut in the middle of New York City!" remembered a student of Lucy Sprague Mitchell. "Mrs. Mitchell" asked them to stand on a corner and observe a road for fifteen minutes, close their eyes for five minutes, and afterward record everything they could about the road.[1] To extend the assignment, Mitchell asked them to review their notes at home and "write about anything that interested them." Many of the students from the 1930s through the '50s whom I interviewed talked about the importance of this simple activity, perhaps because it symbolized what was being asked of them. They felt they were recapturing the freshness of learning from experience. One student said that "the idea was, you don't just learn things out of books, that children learn things by doing, feeling, seeing, smelling, and that we should be exposed to all that."[2] Leonard Marcus described what Mitchell was attempting with the student teachers in his biography of the celebrated children's author Margaret Wise Brown, who had been an adult student of Mitchell at Bank Street. He said, "It was one thing to strive for an intellectually complex understanding of children's complex behavior and development; it was quite another to reconstitute within one's self a semblance of the actual framework of childhood—to see the world, as it were, through a three-year-old's eyes."[3]

Some students recalled that in the mining area of Pennsylvania, once they exited the bus, they were asked to close their eyes and "listen the way a child would."[4] Another student also recalled that they were asked to do this at each different area they visited on the long trip, to feel the soil, smell the air, feel the breeze on their faces, as well as hear the sounds. They were asked to be fully present in the world and experience the uniqueness of place.

I thought of this assignment when I attended a current long trip to the Sea Islands off Georgia. It was the light that struck me, especially as it filtered through the huge trees all hanging with moss. It was like nothing I had experienced before. And I felt a different kind of closeness, an immediacy to the events I learned about—how the Union Army freed the people enslaved on those islands before anywhere else in the country and how the first school for newly freed men, women, and children was established there.

I tried the "Roads" activity with students in the curriculum class I teach. On a windy spring evening, we stationed ourselves on the corner of Broadway and 110th Street—and we did attract some interest, especially when all the students closed their eyes. Back at the college, they described what they experienced with their eyes closed: the freshness of the wind hitting their faces, the fact that it was blowing from the west, their hair and clothes being pulled, the sounds of wind-blown papers scraping the pavement around them, the deep rumble of the subway under the sidewalk below them, sounds of shoes hitting the pavement as their wearers sped past them, the rumble of trucks speeding by, bits and pieces of loud conversation. I asked them why we did this activity. So many said it was to become more aware of the world around us, to be more conscious of "where we are," to understand how children experience the world, and to "see" what we miss when we are only seeing. Their comments were so similar to those of students in the past, who saw it as "a fine-tuning of awareness that is a tremendously important thing to do with children."[5]

"Roads" was the first of three assignments, done in rapid succession as a kick start, a way to activate a process of thinking and learning, for students in Mitchell's environment class. From her students' responses, they understood her intentions—to spark their interest in the everyday workings of their environment; to sharpen the use of their senses so they would experience their surroundings freshly, like children; and ultimately to "learn how to explore an environment so that they could use it with children."[6] The assignments cumulatively placed the students in a position to understand the relationships among human work; how work fulfills the human need for food, shelter, energy, transportation, clothing; and the use of natural resources, such as land, climate, coal, oil, water.

Besides "Roads," there were "Houses," "Food," and the culminating assignment, "Community Work Patterns." Each was designed to move the students progressively outward from their immediate world.[7] The long trip would extend the process further.

Mitchell must have been acutely aware of what students were *not* seeing; she had witnessed, within the short span of time following the First World War, how science, technology, and industry had transformed roads, houses, and work patterns into increasingly complex networks of interdependency. In 1934 Mitchell wrote how a child "lives in a world of end products,"[8] to a great extent removed from the processes and people who enable their world to function. Through these simple assignments on roads, houses, and food, Mitchell was offering adult students the opportunity to begin to penetrate the end products.

For the houses assignment, Mitchell asked the students to do a "case history" of any kind of building. Similar to the roads assignment, she was trying to get them to investigate what appeared obvious and to examine how the house related to the larger community. Florence Krahn, a student in 1937–'38, felt as though she were "taking some inanimate object and creating a story [that related] all of the forces that were involved in making it the way it was."[9]

Krahn had saved all of her course papers. The "Houses" paper showed how the house was connected, through its need for services, to the surrounding area and nearby cities: "The heat is supplied by steam which is piped through the house terminating in the various radiators. A coal furnace supplies the heat for the hot water tank in the basement. The coal comes from the Mahers coal company which is located right on the Sound and receives its supply from barges coming up the East River and the Sound." From her detailed observations and interview with the owner, she penetrated the obvious as Mitchell had hoped, attending to the question of *why?*: Why does the community incur the greater cost of having its gas pumped from a nearby city rather than locally? Why is there a stone wall between the front yard and the street? Why do economic forces of the local community have a bearing on the house? And so forth.[10]

Krahn found that after doing the assignment, she thought about the structure as though it were a living organism. She said, "I took on the house's point of view, and ordinarily, you wouldn't do that if someone hadn't put you in a position to do so."[11] Many students considered the old 69 Bank Street building itself part of the study of environment. It had been a Fleischmann's Yeast plant, and all the pipes were exposed. One student commented, "Lucy Sprague Mitchell had all the pipes painted. All the hot water pipes were red, and all the cold water pipes were blue, and all the ducts were yellow, and there were arrows on the floor. The whole place was an educational experience."[12]

I had a small glimpse of the power of this type of activity first with children and years later with graduate students. On a bitter cold winter day, the heat went out in the elementary school where I was teaching, and it was so cold in that old building that children were blowing smoke from their breath. The caretaker, Mr. Woodson, ran from room to room, examining radiators. Some children had constructed an elaborate block building close to the radiator, and, no matter how he tried, Mr. Woodson was unable to get close enough to examine the radiator. In an angry voice he shouted, "This should not be here." The class stopped what they were doing. They were silent, and every eye was on Mr. Woodson. In sheer frustration—and I think exhaustion—he just whacked it down. Given the silence, the sound seemed deafening. As though a chorus, the children gasped, "Huuuhhhh!" Then, to each other, "Did you see that!" The two children who constructed the building ran up to me and said, "Did you see what Mr. Woodson did?" "How could he do that?" I said that Mr. Woodson was caring for the entire school, and that this was an emergency. I said I'd help them stack their blocks so they could rebuild in a different location. And they went back to their work and somehow didn't mention it again. But I knew I had to come back to what had happened. I had to find a way to help them understand just how important Mr. Woodson's work was to every one of us.

The next morning, as soon as we entered the building we felt the difference; the heat was on again. When we came together for a morning meeting, I asked them how they thought the building was heated? They knew there was a heater and that it probably was in the basement, but little more than that. I asked what they thought the boiler room was like. Some children had seen a burner for a small house and thought it would be similar, only larger. I asked them how we could find out. They all said we should ask Mr. Woodson. We wrote and hand delivered a class letter to him, asking if we could visit the boiler room to find out from him how the school was heated. When he passed the room, he stuck his head in the door, said it was fine, and gave us a time. We developed some questions to ask him.

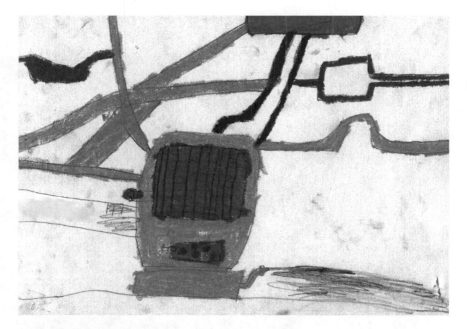

In this six-year-old's drawing, the old furnace seems alive, with pipes growing from it. He wrote: "This is the heater. It gives us heat. Mr. Woodson fixes it. He opened the pipe. We saw steaming water come out [lower right] because Mr. Woodson showed it to us."

All of us were surprised as we entered the boiler room. We were immediately struck by how hot it was in there. The low ceiling was a spiderweb of pipes and the boiler was huge. With little adieu, Mr. Woodson immediately addressed our reason for being there. He went straight to the burner and opened the door so that we could see the fire blazing inside it, the source of the warmth we now especially appreciated. From that dramatic introduction on, the children were in awe. He then showed us his tools, how he used them, and how he had to regulate the different gauges. He showed us where the oil entered the building, its storage unit, and its route to the burner. The children asked him how do we know when we need more oil, how does it get to the school, and where does it come from. He said he'd let us know when the next delivery would be made so that we could see how it gets into the building. He showed us which pipes carry the heat through the building to the radiators, and then walked us up the back staircases showing us the exposed heating pipes working their way through that old building. Then he said he had to get back to work. We thanked him, and the

After showing us the burners and where water, gas, and electricity entered the building, Carlos Lenis paused to answer the students' many questions. We were taken with his knowledge and skill, but especially with his obvious love for what he did. (Photograph by author)

children applauded. He was surprised and touched by our thank-you notes and the book we made that included the children's writing about the trip and their drawings, some of him at work. From then on, when he passed our room, he'd stick his head through the door and say, "Keep up the good work." Before this visit, I don't think he spoke with the children, and for the children he was background. That changed.

When I led graduate students in the curriculum class to the Bank Street College boiler room, I was amazed at how similar it was to that visit with Mr. Woodson—how our greater understanding of the workings of the building helped us become aware of and care about the people and services we took for granted. Carlos Lenis, the college heating and air-cooling engineer, was our guide. The boiler room was hot and pipes laced the ceiling and walls. We saw where city water, gas, and electricity entered the building and the pipes through which waste left.

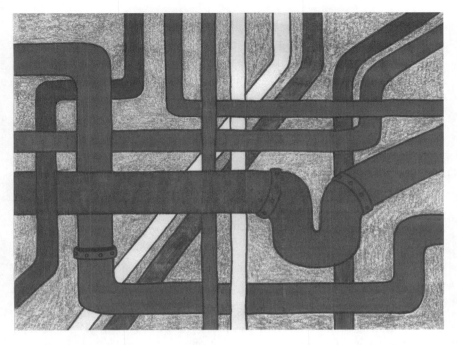

A graduate student's rendition of "The Room of Pipes." (Drawing by and courtesy of Mary E. Calabrese)

We learned about the incredible amount of water our building used in a day and began to think about its use across the city. Like the children, the massive size of the burner and the fire blazing inside it surprised us. We traveled to the top floor of the building to examine the air-cooling system. We experienced the complexity of the building's air-filtration system by walking into a series of near-pitch-black chambers with air rushing through. It felt like being on an airport runway. And also like the children, our experience stimulated so many new, more penetrating questions. They wanted to know what Carlos did when part of the system broke down? Did he call someone in? We all were surprised to learn that he took care of *all* the problems himself, that he found the teasing apart of what was wrong and what needed to be done like solving a puzzle, which he found satisfying. We were taken with his knowledge and skill, but especially with his obvious love for what he did. I am sure Carlos didn't realize that he presented to teachers a model to emulate—of a professional, of caring, diligence, and *being a learner as a critical aspect of one's work.*

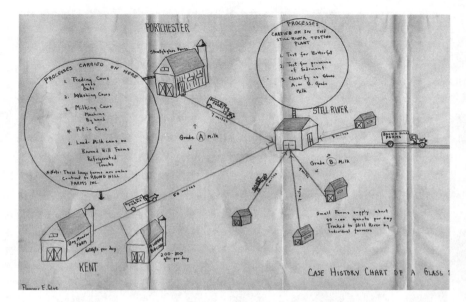

Mitchell asked graduate students to trace a food to its source. For Florence Krahn this assignment emphasized "how you never got to the bottom of something if you didn't get down to its source." (Chart by and courtesy of Florence Krahn)

After that visit, Carlos said that he knew the students were smart but never expected them to be so interested in what he did and to have such good questions. He said that in the twenty years he worked for the college, he had never had this kind of exchange with the students. During our next class session, one student said, "I can't believe I never noticed Carlos before. Now I think I'll never forget him."[13] And the students discussed how that visit could extend outward to how energy is brought to the building, with a focus on the people who make it possible. I believe that the power of their exchange with Carlos led them to focus on the people as the way to understand the work more deeply and personally. They saw how with older children and adults it could lead to a study of the current daunting ecological and political issues of energy.

The next of Mitchell's assignments focused on food. She asked that the students start with a food they had eaten, trace it to its source, then chart the process visually as well as describe it in writing. Krahn entitled her chart "The Case History of a Glass of Milk, Which I Drank." The chart depicts the full process, clearly showing a chain of interdependence. It is also a chart of Krahn's firsthand investigations of dairy

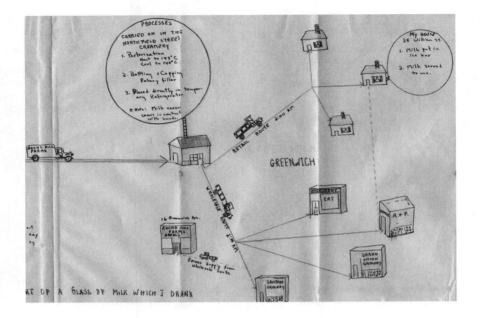

farms, processing plants, and local stores. Because it is a chart, it does not show what she conveyed in the interview how each of the stages in the process came alive for her through her exchange with farmers, truckers, vendors, and other workers. If it were today, she probably could get all the information from the Internet and stop there, but it would be just that, information. As Krahn proudly examined the chart during our interview, she said, "The *source* of things—that word was very important because you never got to the bottom of something if you didn't get down to the source. *Things didn't just happen.*" [14]

In the current curriculum class, for the final assignment many students develop studies of how we get our food. Perhaps nothing strikes us as more primal than the need for food, and nothing evokes home, family, and culture as food does. The studies lead to an exploration of the nature of an island city, to which food travels from across the world, the country, and the state. The studies lead to the roadways and conveyances that invariably spark children's imaginations—the many tunnels and bridges food must pass through and over, and the trucks, trains, boats, and planes that converge to deliver food. The studies lead students into the neighborhood and beyond, to farmers and farms and farmers' markets, workers and large wholesale markets, managers and supermarket storage rooms, grocers and small neighborhood grocery stores, bakers and bakeries, to truckers and their trucks, and even street food vendors. The proliferation of farmers' markets throughout the country has made speaking directly with farmers more accessible to teachers and children. Although the adult students are reluctant to approach workers they most likely don't know, they invariably discover that there are magic words of introduction: "I am a teacher and . . ."

A student in the current curriculum class, Ronnie Igel, who was developing a study for second graders of how the city gets food, planned a trip to the massive Hunts Point Meat, Produce, and Fish Wholesale Market in the Bronx. The wholesale market was one important link in the learning opportunities she planned that followed a path from farms to wholesale market to local stores. Thoughtfully, she included a visit to a local common pantry that served the food needs of families in need. Throughout the study, she integrated science, math, writing and reading, art, and, being a study of food, cooking. And discussion was central to everything she planned. Though the study is consistently thoughtful, Igel's description of her visit to the Hunts Point Meat market area is particularly poignant.

Although this was not peak time (night and mornings until 11:00 are), the entire area was full of huge refrigerator trucks. I did not feel physically safe. I decided to approach a driver who stood by his truck and didn't seem to be as busy as the others. I explained what I was trying to do, and he was instantly friendly and helpful. He guided me to an area alongside his truck and began to answer my many questions.

Angelo explained that his route originated from Palm Springs with stops in Denver, Nebraska, New Hampshire, and New York. The trip took two and a half days with basically no stopping for sleep.

He was free to speak with me now because he was waiting for his turn to unload his cargo of beef. His truck was backed into an unloading dock. He showed me the inside of the truck. There is the "cab," which consists of a surprisingly large sleeping area located behind the driving area. The cargo section of the truck is refrigerated and detachable. It is loaded with both cartons of beef and huge whole parts of beef suspended from hooks.

Angelo demonstrated ways he cooked his own meals while on route. He has a hot plate but usually uses a truck driver's version of a TV dinner (purchased at truck stops). These microwave themselves when water is simply poured over them. He demonstrated this right on the ground in the parking lot. He gave me the box to show the children.

He explained his route from start to finish: what he picks up, what he drops off, how he is paid, how his company is paid, etc. He showed me the inside of the warehouse, where his cargo is stored until it is picked up and trucked to its final destination, which could be anything from a giant supermarket to a tiny bodega. The warehouse was like one giant building-sized refrigerator. It is freezing in there. He discussed federal inspection, processing plants, unions vs. freelance, pitfalls of life on the road (crime and corruption among others), country driving vs. city driving, mechanics—you name it, he had something to say about it. Most important, he said, was getting back home in time for Thanksgiving.

Although I was fascinated by the things Angelo showed me, I was more fascinated by *him*. It was through him that I got a feel for what the job was about. I got a real sense of what his life was. *He genuinely moved me.* When I was finished interviewing him, he suggested that I give him the school's address so that he could send us postcards from his various stops. I offered to pay the postage, which he refused. He said he makes runs to Hunts Point often, and we could prearrange for the class to meet him.[15]

This type of experience is just what Mitchell had wanted for adults and children: a deeper understanding of the complexity of a process that links us to others, to people we depend on, yet whose lives and fate are largely invisible to us. More than understanding, she sought an emotional connection to the worker, which she believed comes from *person-to-person* exchange—as the first and second graders experienced with Mr. Woodson and the graduate students with Carlos. If Mitchell's statement that we live in a world of end products was true in 1934 when she wrote *Young Geographers*, how much more true this statement is today, not solely for children but for adults as well. It is not just that we miss important processes that have bearing on our lives, we also miss the connections to the people whose work sustains us. Ronnie Igel and Florence Krahn demonstrate how powerful it is when we begin to penetrate the "world of end products" and begin to understand children's interest in "how things work" and in the people who make things work.

The fourth and last of Mitchell's kick-start assignments was "Community Work Patterns," which built on the first three. One student of Mitchell's environment class described community work patterns as a series of concentric circles moving outward from the neighborhood, showing the relationships among work, human needs, and natural resources—essentially human geography. She said Mitchell viewed work patterns as a way for children and teachers to "make sense of their world."[16] For Mitchell and other educators, World War I fueled the study of human geography. The war was pivotal in making clear on a world scale the fundamental interdependence of human needs, human actions, earth resources, and people's work. Geography texts for teachers and children from the 1920s and '30s focused on basic human needs of food, shelter, clothing, light, and energy; how these were met in children's own environment; and how the local community served the needs of other communities.[17]

For the work patterns assignment, she asked them to select a basic need, such as energy, and, with as much firsthand investigation as possible, follow a chain of interdependence that leads from the neighborhood outward to the source. If a student focused on energy, the study might trace the use of coal from coal burners and coal bins in the home to the trucks and truckers that deliver it, to the warehouses from which workers distribute coal, to the barges and trains and workers that transport the coal to the city, eventually to the coal mines and coal miners of Appalachia and to the effect of the work on the worker and the environment. Mitchell believed that the cumulative study of "environment" revealed the root causes of most social issues.[18]

The Trips

As students progressed through the four assignments, the connections between human needs and geography grew increasingly apparent, as did the connected social issues. For example, tracing a pair of cotton pants to its source might lead to stores and salespeople, trucks and truckers, factories and the conditions of labor, to union organizing, to cotton fields and migrant labor, child labor, and the use and abuse of the land. In a sense, the trips she planned for her adult students were to illuminate work patterns in their immediate and extended environment and to enlarge students' circles of understanding of the world around them; and she believed and hoped these experiences would enlarge students' circles of caring—the kind of caring that led to commitment.

When the adult student said that they "went on trips morning, noon, and night," I never imagined that she meant it *literally*.[19] They followed Mitchell to downtown docks that served coal barges, ocean liners, and ferries to Staten Island and Brooklyn. One student recalled how

Mitchell, then not a young woman, just jumped onto the mountain of coal on the coal barge and invited them to do the same. Though she had taken these trips before, her excitement was evident. To her, the city was "magic," as she believed it was for children. She wanted her adult students to experience "the smiting beauty of skyline, the supreme vitality of its dock-lined rivers, on its streets, even in the noisy subways."[20] She wanted them to rediscover the excitement, adventure, and romance she believed children experience.

They visited noisy railroad terminals, observed workers unloading freight, and descended deep into the tunnels to explore the underground powerhouse and the switch tower, where they learned the signals and how to use the switch controls. They explored the sources of the city water supply. Similar to the way Trish Lent, using an outline map, asked her second and third graders to determine where the city's bridges might be located, Mitchell's adult students determined suitable places for reservoirs on geophysical maps. Then they traveled north to a major reservoir. They followed the process of how the city gets its food and visited large distributing centers. When most people were asleep,

Mitchell (center) is directing students' attention to aspects of a new building being constructed. Jean Hubbard, who is among this group (Class of 1944), said, "When Lucy Sprague Mitchell took us out onto the streets of New York, we felt the joy of being alive." (Photograph courtesy of Jean Hubbard)

NOTES TOWARDS A CHART OF THE DEVELOPMENT OF GEOGRAPHIC THINKING AND TOOLS
Each Stage May Include Some or All of the Preceding Stages

Stages Approximate Age Zones	Interest Drives. What children observe in their environment	Orientation	Tools and children's methods of expression	Curriculum implications. Trips and Maps
1st Stage Before walking and talking to 14 months	Attention to and experimentation with qualities of things (including own body)—distance, weight, size, color, texture, etc.	Relationship of self to not-self. Space relations in things. (Foundation of locational geography maps.)	Senses and muscles used for exploration in direct experiencing, such as handling, tasting, throwing, seeing, smelling. Associational process becomes active = discovery of relations. Pre-word symbols, such as bottle of milk standing for taste of milk. Expression is through motor and sense activities = play.	Much material for sense and motor experiences. Relationships within single object, and around self. Motor exploration.
2nd Stage Walking and talking begin 14 months to 3 years	Experimentation with own body, such as stepping, running, jumping. Things used to increase sense and motor experiences. Further exploration of qualities of things. Sociability without cooperation.	Position of things in room begins, such as clothes, toys, etc.	Words still largely direct language. Tools are elaboration of first stage. Expression as in first stage + motor and sense recalls = play.	First stage elaborated. Color as symbol, to designate own possessions as towels, basket, etc. Much space. Block play and crayons beginning on sense and motor level.
3rd Stage 3 years to early 4th year	Environment widens to domestic still with self as center. Interest in moving things begins. Also in growing things.	Orientation in room and building becomes more elaborate.	Word elaborated. Toys as symbols of own experiences. Domestic play with own experiences recalled. Often superimposed upon moving inanimate objects. Traces of representation in block building and crayons.	Trips in house. Much space. Dolls and domestic set-up. Own crayons. Materials narrow to specific toys. Block play develops. Exploration of living things in immediate environment.
4th Stage 4 and 5 years	Widened interest in external moving objects, such as autos, animals, boats, trains. Relationships largely in terms of sense and motor expressions; e.g., a train moves, is hot, etc.	General sense of direction on streets from home to school and other familiar places.	Images in crayons and clay. Dramatic play extends to moving objects in domestic setting. Symbols for image recalls often have little representative value. Cooperative play begins.	Trips extend to familiar streets. Orientation after trip. Pipes in building, etc. Widened exploration of living things. Blocks indoor and outdoor. Clay. Crayons. All develop in representative qualities though design persists.
5th Stage 5 and 6 years	Moving objects begin to function. Relationships begin to include functional; e.g., train related to track, station, freight, etc.	Familiar places crudely placed in space relations. Street environment and house environment. Rough block-building maps.	Dramatic play much elaborated. Representative symbols more important. Cooperative play elaborates.	Motor memories still dominant. Oilcloth for rivers. Chalking in street. Airplane views. Perspective map. Trip to high building to see many things in their space relation.
6th Stage 7 and 8 years	Beginning to leave the "here and now." Distant and long-ago still has to be closely connected with the here and now. Interest in skills and techniques begins.	Rough maps with crayons. Orientation begins in relation to distant and long-ago.	Symbols of general ideas begin. Still closely tied up with direct images. Books. Source material written and in map and chart form.	Use of compass. Pilot maps. Practice in scale relief experiments. Out-of-door maps. Concept of erosion—rivers and sea-drainage —growth of living things conditioned by earth forces. Tool maps of oilcloth. Trips in connection with here and now. Photographs of far-away. Stories about far-away in which dramatic control is geographic; e.g., grass or earthquake.

By labeling this chart "Notes Towards a . . . Developmental Continuum," Mitchell emphasized that these were *her* findings. She wanted students to add to this chart using their own experiences with children. (From "Notes Toward a Chart of the Development of Geographic Thinking and Tools," in *Young Geographers*, by Lucy Sprague Mitchell. Reprinted by permission of Bank Street College of Education, © 1991 by Bank Street College of Education.)

they set out for the dock terminal markets to observe the auctioning of vegetables and fruits—from midnight to 3:00 AM. They forced themselves up before dawn to get to the Fulton Fish Market along the East River by 5:00 AM. There they felt the cool breezes from the river and smelled the sea. With excitement, they heard the shouting and saw the constant movement as boats docked at the market, as fishermen unloaded bushels and bushels of freshly caught fish, and as the fish were carted and loaded into the series of huge bins. These stretched for at least a block to which wholesale and retail buyers would come from across the entire city.[21]

One of the students believed that the course assignments and trips "just touched the surface of what makes the world go round."[22] It is likely that Mitchell would have agreed with her. However, she believed that the impact of the course would evolve for the students over years. Like Dewey, who believed the measure of an educative experience is the direction it takes the learner,[23] she was most interested in the directions in which they were moving. And she believed that the students had begun to understand children's interest in "how things work," to think differently about the relationship between the earth and human work, and had begun to connect patterns of work to social problems. She believed that all these understandings would give a framework for their work with children.[24]

Studying Children's Relationship to the Environment

The course assignments and trips were done on an adult level. Though the connections to their work with children grew increasingly clear, Mitchell wanted her students to make an *explicit* connection to the children they were teaching by observing and charting children's relationship to their specific environment. She asked them to use the categories of the developmental continuum in *Young Geographers* as a guide. (See chart.) What was implicit was that children and their communities were not generic or disconnected. Mitchell wanted the students to follow the same process that led to the developmental continuum in *Young Geographers*, to *Young Geographers* itself, and in many ways to the concept and process of the environment class: taking children on trips and systematically observing and recording their behavior at each age level. Through this process Mitchell grew convinced that throughout the elementary years, a child's environment offered the integrative and cumulative source material for curriculum:[25]

> It is obvious that the environment can be a field of exploration from a time when a baby has not discovered that his toe belongs to his body, to the time when he discovers that the social thinking of his family or his nation is one of the many kinds of clan thinking produced by cultures in differing environments.[26]

In the course, as well as in *Young Geographers*, Mitchell traced a child's relationship to the environment. Her developmental continuum reflected a younger child's solid grounding in the "here and now" world and an older child's social thinking—at each stage considering the child's intellectual and emotional development and implications for curriculum. For Mitchell, with growth and experience, a person's environment expands in time, space, complexity, and group affiliation; it grows to include events in the past that organically connect to the present.[27] As children reach preadolescence, when they are able to assume another's perspective, Mitchell believed the focus should be explicitly on the worker as well as the work, on the effect of the work on the worker and the natural environment.[28]

Although the Study of Environment class was designed to illuminate the sources of social issues, Mitchell and her colleagues believed it wasn't enough. They knew that classroom teachers and the student teachers in the program struggled to make sense of the problems of the Depression but, most important, the teachers were looking for guidance when moving from knowledge of an issue to addressing that issue with children. In response, for the 1934–'35 academic year, the year of the first long trip, they offered an additional environment class that focused specifically on social and economic aspects.[29]

Eleanor Hogan's Social Environment Course

The differences in background between Eleanor Hogan and Lucy Sprague Mitchell could not have been greater. Born in 1878, Lucy Sprague was the child of one of Chicago's "captains of industry." A student described Mitchell as "an Eleanor Roosevelt type lady"—tall, patrician, with "lady-like bearing and speech."[30] Like Roosevelt, Mitchell came from a world of wealth, privilege, and power. Mitchell's self-confidence, her elite education, and even a sense of entitlement to express her views came from that world.[31] And also like Roosevelt, she was compelled to move beyond it. She yearned "to live in a really living world."[32] And Jane Addams, founder of Hull House, the Chicago settlement house, symbolized that world, "the real world—a world of work and people that [she] longed to reach but could not."[33]

In striking contrast to Mitchell, Hogan, born Eleanor Pedersen in 1898, grew up in Brooklyn, a child of poor Swedish and Norwegian immigrant parents.[34] To assist her family, she left school in the ninth grade to work as a secretary. She and her older sister helped raise their four younger siblings and earned the money to send two of them to college. Hogan later received her high school diploma through an extension course. She began her career in education with her enrollment, as a special student because she lacked a BA, in the first class (1930–'31) of the teacher education program Mitchell and her colleagues created, the Cooperative School for Student Teachers, which became Bank Street College. After completing the program and teaching for two years in experimental schools, she joined the small, intimate faculty of the Cooperative School. Ten years of evening study later, she received a BA from New York University. Although to many students she was "imposing," "strong," "a brilliant teacher," she struggled with a sense of insecurity among her highly educated, frequently wealthy colleagues at the Cooperative School.

Mitchell must have seen special qualities in this attractive, intelligent young woman who had not even received a BA—perhaps it was her intense identification with the labor movement, her social philosophy. Perhaps she was aware of Hogan's highly developed administrative abilities.[35]

Mitchell and Hogan shared a worldview that impressed many of the students, and it was this, as much as their dramatic differences, that made the teaching partnership dynamic. Similar to progressives at the turn of the century who grappled with the problems of the new industrial society, Mitchell and Hogan and many other progressive educators of the 1930s believed in both the power of education and political action to create a more just and equitable society. And their concept of a teacher's role was tied to this vision of a changed society, to the kind of people who would create that society. However, unlike Mitchell who embraced labor's struggle through conviction, the struggle of labor in the 1930s was Hogan's personal struggle.[36] So it is not surprising that Hogan was asked to develop and teach a social environment course that focused on social issues.

The Assignment

In her March 4, 1939, diary entry, Elizabeth Helfman, a student in Hogan's class, wrote, "A good morning spent taking around a Tenants' Petition about stopping rent raises. Much success!"[37] In the neighborhood where she student taught, people who lived in cold-water flats in a number of buildings owned by the same landlord found it impossible to pay the rent increases recently levied on them. They called a rent strike. It was winter when Elizabeth and Janet Greenwell, another student who student taught in the same school, went from one freezing apartment to another talking with the people. The tenants were mostly

Italian and mostly women, who were "very happy to talk with [Elizabeth and Janet] about their problems with the landlords" and what they wanted.[38]

Elizabeth and Janet did this as part of an assignment that asked them to grapple with a social issue of importance to the children and families of the schools in which they worked. The underlying assumption was that the education of children could not be separated from the social conditions around them. Hogan wanted them to understand what the issue meant in the lives of the people of that community and, with additional research, to present to their peers a report of their findings and recommendations—which were to be practical, not solely platitudes. Elizabeth became aware of a bill before the local legislature that would institute rent control in the area. She and Janet and a number of tenants wrote a petition, and on March 4, 1939, brought it from apartment to apartment and sent it off to the legislature. They also attended the legislative hearing about the bill, and shared the tenants' excitement when the bill finally was passed.

The Trips

To deepen students' understanding of issues discussed in class, Eleanor Hogan led students on trips in the Greater New York area into the frantic work pace of garment factories, cigarette-smoke-filled meetings of trade unions, a somber children's court to hear cases, a crowded relief office filled with people desperate for work, slum tenements, brand-new subsidized housing, detention centers, children's bantering at recreation projects, and heated political rallies.[39] (It was on a trip to the headquarters of the New York Transit Workers Union that Eleanor first met her future husband, Austin Hogan, head of the union.[40]) Whenever possible, situations were viewed from a variety of perspectives: they spoke with leaders of the United Garment Makers Union, then visited a factory, observed the work conditions, then spoke with management; when they visited tenements, they spoke with the tenants and, on another occasion, spoke with the landlords. Though Hogan had a point of view, she wanted students to understand the complexity of the issues and not fall back on "pat solutions."[41] Also, these local trips never focused solely on what was wrong. Always there were trips that showed how people, in concert with others, worked to redress social conditions and were making a difference.

Hogan believed that with firsthand knowledge of an issue, such as juvenile delinquency or substandard housing, teachers would be better able to think through how to discuss such an issue with children. It is not surprising that teachers avoid discussing social issues with young children. In general, teachers care deeply about children's well-being, but feel at a loss when confronted with the harsher aspects of children's lives and the world around them. Admirably, many teachers try to make their classrooms havens, yet in so many cases it is the children themselves who bring the issues into the classroom. And even when we as children's teachers do not deal with social issues in school, it does not mean that children don't deal with them in their lives. It is interesting how many children get the message that certain situations, though they might be right out on the street for everyone to see, should not be talked about in school. A teacher I know who was studying transportation with first graders related how for her children homelessness fell into this category, how she became acutely aware of what children were *not* saying. As part of the study they visited New York's Grand Central Station. Like most people they were taken with the sheer grandness of the place, all the people rushing through, and of course the tunnels, the trains, and the conductors. The teacher noticed that as they passed one of the waiting rooms, the children stopped as though frozen, looked silently, then just moved on. The room was filled with people sleeping on the benches or just sitting alone. Their clothes were dirty and they had some belongings in torn shopping bags.

The next morning, when they discussed the trip, no one mentioned the people in the waiting room. Children wrote about the trip, did drawings, and created models of aspects of the station using blocks. They built tracks, trains, and tunnels; the large open space with ticket booths; and three children built the waiting room filled with toy figures of people. When the children spoke about their structure, they said simply that it was the waiting room. The teacher realized that she could think back to a time when homelessness didn't exist or at least wasn't prominent. And for her, this should not be. She was overwhelmed by it. But she also began to realize that the children she taught had no such perspective. Homelessness had always been a part of their world, and it must have been peculiar to them that important adults in their lives didn't speak of it.

She accepted her discomfort and brought it up at the next morning's discussion time. She said to the class that everyone should have a home to live in, but on the trip she saw people who were living in the station. That was all she said, and it was as though the floodgates had opened. They described what they saw, and their questions were an indictment of a society that allows these things to happen: "How could this be? Doesn't anybody care?" She let them express their thoughts and felt freed that she didn't, as she had thought, have to offer them a neat solution. But she took their questions seriously and researched efforts in the neighborhood to help people who lacked the means to obtain shelter. Her research led her to a soup kitchen just three blocks from the school and a residence for elderly women. She spoke with the head cook at the soup kitchen and found that he welcomed speaking with groups of children about his work and the work of the soup kitchen in general. They arranged a time for the visit when people would be working in the kitchen preparing for the afternoon meal. She didn't want their visit to intrude on people's privacy as they waited to eat or were eating.

The morning after their visit, when they discussed the trip, children said they wanted to do something to help the soup kitchen. She asked them to think about what they could do. One child said they could ask people in the school to bring in food from home, and they could deliver it to the soup kitchen. Another child said they could raise money. She asked them how they might do that. A number of them mentioned how the eighth graders had had a bake sale to help pay for an overnight trip. This idea seemed to grab them, and it became clear that they were more interested in running their own bake sale.

Once they decided on the bake sale, there were so many decisions to make: what they should bake, who should be invited, how they should advertise, how much they should charge. The teacher told them they'd have to earn enough money to cover the cost of the ingredients, which the school would lend them. They decided on baking small loaves of bread—banana, pumpkin, and zucchini. Each loaf would cost a dollar. They looked up recipes and, with their teacher's help, began to work out how much of each ingredient they'd need for many loaves of bread. They divided into teams to shop, bake, make signs, and write letters to parents and to other classes. Then, they became serious bakers, and worked for days baking and freezing many small loaves of bread. The sweet smell of their breads wafted through the school hallways for days. Using math manipulative materials, they worked on how to give change. When their bakery opened, the children were brimming with excitement. The breads were such a hit, they sold out before every class had a chance to buy something, so they continued baking and selling. I visited their bakeshop, and the three sellers tripped over each other to wait on me. I bought three loaves, one of each flavor, and they were delicious—the best deal in town. When it was over they worked on counting what they earned, which was quite a math problem given all the change.

Once it was all counted and double-checked, they worked on subtracting the cost of the ingredients, which the school had lent them. They were thrilled to see that they had earned a large amount of money for the soup kitchen. The entire class went to the bank to buy a bank check made out to the soup kitchen, then proudly delivered the check to the soup kitchen chef.

Their teacher was freed to act with the children when she realized that she didn't have to offer them *the* solution, instead she helped her six-year-olds find ways in which *they could make a difference*.[42] And making a difference was what Hogan and Mitchell wanted and expected of teachers. To do this, teachers had to not simply "know about" what was happening around them, but "know" through getting to know people person-to-person, through their own experience.

Another trip Hogan led was spurred by an article in the newspaper, describing how a Ford plant in New Jersey had sped up the assembly line. In a diary entry dated March 9, 1939, Elizabeth Helfman recorded, "A trip to the Ford Plant, Edgewater, N.J., miracle of mechanical efficiency, precision, timing—meaning what to the workers?" Following the trip, Helfman represented what she thought it meant to the workers by creating a dance drama, *The Speedup*. Florence Krahn remembered how the entire class worked together to perform it. Just as she had saved many of her assignments, she saved a copy of Helfman's narration. It was a drama produced in three episodes: "The Speedup," "The Layoff," and "The Strike." Like Martha Graham's "American themes" of the mid- to late 1930s, the dance was essentially a documentary with narration:[43]

The Speedup

What do they mean by the speedup? Pushing, hammering, bending,
   hammering, pushing, moving on, on, on.
Don't fool yourself, we know what they mean.
They mean doing just what you are doing now, only quicker.
Bend and hammer and push and bend and push, only quicker, quicker.

Hurry, you fool, quicker!
Hurry, hurry, hurry.
Yes, we work on the belt, Yes, this is a speedup.
Hurry, Faster, you fool! Hurry. Screw it in quicker, now, push, now, bend.
   Hurry.
Faster and faster, our heads whirl and we move because we must and we
   hardly know what we move.
What is this that is happening? What is this?
(Hurry, brother, faster, or they'll get you.)[44]

For Helfman and Krahn, the dance personalized their encounter with another's reality and forged a "very real" connection. When Krahn moved to Dearborn, Michigan, seven years later and visited the Ford plant there, she experienced it through her memories of that dance. In the interviews and questionnaires many of the students traced a sense of responsibility and resulting political action to the deep connections forged through such experiences.

Helfman's dance drama, the children's re-creations of Grand Central, Trish Lent's class model of the Brooklyn Bridge and their poetry bridge, and the writing of Laura Gerrity's students were tangible, public expressions of their experience. Mitchell called these follow-up experiences "outgo." When Mitchell had taken children on trips, she became aware that children expressed their experience of a trip most articulately in their play, not with words but physically, in their block buildings, paintings, clay work, and drawings, and through music, movement, and drama. When she asked adults to reflect on experiences in similar ways, she came to the conclusion that the learning process was essentially the same for adults.

For Mitchell, there were two major aspects to the learning process, not to be separated in a teacher's thinking or in classroom practice: "the intake," a learning experience in which information is acquired, and the outgo. To separate the two would be "like separating two halves of a pair of scissors: you no longer have scissors left—just two blades."[45]

Like Dewey, Mitchell believed that learning would take place only if an experience is transformed, if a new relationship is drawn and expressed. Given the similarity to current computer processing terminology, intake and outgo might sound mechanical. However, Mitchell envisioned outgo as an individual expression of experience, a personalized form of crystallized remembrance—"which is essentially a creative, active thing."[46]

The Work

Hogan arranged what she and Mitchell called a "social experiment," whereby the students would spend one morning a week for one semester performing some form of work in a setting in which they would confront social issues, such as "the left-wing League of Women Shoppers and the League for Industrial Democracy as well as such community groups as the Lower West Side Federation on Housing and Employment."[47]

When reflecting on their experience of Hogan's class, students said that it gave a portrait of the society, of "how Americans lived." They viewed the work in social service agencies, the trips, and the assignment as different from anything they had done before. These experiences placed the teaching role in a larger context, as stemming "from a philosophy of teachers being trained in the big picture, not just the classroom."[48] They saw themselves as players in a larger field, and their work as teachers grew more important. They learned that to address issues with children, they, like the first-grade teacher who brought her children to Grand Central Station, had to confront these issues themselves.

One student, expressing the opinion of so many other students, said, "What was different and important about the environment classes was that Lucy Sprague Mitchell and Eleanor Hogan were trying, above all else, to open our eyes to see things we had never seen before."[49] Mitchell and Hogan wanted the students to understand with an expanded perspective, to see the world through another's eyes—of an autoworker, a garment factory worker, a landlord, a union organizer, a social worker, a politician.

The Environment Classes Within the Total Program: "An Orchestrated Experience That Moved Outward"[50]

The environment classes were designed to integrate all aspects of the teacher preparation program that Mitchell and her colleagues spearheaded. In each aspect of the program, the focus was on the *person* who teaches. Mitchell was most interested in attitudes, not solely toward work but toward life itself. She characterized the attitudes she so passionately

worked to cultivate as those of a scientist and of an artist. She believed that trips offered the opportunity to follow a scientific process—
exploring, "eager alert observation," questioning, analysis, forming
hypotheses, testing of one's perceptions through the exchange with others, and using what was learned in future explorations. Trips also offered
the possibility of acquiring attitudes and ways of being she associated
with an artist—of "emotional drive" and "relish," active participation in
a "creative phase of work," and a sense of "joy" and "beauty." [51]

The Cooperative School for Student Teachers, the teacher education program that eventually became Bank Street College, grew from
the work of the Bureau of Educational Experiments, which Mitchell
headed. The bureau was an interdisciplinary research organization that
kept track of and supported experiments in education. To avoid the trap
of believing that the bureau had found "the way," Mitchell relied on the
"joint thinking" of the directors of eight experimental schools and of
bureau staff. It was the directors of these schools that asked the bureau
to create the program for teachers that was piloted in 1930, and they
helped set its policies and curriculum.[52]

The experimental schools were located in urban, suburban, and rural
settings in the Greater New York area. The teacher education program
reflected the differences in student backgrounds, curriculum concerns,
and physical environments.[53] Among these schools was a residential
school for orphaned girls in Flourtown, Pennsylvania; the Little Red
School House in NYC, then an experimental public school; and the
City and Country School, also in NYC, whose director created the children's wooden building blocks that are seen in early childhood programs
throughout the country. The "cooperating schools" were sites of research
in child development, curriculum development, educational materials
development, and in studying educational environments that support
children's growth. Students did apprentice teaching primarily in these
schools and attended classes at the bureau's new site, 69 Bank Street.

Mitchell's early description would characterize the program right
through the early 1950s. She described three interrelated aspects. The
first was "the development of the student teacher's personal powers." [54]
On an adult level, teachers would experience the kinds of things they were
being asked to do with children, such as to explore the physical and
social environment around them and to express their experience using
art materials, music, dance, and drama—as they did when they visited
the Ford plant assembly line and created the movement drama. In their

student-teaching placements, they followed a parallel process with the children by taking class trips into New York and examining what makes the city work. When recalling their student teaching, many adult students spoke of the children's and their own excitement as they ventured out together to explore noisy construction sites, the boats on the rivers, busy markets, massive power plants, and a whole world of activity under city streets. Many also recalled how following a trip, children thoughtfully discussed their experience and reflected the experience by using movement and drama, painting, writing stories, and, most dramatically, by painting large maps of the city directly on the floor, over which they constructed with blocks so much of what they had encountered.[55]

The desired results would be an understanding of relationships that connect that environment to them and to a larger world, and an understanding of how children might see and use that environment. Ultimately, through the broadening of their environment and perspective, Mitchell and her colleagues hoped the student teachers would see themselves "as part of larger and more significant groups."[56] Mitchell believed identifying with others came not from sitting in a classroom but by getting out into the world and being a part of what

This is an example of how the "Sevens" (second graders) at City and Country School used blocks to represent human-geographic relationships. This block-building scheme shows how the children represented relationships between Manhattan and the surrounding areas. (Photograph courtesy of Harriet Cuffaro)

was happening—by going to the street corner, the factories, the train stations, the union halls, and the coal mines.

From the second aspect of the program, the understanding of children, Mitchell expected much more than textbook knowledge. She wanted the student teachers to develop through their firsthand experience in student teaching a deep understanding of the specific children they taught. She wanted them to be able to see how individual children of a particular age range in a particular school and neighborhood use their bodies, play, use language, engage with their peers, and use materials. In essence, student teachers needed to know how the children understand and act on the world. To do this they would both study child development and acquire the skills of observing and recording children's behavior.[57]

Knowledge of children and of the environment would be used in service of the third aspect, curriculum knowledge. Included here was mastery of teaching the basic subjects, the 3 Rs (reading, 'riting, and 'rithmetic), but what was central and emphasized was the student teacher's ability to create a learning environment and plan a cohesive, integrated, and "organic" curriculum. This ability was essentially the agenda of the environment classes. The studies created by Laura, Trish, and Karen can be considered latter-day versions of what Mitchell was aiming for. What we today call "the skills" (reading, writing, and mathematics) are often taught in isolation, with little connection to the world in which they are used. Too often these subjects have become the mainstay of an education devoid of content and the focus of many teacher education programs. In contrast, Mitchell viewed academic "skills" as "tools" to be used by children in the service of a deeper understanding of their environment.

Chapter 6

"A Way of Feeling into Another's Life"

"Do I Have a Point of View? Where Did It Come From?"

Willie Kraber said that on the 1941 long trip she finally realized what she thought she knew already, that "there are many kinds of people in the world." And she asked herself, "Do I have a point of view? Where did it come from?" She said that realization and these questions she asked herself influenced all her work as a teacher of children and school administrator. With those comments, Willie ended our interview.[1]

She was one of the students in the long-trip photo in Bank Street's lobby, the photo that sparked my interest in the trips. With the introduction from a senior retired faculty member, I called Willie to set up my first long-trip interview. On the phone she said what I was to hear over and over again: "I don't know how much help I can be. This took place a *long* time ago." As I approached her Brooklyn apartment, I didn't know what to expect. Aside from the bits of information in Mitchell's autobiography and Antler's biography of Mitchell, I knew little else, except that the trips remained part of the folk history of the college.

Willie welcomed me into her home, offered me tea or coffee, and began the interview by describing the moment of leaving. She said the sun was shining, and everyone seemed excited, but she felt uneasy saying good-bye to her husband and four-year-old son. It was the first time she had traveled apart from them. She entered the bus and waved to them through the window. She saw how tightly her child clung to his father. When she made eye contact with him, he grabbed the tassel of his knitted hat and pulled it tightly over his face—and with that image Willie began the long trip to the coal mines and steel mills of Pittsburgh. She said that it was hard for her to think or talk about that trip in a theoretical or objective way because the experience was so personal, yet her detailed and nuanced portrait evoked the time, place, people, and events. I sat with rapt attention listening to this eighty-five-year-old woman, as she, with little prompting, spoke for an hour, vividly re-creating events from more than fifty years ago.

This beginning led to my own long trip into the experience of students who followed Lucy Sprague Mitchell and Eleanor Hogan into corners of the world they might never have confronted. After interviewing twenty-two people who attended the trips, I knew what I had suspected, that Willie's comments were not unique. My goal was to interview at least two people from each of the sixteen trip years, which wasn't possible for the earliest trip years because many of the participants were deceased. Using the college admissions records, I cast the net as broadly as I could by sending questionnaires to everyone I could not interview. Of the 136 questionnaires I sent out, I received 101 responses—an unusually large response for questionnaires, especially given the advanced age of many of the trip participants and that the events had taken place from forty-five to sixty years ago. More important, many were detailed, substantive statements of what remained outstanding from the experience and of the perceived impact, a testament to the power of the experience. One might question the validity of retrospective accounts of events experienced forty-five to sixty years ago. Yet the recall of events from over the long span of a person's life offers a distinct vantage point for making sense of and integrating life experiences, in a way that could not have been done earlier.[2] For my purpose, the "accuracy," if there is such a thing in relation to memory, was not as significant as the subjective meaning given to events, the meanings that influenced thoughts and actions.[3] Yet, very early in the process, I saw how the accounts corroborated each other repeatedly.

"Contacts More Real"

Mitchell said that the major goal of the long trips—and teacher education in general—was the enlargement of the groups to which the student teachers belonged, so that they, as teachers, would work to enlarge the groups to which *their* students belonged.[4] The goal was nothing less than to expand the adult students' circles of knowing, caring, and commitment. Mitchell had struggled with ways to help her students move beyond their familiar worlds and what they had been conditioned to see and believe. She grew convinced that "social insight, the understanding of groups other than our own . . . will have to come through contacts more real than can be made through words,"[5] that to care enough to have commitment to groups different from one's own, you need to *know* the people firsthand, not just *know about* them. Mitchell and Hogan believed that the future of a democratic society lay in the balance—and seventy years later it continues to lie in the balance.

Many of the trips taken in the environment classes had the same goal as the long trip, to enlarge students' circles of knowing, caring, and commitment, but the long trip moved the students further outward into American society; it was "big league" by comparison, the "top and the end," a dramatic extension and "culmination."[6] To a much greater extent than the local trips, the long trips took them out of the comfort and routines of their familiar world, and, unlike the class trips in the city, they couldn't go home for the evening. They were immersed together in another's reality for a week to ten days. (See chart.)

Pre-WWII Long Trips	Post-WWII Long Trips
1935-1941	1948-1951
Led by Lucy Sprague Mitchell and Eleanor Hogan	Led by Eleanor Hogan Assisted by Sheila Sadler (1950 & 1951 trips)
Focus	**Focus**
Labor/Unionization Government Efforts on Behalf of the People Use and Abuse of Natural Resources	Civil Rights Labor/Unionization Government Efforts on Behalf of the People Use and Abuse of Natural Resources
Major Sites Visited	**Major Sites Visited**
1935–1936: West Virginia	1948-1951: Tennessee
Coal Mining Towns	Tennessee Valley Authority (TVA)
New Deal Resettlement Community: Arthurdale	Ducktown
1937-1941: Pennsylvania	Highlander Folk School
Coal Mining Towns	African American Farming Community: Bakewell
Steel Towns	

The span of prewar and postwar trips.

The trip was positioned in the program as the "last phase" of the students' study. For Mitchell, the last phase was to be a *beginning*. Her question on the value of the long trip was not: How much did students learn?

What she wanted to know was: "Has it started social growth?"[7] She believed the full impact of the experience would take not "hours but years. For growth is slow and growth is individual."[8] Mitchell would be gratified that forty-five to sixty years later, across years of work and family life, the statements of many of the students show that her goal was realized.

On the long trip, ideas about teaching and the role of a teacher in American society—ideas that were fundamental to their course work and student teaching—assumed a new immediacy. This chapter and the next focus on the long trip, on what remains important for the students and the impact they believe it had on them. This chapter focuses specifically on the students' experience of:

- Mitchell and Hogan's planning
- how their group became a tightly knit community
- how the places visited revealed a dramatic connection between people and their environment
- the power of reflecting on and expressing experience through the arts
- encountering social issues and social change.

Mitchell and Hogan's Planning

Any consciously designed curriculum reflects a view of what knowledge is most worth knowing. For Mitchell and Hogan, that knowledge was not divorced from the context in which education takes place—the world in which children lived. What they selected from that world and the seriousness with which it was planned and taught revealed their values and a vision of the kind of teacher they wanted the students to become. Unlike the popular stereotype of the progressive teacher interested primarily in *how* one learns with only perfunctory concern for *what* is learned, the trip leaders believed that knowledge of the working world of American society and the relationship of that society to the natural world was *essential*. They believed the students, as teachers of children and as citizens, had to understand social, political, and economic currents. Otherwise, how would they guide children to become responsible citizens? If it were an academic exercise, it could have come from books. They wanted the kind of knowledge that would move the students outward from familiar worlds, to find out "in their muscles" that "the world indeed had corners [they] had not yet experienced before";[9] that the United States was a nation of profoundly different physical and cultural regions; that there were human commonalities that transcended differences—all of which had implications for the education of children.

Just as in the curricula designed by Laura Gerrity, Trish Lent, and Karen Kriesberg, the *how* and *what* of the curriculum was an instrument of Mitchell and Hogan's aims. And throughout the long trip they modeled the kind of teacher they hoped their students would become.

Planning for the Exchanges with People

A photograph taken on the 1948 trip shows a group of men from the all–African American community of Bakewell, in Soddy, Tennessee. In front of them, though not included in the photo, are the men and women of the community and the long-trip participants. A student's journal

Lucy Sprague Mitchell and Eleanor Hogan enjoying a moment of rest at a stop along the Pennsylvania Turnpike. Students of the 1941 long trip fondly remember this photo. (Photograph by and courtesy of Elizabeth Olesen Garvais)

entry says it is a civil rights meeting. A tall, lanky man with a shock of white hair is speaking. He is a minister, the Reverend De Jarnette. And among the men is Eleanor Hogan. A student commented that "it's not a coincidence that you see Eleanor Hogan right there with the people who are the main characters in whatever drama was involved in each of the places we visited."[10] She and Mitchell cultivated relationships with the people they would visit on the trip. In this case, it was Reverend De Jarnette who was Hogan's connection to the community.

The Reverend De Jarnette (right) addresses members of the Bakewell community and the long-trip participants. Through the Highlander Folk School, Hogan had long-standing connections with Bakewell and De Jarnette. (Photograph by and courtesy of Emil Willimetz)

Each time the students arrived at a new setting and were introduced to people—be they miners, mine owners, union organizers, or the people of Bakewell—they became increasingly aware of the time and thought that went into making the arrangements. They never just turned up anywhere; wherever they went they were expected, welcomed, and the people they visited seemed to have looked forward to their coming. They were impressed that teachers from so far away had come to meet and speak with them, and considered it important that people who would influence the minds of children understood their struggle from their perspective, which wasn't necessarily conveyed in newspapers.

Mitchell believed that observing external differences among people frequently strengthened feelings of strangeness and separation. For this reason she felt that moving from books to firsthand contacts with people whose lives are different from one's own required more maturity than did trips that focused primarily on the work itself. To move beyond external differences and "protect the human relationship," she did not want them to *observe* the people; she wanted her students to *interact as human beings*—"person-to-person." And students recalled that they didn't have any prescribed interview procedure and didn't have a little pad to take notes. They were asked to get to know the people they visited in the ways they usually do.

Many spoke of how Mitchell and Hogan modeled the person-to-person interactions they expected from the students. One student recalled that "Mitchell got along so well with the miners. She was so down to earth." It impressed the student that Mitchell never asked miners working at the legal mines what they thought of the bootleg miners, who dug their own mines into land left vacant by its owners—even though she had asked managers and bankers and union people for their opinions. She was not asking workers to pass judgment on their peers or admit to agreeing with illegal actions.[11] Elizabeth Helfman and others believed that the workers took them so seriously because of their "very able faculty" who seemed to know what questions to ask.

At the civil rights meeting that Hogan and the people of Bakewell planned, it was clear to the students that "Eleanor was very concerned that [they] appreciate what Reverend De Jarnette was saying and understand the significance of the man's life and work. He was a person of real convictions."[12] Allen Ohta described him as a "homebred southern religious radical" who had taken difficult assignments and "understood how you could achieve things" in the South. And the minister had accomplished a lot "in terms of getting people to take ownership of their own situation." He had led a strike with parishioners of a nearby community, bravely leading the picket line of strikers right down Main Street. For that he lost his collar, but he remained the "much beloved" pastor of his parishioners and was well respected at Bakewell.

As the students met the key players in each new setting, they became increasingly aware of how important these exchanges were to their faculty, and how their faculty viewed the people as having conviction, the courage of their conviction, and the knowledge and drive to make a difference—all qualities for teachers to emulate.

Planning Everything Else

Thoughtful planning was not evident solely in the arrangements made with the people they met; it was evident in practically every other aspect of the trip. Like Laura, Trish, and Karen, Hogan and Mitchell went on the trip themselves in advance; however, their planning led them one thousand miles away. At the time of the postwar trips (1948–51), Mitchell was in semiretirement and Hogan led the trips herself. Sheila

Sadler, the faculty colleague who assisted Hogan on the last two long trips, said Hogan carefully mapped out the routes, chose the motels and restaurants, "even the comfort stops, which were always at the crossroads, so that there were four gas stations to go to." [13] The detailed itineraries she prepared for the students listed each of the places they would be visiting by day, hour, and distance from New York. Like a daily schedule posted in a classroom, the itineraries enabled students to feel in control and gave a sense of security. (See appendix.)

The Preparation

Just as Laura, Trish, and Karen had thoughtfully prepared their students for a trip, Mitchell and Hogan crafted the trip so that the stage was set for the students' experience. Not surprisingly, for the prewar trips (1935–41), Mitchell and Hogan focused on the implications of industry trends for the coal miners and steelworkers and for the natural environment. For the postwar trips, which started in 1948 and ended in 1951, Mitchell, who did not attend these trips, focused on the relationship between people's lives and work and the natural environment. In their science class, they did experiments about dams and water cycles. In fact, the trip was discussed in all of their courses. Hogan discussed the role of the TVA in renewing the economy of the agricultural South through educational assistance to farmers, soil renewal, conservation, and electrification. Sheila Sadler felt that Hogan was clearly a believer in the concept of regional development sponsored by government, although Hogan was also very sensitive to the resulting displacement of people because of the dams.

It is interesting to consider what stands out as distinct events fifty and sixty years later. In retrospect, many considered the trip a natural extension of the program, and though many felt that they had been well prepared or "must have been well prepared," few remembered the particulars. The course notes that some students saved reveal the depth and detail of the preparation. [14] Perhaps Mitchell and Hogan's lessons modeled careful preparation, set a framework for what they would experience, and, over time, were assimilated into students' memory of the trip. Above all else, it was the experience of the trip that remained outstanding. A student who participated in the 1937 long trip said that "the very things Lucy Sprague Mitchell talked about are the things that last, the things that are typical of young children, the five senses, what you smelled, what you ate, what you saw, what you touched, and what you heard."[15] Similarly, what students highlighted of the follow-up to the trip were the activities that engaged them physically and emotionally. When one considers the overwhelming extent to which children's learning in schools is primarily comprised of textbook reading, verbal lessons, and written question-and-answer activities about something they may never have seen, heard, felt, smelled, or tasted, it's little wonder that many adults, when looking back over their schooling, see grayness.

There was, however, one aspect of the preparation for the postwar trips that nobody forgot. It was Mitchell's lesson on the geography they would be traveling through. Sheila Sadler described part of the lesson.

> Lucy Sprague Mitchell took different colored plasticine bars and rolled them out so that they were layers—maybe half an inch thick—and piled up these layers of colored plasticine, and in a low voice and slow pace she said, "These are the strata that make up the crusts of the earth. Are they flat? No! The earth is round." In a progressively louder voice and faster pace, she continued, "It *moves*. It *breathes*. It *upheaves*, and then there are *volcanoes, shiftings, earthquakes*. And what happens to these layers?" And she would mould the plasticine with her hands and stare at us with her big, intense eyes, holding the plasticine so that you could see.[16]

One student said he "can still see her there, tall, intense, wielding a huge butcher knife, swinging her arm back as though about to chop wood, then with great force slamming the knife through the plasticine. Everyone jumped at the sound as she chopped off the top of the mountains"[17] to illustrate centuries of change.

Mitchell then directed their attention to the specific geological formations they would be passing through as they traveled: "Now when you go over to the Palisades Parkway, where they have cut the highway through, look at the layers, and you will see a fold, you will see a fault. And you will see where it's sharp, which is the fault. The folds are the rounded ones, where the layers actually shift."[18] With these last statements, Mitchell set the stage for what they would discover while traveling on the bus.

From their experiences before, during, and after the trips students realized that good teaching grows from careful attention to detail, from a commitment to what they are teaching, from research, hard work, from *thoughtful planning*. Just as important, Mitchell and Hogan never defined the students' experience, never told them what they should learn from the experience, never told them what to think, and never gave them a list of behavioral outcomes—which today seem to be a driving force in the education of children and teachers, too often limiting the learning process. Mitchell and Hogan set the stage and gave the opportunity for each individual to have an experience, and created a forum for sharing their experiences and for the students' own questions to emerge. My colleagues and I who worked on current long trips faced the high and exacting standards set by Mitchell and Hogan. (See appendix for itineraries of the 1950 long trip to TVA areas and of the 2009 long trip to New Orleans.)

A Tightly Knit Community Was Formed

On each long trip a new class identity developed. Together the students and faculty experienced a "whole other world." They shared experiences that enveloped them physically, as they crawled on their knees making their way through a seam in a coal mine and felt the heat of steel cauldrons, as they experienced the danger of a steelworker's strike, as they were overwhelmed by the grandeur and lushness of the TVA region and, in direct contrast, by the complete destruction of land that had been denuded by industry. Through eating together, sleeping in the same hotel room, being rattled around on the bus together for hours, and the sharing of intensely emotional responses to what they encountered, their interactions with each other grew more casual and at the same time more intense. As they traveled further and further into the trip, their sense of belonging together grew stronger.

It's interesting that for every trip year, except for three in the late 1930s, students spoke consistently of a new sense of belonging as a major aspect of the trip. These were the years they traveled by car in small groups instead of together by bus. Faculty and students volunteered their cars to reduce the cost of the trip. What was it about the bus that was so critical to an emerging sense of community?

As the interviewees spoke of the singing, eating, fun, and serious discussions they shared on the bus trip, I recalled so many of the bus trips I had taken as a child, of singing the endless "One Hundred Bottles of Beer on the Wall," of the silly jokes, of seeing what each other had brought for lunch, and of getting to know the person next to me so differently. I also recalled when I taught at a small Head Start center a time

No long-trip participant forgot the drama of Mitchell's lesson on the geological formations they would be passing through on the long trip. (Photograph of Lucy Sprague Mitchell from her book *Young Geographers*. Reprinted by permission of Bank Street College of Education, © 1991 by Bank Street College of Education.)

when parents and grandparents and siblings accompanied the children on a bus trip to a state park for a picnic. A child's grandmother had baked cookies and kept passing them around. I got to know the children's parents so differently. They spoke about their lives. I felt closer to the children's families, and they felt closer to each other.

As I listened to Mitchell's and Hogan's students talk about the bus and thought about my own experience on bus trips, including the current long trips, I realized that the bus was part of the trip, not simply a way to get there and back. The long trips, however, had the added dimension of recurring stretches of uninterrupted time as they traveled from one trip site to the next.

Mitchell and Hogan had encouraged the students to talk among themselves about what they were seeing. And like the children's families on the Head Start trip, they emerged as individuals as they spoke with each other about their lives in ways they hadn't before. As they revealed more of themselves, their differences became source material for understanding each other as well as for understanding what they were experiencing together. Many had grown up in families that saw unionizing as the downfall of America, some in families that were staunch advocates of labor, and some of the students had been union organizers themselves. On the bus many discussed how "shaken up" they were by the actual experience of a strike, of workers at a union meeting, of speaking with management—all so different from what they had expected.

And they didn't always agree with each other. A student recalled often in later years the argument she had with another student following their visit to a nursery school in West Virginia. The student, whose husband was African American, was appalled to see a copy of *Little Black Sambo* in the class library. Another student had great affection for the story and argued that "children should be allowed to make identifications with characters in books without adult interference."[19] In later years, she was to recall this conversation often as she considered the complex issue of stereotyping when selecting books for children.

When they discussed segregation, many were surprised that a classmate who had grown up in the South seemed to accept what was such a shock to the others. Another student said that through these discussions she gained insight into how people are conditioned by their environment, "how you don't fight the things that are just part of your environment, because when you grow up accepting them, and seeing everybody around you, and people you love, accepting it, then, obviously, it can't be that terrible or that wrong."[20] Students said these types of discussions, which occurred on the bus, contributed to their radicalization and were therefore "more than educational."

The unmasking of the forces that condition people had been one of Mitchell and Hogan's aims for education in general—and for the long trips in particular. If Mitchell and Hogan's goal was to create a democratic community among the students so that they, in turn, would do the same with the children they would teach, the bus offered the stage. As the predictability of the world they left behind was replaced by the routine of the trip, the bus became for many a supportive critical container. By venturing outward the way they did, they showed trust in their peers as well as in their faculty. John Dewey emphasized the centrality of communication to democratic living, of an exchange among people that would leave each member's world enlarged.[21] For many of the students, this level of communication emerged on the bus as they shared their own feelings and understandings of what they were experiencing together. Like the daily discussions in Laura Gerrity's and Trish Lent's classes, the bus served as the "intentional" learning environment, offering the time and place for casual and serious discussion to occur.

A Dramatic Connection Between People and Their Environment

It is significant that before they experienced the trip destinations, they had spent all that time on the bus getting to know each other. It was a different group that descended into the mines together.

West Virginia and Pennsylvania Coal Mines, 1935–41;
West Virginia Coal Mine, 2006

Many feared that they would struggle to breathe, that the claustrophobia would be overwhelming, *that the mine would collapse*. Though most were "not anxious" to go down into the mine, they knew they'd be sorry if they didn't. Some felt excitement. Most experienced both emotions as they put on miners' lamp caps. They hadn't expected the elevator to be rickety. As they descended the shaft they held each other's hands as they listened to the loud clanking of the pulleys and felt the vibration through their bodies. Somehow they never expected the descent to take so long or the mine to be so deep—it seemed to take forever, as though to "the center of the earth." They expected the temperature to grow colder as they descended, but it became uncomfortably warm. Water kept dripping around them. It grew darker and the air became thick. When they walked in the tunnel, they couldn't stand fully upright, and they realized how fatiguing it must have been for the miners to work for such long hours bent over. To get through certain tunnels, the students had to crawl on hands and knees, and they prayed they "wouldn't hear a rumble." They kept their eyes on the canaries that had been brought down by the miners. If the air became dangerous, the canaries would die.

As they left the elevator they realized that they were completely enveloped in coal. Florence Krahn recalled that everyone there had known that miners worked underground, yet experiencing the reality of it was a surprise and became "something you really thought about." As they walked through the tunnel, they felt the texture of the "brilliant black surfaces" and pried off pieces and examined their structure. Being there fueled an interest in the process of mining. In our interview, Helfman spoke of the excitement of walking along a tunnel full of coal, seeing miners actually doing their work by hand with pickaxes.

The students experienced mixed emotions as they approached the mine elevator. (Photograph by and courtesy of Elizabeth Olesen Garvais, 1941 long trip, Coverdale Mine, PA)

By meeting the miners themselves, students moved beyond one-dimensional images of the oppressed worker. They remembered the miners as friendly, "appreciating [the students'] interest." Krahn realized that mining "got not only in their lungs but it got into their blood," that "even though it was hard work, there was something that pulled them to it."[22] However, they told the students that for their children they would want a different kind of life.

Decades later, as part of the 2006 long trip to West Virginia, we also descended into a coal mine. Even with all the time I had spent listening to and thinking about the dramatic accounts of students' mine experiences of the 1930s and early 1940s, it was an eye-opener. I don't know why I had imagined that some natural light would filter into the mines. When the miner who escorted us through the mine turned off his lamp, I could not even see the person right next to me. I had known the ceilings might be low but didn't expect my head to touch the ceiling. Taller members of the trip had to stand bent over. The ground was covered with water, and I pictured miners working all day standing in water. What was most surprising to me was the narrowness of some of the seams, about eighteen inches high and twenty-four inches wide. Men would lie down on their backs or stomachs on skateboard-like conveyances and push themselves into the seam. With their clothes wet from the ground, they would stretch their arms awkwardly for hours, day after day, to extract the coal.

Mitchell's students remembered that the mountains of slag, the coal grit left from the processing, seemed to be everywhere in the mining towns. They had learned that the slag was full of dangerous chemicals, and gasped as they watched children playing on it as though it were rock and soil. Coal grit blew from the heaps of slag and from the processing plants, leaving a film in school classrooms, school yards, and people's homes. That was over fifty years ago. On our current trip to West Virginia in 2006, we didn't see slag heaps. Now the debris is "impounded" into giant empty holes in the mountains. An impoundment is a dam constructed from mine refuse that holds the sludge left over from the washing and processing of coal. It contains carcinogenic chemicals used to "clean" the coal and toxic heavy metals that are present in coal—arsenic, mercury, chromium, cadmium, boron, selenium, and nickel. We saw an elementary school that was directly below a sludge impoundment of more than 2 billion gallons of thick toxic black liquid.

The impounded sludge has leaked into the water supplies, polluting the Coal River and the area's drinking water. A resident of the area showed us just how contaminated the drinking water has become. He filled a bucket with tap water, let it settle, submerged his hand into the water, and scooped from the bottom. When he opened his fist, all of us were stunned to see a handful of bright orange grit! He told us that he and his neighbors live with the constant fear of the impoundment failing completely, bringing down upon them a tidal wave of sludge.

The same elementary school that was built below an impoundment stands right next to a massive coal preparation plant, where coal is "cleaned" and processed for transport and distribution. Just as it was in the coal towns of the 1930s, children are breathing coal soot from the processing plant every day, all day; it is in the ventilation system, on the children's climbing equipment, and on the grass. We learned from residents in the area that the exposure to the coal dust and the chemicals in the air and water has caused an inordinate number of cancers and other serious illnesses.

When we learned that almost 60 percent of the electricity used in the United States is generated from burning coal, we began to realize the magnitude of the resulting environmental issues. Turning on a light will never be the same for any of us who attended that trip. These are critical realizations for individuals who will influence children's attitudes—and critical to a citizen's sense of responsibility for the human cost of the use and abuse of natural resources. As it had for our colleagues in the 1930s, the issue of coal mining would forever after evoke an emotional and physical response, a new identification.

The TVA, 1948–51

Joie Willimetz, who grew up in the South, remembered that as a child she would hear about "those horrible floods wiping out so many people and doing so much damage to the region."[23] She remembered hillsides completely washed away and vast fields eroded through overplowing and the floods. On the 1948 long trip to the TVA region, she saw how the area had been transformed. It was the nation's largest government effort to reclaim a vast regional area and end the cycle of everlasting indebtedness. TVA "took mountain lands and rivers and reorganized the world."[24] Before each postwar trip, students discussed the controversy of the TVA in the environment classes—the flooding of farmland to create lakes, the raising of mountains for farmland, the forced relocation—albeit for compensation—of populations for whom the area had been their home for generations, and of the construction of great dams to harness the power of the Tennessee River to generate electricity. Some students had never realized that people could be placed in a position where they had "no control or say-so about their lives." and wondered how they "would have felt in the same circumstances." One student did know what it felt like. Although she saw the "economic and social advantages" wrought by the TVA, she had also seen "the anger and dismay of relatives." The TVA had "flooded part of the town where [she] was born."[25]

Some of the students were wary that it wouldn't work at all; however, when they saw the majestic dams, lush green forest areas, crystal clear lakes, attractive farm houses and barns, and crops growing along vast swerving contours of land to prevent erosion—all of which had been created or influenced by the TVA—they couldn't help but be impressed. On the bus, they had driven through nearby mountain areas and had seen the poverty that went along with acres and acres of eroded farmland. These were areas untouched by TVA.

Wilbur Rippy, who participated in the last long trip (1951), had grown up in that region. In our interview he recalled his father pointing to a light shining way in the distance and saying, "Now see that? Those folks over there got electricity." He said that to this day he "couldn't eat a piece of corn bread without tasting kerosene."[26] He and many of the students saw hope in the giant electrical towers "marching like an army" into the region. Rippy said he and other students realized that the world could be changed, that "it doesn't always have to go on. People don't have to have a damn kerosene stove blow up in their face." Mitchell and Hogan did not accept the world—and education—as it was. And on the trips, they wanted their students to open their eyes to painful realities of people's lives and, just as important, to the possibility for change. They wanted their students to work for *what could be.*

Probably nowhere would students see such a dramatic illustration of human conditioning of the natural world for the social good of many. Government was taking action on behalf of the people of an entire region of the country.[27]

Ducktown, Tennessee, 1948–51; Kayford Mountain, West Virginia, 2006

The student said, "We went from springtime, normal, lush green, growing, vital countryside, gradually into death."[28] The memory evoked a visceral response in this student and in almost every student who participated in the post-WWII trips. She was describing their gradual progression from the lushness of the TVA into Ducktown, Tennessee. The copper smelting plant there was still working and belching out smoke. When it rained, it turned to sulfuric acid.[29] It was as though the land had been flayed alive, leaving a red raw wound that stretched endlessly. It felt like they had landed on the moon. They could not believe the devastation; "it was terrifying."[30] Nothing grew there. A student remembers seeing nothing but a broken-down fence "looking like it was sticking up from a bald man's head." The students knew they were there to see the "opposite of taking care, a way of doing business, grab what you can, eat up the land, don't regulate."[31] By comparison, what the TVA had achieved looked "like a miracle."

When I saw Kayford Mountain, West Virginia, I felt like I was reliving the postwar students' experience of Ducktown. It was on the 2006 long trip to mining areas of West Virginia. These current long trips began in 1995. Unlike the earlier trips that were an integral part of the teacher education program, the current trips are offered by Bank Street's division of continuing education and are open to the extended college community: faculty, students, graduates, board members, and affiliated educators. Like the prewar long trips, the focus is the environment, social justice, and, just as important, the implications for children, their families, and schooling.

On the recent West Virginia trip, we witnessed how the lives and fates of people living in coal regions are still tied intimately to issues of coal mining. In Appalachia, mining coal in deep tunnels dug into the earth is only one form of mining, considered by many coal companies as outdated. A current method, described as "more efficient," is more insidious—mountaintop removal. This method goes beyond strip mining, which removes the earth around the perimeter of mountainsides. With mountaintop removal, the top of an entire mountain is blasted away so the coal can easily be excavated. When the coal is depleted, the company moves on to the next mountain. This method is decimating the Appalachian Mountains, wreaking havoc on the environment; poisoning the water supply; and destroying people's health, homes, and way of life. At the current pace of mountaintop removal, the land affected soon will be larger than the state of Rhode Island. Already, one thousand miles of streams have been contaminated by the chemical-ridden, blasted, and scooped-out topsoil and rock, which has contaminated the water table.

As part of that recent trip we met with Larry Gibson, who is the prime mover of the Keeper of the Mountain Foundation, an organization that works with other organizations to fight mountaintop removal. We visited Larry at his home on Kayford Mountain. The family cemetery, close to his home, showed us that his family has lived on or near Kayford Mountain in West Virginia for over two hundred years. An environmentalist described Larry as a man who casts a tall shadow, and we learned why. At great personal risk, he is fighting the coal companies by refusing to sell his land to them. He is the last holdout on Kayford.

Larry showed us a model of how Kayford was being destroyed layer by layer to reach the coal. Then Larry led us to the mining site. We slowly walked through the loveliness of his side of the mountain—covered in spring's first green all dotted with red bud—until we came to a clearing that overlooked a scene I'll never forget. We had walked into a

At great personal risk Larry Gibson fights the large coal companies by refusing to sell his land on Kayford Mountain in West Virginia. Using the model, Gibson showed us how Kayford is being dismantled. (Photograph by author)

vision of hell, a scene from Dante's *Inferno*. We saw three trucks in the distance. Though each carried one hundred tons of coal, the vast scale of the scene dwarfed their massive size. And though the excavator was as large as a square city block, it appeared as a speck. Many people once lived there. The area had been blessed with a wide diversity of trees, flowers, fish, animals, and other creatures. The Appalachians have been considered the nation's rain forest.

Gibson led us from his part of the mountain to the site of mountaintop removal. We stood in disbelief. It was as though we were witnessing a scene from Dante's *Inferno.* (Photograph by author)

I helped plan this trip and had researched mountaintop removal. I had read the *National Geographic* feature article on the very sites we would visit and the people we would meet;[32] read books on the topic;[33] seen striking aerial photographs of it on the Internet; spoken by phone with community activists, environmentalists, lawyers, and public officials, all of whom are fighting mountaintop removal; and seen a documentary movie about it. None of these prepared me for the enormity of what Larry Gibson showed us on Kayford Mountain.

As I stood before that panorama of devastation, Lucy Sprague Mitchell's belief that direct experience is "smiting" really hit me, how it was a world apart from hearing or reading about someone else's experience, and what she meant was right before me. I realized that this is what Mitchell had wanted, for children and their teachers to learn from their own unfiltered experience in the world. On Kayford Mountain, suddenly the "inconvenient truth" of irreparable environmental damage became real and personal and horrifying, and I saw how education on all levels had to embrace environmental consciousness as a mandate. Through being there and meeting those courageous people, I am connected to those people and their struggle. Just as with the student teachers of the 1930s, '40s, and '50s, our circles of knowing, caring, and commitment had enlarged. Even though we came together for a short while, our lives had touched.

Reflecting on and Expressing Their Experience Through the Arts

When the students returned to the college, they discussed their experiences and wrote about them. They designed curricula for children of the areas they visited, considering the children's specific life experience and physical environment. Similar to the preparatory lessons, many follow-up activities paled in most memories and were remembered as part of the program in general rather than as separate events. One might assume that the discussions, writing, and curriculum projects influenced the ways students understood and remembered the trip.

What did stand out for students were the more intense and dramatic forms of follow-up, the artistic expressions of the experience, the books they wrote for children, the plays they wrote, the murals and maps they created, and the dance dramas they created and performed. For many, while in the process of creation, images of the classrooms in which they had student taught flashed across their minds. Their own experience resonated with how actively and eagerly the children worked together to reflect their experience in blocks, how the children's writing seemed so alive, how the painting and movement and dramatic play enabled the children to understand their experience in new and deeper ways.

Following the long trip, Florence Krahn created a book for children that she eventually used in her teaching. It is a simple story for ten- to twelve-year-olds about a child of a coal miner who, more than anything else, wanted to take his place next to his father in the mines: "He thought nothing could be more fun than to ride down the pitch in the cable car and then walk through the long gangway with water dripping from the rock overhead, deeper and deeper into the earth until he should come to his own tunnel. He would drill through the hard rock and plant dynamite like his father."[34] When Krahn read the story to her students, she was moved by their wide eyes intensely focused on her, by their obvious interest in the boy's life. It was an important moment for her because she realized that she could create materials for children and that she could use her own experience directly in her teaching. Krahn saved the book, just as she did her assignment papers. For Krahn, the vividness of the story and the reality of the father and son grew directly from her interactions with the miners at Hazelton, Pennsylvania.

Willie Kraber recalled the dance drama she organized. It was of the murals covering the walls and ceiling of the Croatian Church of Saint Nicholas in Milevale, Pittsburgh. Kraber was the one person to speak of the dramatic murals. She felt as though she entered the world of those murals, which seemed to emerge from the dark walls and ceiling of the church. The twenty murals, done in the 1930s, blend religious and cultural symbolism with vivid scenes candidly showing the exploitation of Croatian immigrants—dead coal miners and a smug, self-satisfied industrialist cover the walls. (Today these "industrial murals" are celebrated as a memorial to the Croatian workers.)[35] Kraber was overwhelmed and realized that just as in the paintings and statues of the old cathedrals, "these are the faces of real people," the people who actually work the steel mills and the mines. In our interview, as she recalled the sorrow evoked by those images, she said, "I was immensely proud of that dance."[36]

Like Krahn, Kraber discovered capabilities in herself she hadn't been aware of. And Mitchell saw something new in the student's work, a new intensity that she attributed to the power of a group experience "profound enough in both intellectual and emotional quality."[37] And she saw it spill out into almost every organized area of the curriculum. For Mitchell, the power of the experience in the students' minds and imaginations enabled them to venture out in new ways and grow as individuals, as a community, and as teachers. As educators, it's worth reflecting on the fact that it was through the arts that the full emotional and intellectual power of the experience was expressed. Unfortunately, in the education of children, and in many cases of teachers as well, it is all too common to hear the arts spoken of as a frill, an expendable addition—and not as an essential way of knowing. We give lip service to individual differences in children, different learning styles, "multiple intelligences," yet in practice "real" learning means reading, writing, and mathematics—most often abstracted from the world in which these skills are vital. We have narrowed the field, diminished possibility, and placed many children, for whom the arts are a natural and powerful form of expression, at a disadvantage.

Like the discussions on the bus, the artistic expressions brought the students together. These expressions of experience revealed their private impressions and ideas in new ways, for themselves and for all to see. And like Elizabeth Helfman's dance drama of the speedup at a Ford plant, these creations personalized their encounter with another's reality and forged an intense, "very real" connection that fostered a sense of responsibility and political action.

Encountering Social Issues and Social Change

A long-trip participant said that two opposing images stand out from her trip: the utter destruction of the land at Ducktown and the lushness of the TVA areas. She was essentially revealing what Mitchell and Hogan wanted the students to experience: daunting social situations they might have read about but had not encountered themselves, and, just as important, the "attempts to do something about them" by people working in concert with others or by government.[38] Hence, students encountered the depression in mining (mines abandoned by owners and resulting massive unemployment) and the illegal makeshift mines dug and mined on abandoned land, the hazardous working conditions in the steel mills and the steelworkers union, and rampant racism and the Highlander Folk School and Bakewell. Many felt that it was the witnessing of both what a "social issue" meant in the lives of people and of people's efforts to address the issues that fostered the conviction that they themselves *must* work to make a difference as citizens and as teachers—and that they *could* make a difference.

The following two examples from the postwar trips focus on the issue of racism: the work of the Highlander Folk School and the all–African American community of Bakewell. For the students on the postwar trips, witnessing overt racism on the streets, in stores, and how some people spoke of African Americans in the most demeaning ways all set a framework for understanding the magnitude of what was happening in Tennessee in Monteagle at the Highlander Folk School and in Soddy at the Bakewell community. The visits to these two places offered a perspective that would influence the thinking and actions of many of the students as they lived through years of struggle to fundamentally change American society—at the voting booths, on the buses, in the schools, at workplaces, and in neighborhoods.

Highlander

Highlander was different from anything they had experienced before. A student described it as "a micro representation of what the world could be—the joy of it." [39] They were struck by the humanity—and modesty—of the people who worked there, how they lived their beliefs and were making such a difference in people's lives.

Jane Addams and John Dewey's vision of education as a fertile means to create a more equitable, just, and democratic society had inspired Myles Horton, who founded Highlander in the 1930s. And like Addams and Dewey, Horton believed this would not happen solely through books and sitting in a classroom—which must have resonated powerfully with Mitchell and Hogan.

The Highlander staff members were not there as social workers or as people who handed things out to a community. They were there to help a community learn how to do things for itself. [40] To do this, Horton offered no preset curriculum for the community groups who attended the six-week training sessions. Horton and his staff members struggled always with the question of how to offer people a framework for understanding their own problems, while making sure the participants led the sessions themselves.

Today, Highlander, renamed Highlander Research and Education and located in New Market, Tennessee, focuses on ensuring the rights of current immigrant groups and cultivating immigrant leaders. In the 1930s, when antiunion action had been most violent and entrenched, Highlander became the official CIO labor organizing school for the South. In the 1940s and '50s, it became "a spark plug for the civil rights movement." [41] Its staff led voter registration drives, ran literacy schools so that people could pass the voter literacy tests, and trained people who would become towering figures in the civil rights movement, such as Rosa Parks, Septima Clark, and Martin Luther King. [42]

From its beginnings in the 1930s, Highlander had been integrated, in spite of official segregation. African Americans and whites ate together and slept in the same rooms. As the students learned about the Highlander staff's way of living and working, the students realized the extent to which people at Highlander risked their well-being to live their ideals. They were repeatedly threatened, called un-American, communists, socialists, and agitators. At one point the state of Tennessee confiscated its land—which Highlander was able to reclaim. And defying Jim Crow as they did in the 1930s and '40s was "a momentous thing." In our interviews, a student who participated in the 1950 trip spoke of how the Highlander people were accused of being communists. She laughed when she said how ironic it was that what they were really doing was reaching people where they were so that they would be able to make the democratic process work for *them*.[43]

Many interviewees described Myles Horton, his wife, Zilphia Horton, and the Highlander staff as educators to emulate. A student described them as "glowing" with the pleasure of their work. Somehow, in spite of the enmity they had endured and their daily struggles, they didn't focus on this or even talk about this. They spoke of what they were attempting and modeled educators who endlessly worked on their own process; whose teaching methods were determined by their goals; who were moved by conviction; who created a community through the social process of living and learning together and ultimately modeled being educators who care. Their work stands in stark contrast to the current focus on standardized curricula and passing tests with lip service to a more just society and little regard for the lives and experiences of the learners.

The students were captivated by the warmth of the place, of people tied to one another, and of the hospitality of Myles and Zilphia. Students spoke of experiencing a "sense of the community of mankind," not solely as a dream but as a possibility. One student said that from seeing black and white working and living together at Highlander, she realized that "this is the way it *has* to be."[44]

On the students' last day at Highlander, as the cool evening descended, they all sat around a campfire and sang union songs late into the night. Music and dancing were an essential aspect of the Highlander process. Training groups came together in new and deeper ways through the shared fun of the square dancing and singing.

In 2005, on one of the current long trips to TVA areas, we visited Highlander. We ate in the dining room and slept in the dormitories. We also shared the fun and serenity of singing into the night with Highlander staff. This was Zilphia Horton's legacy—the singing and music that became integral to Highlander's work. As a songwriter, singer, and musician, she had a full repertoire of labor songs, many of which she had taught strikers right on the picket lines, throughout the South. She believed the songs energized the strikers and strengthened their conviction.

Allen Ohta, who on the 1948 trip commanded his classmates' attention when he stood fixed before the "colored" drinking fountain, said Zilphia had such a beautiful voice she touched everyone—especially with the song no one had heard before. Sheila Sadler was so moved, she persuaded Zilphia to teach it to her, and Sadler wrote it down and has valued that piece of paper ever since. The music was taken from a black spiritual, and the words were written in 1946 by two tobacco workers as the anthem of the Black Tobacco Workers Union.[45] The students traveled home singing that song. A few years later, Zilphia Horton and Pete Seeger made changes in the wording, and Zilphia spread the song that "came in like a wave over Hawaii with the Civil Rights Movement,"[46] and with its title, "We Shall Overcome," it captured the ethos of an era.

After hearing this song for the first time, Sheila Sadler had Zilphia Horton teach it to her. Sadler wrote it down and has valued the tattered piece of paper ever since. A few years later—with minor changes in wording and the new title, "We Shall Overcome"—it became the anthem for a generation. (Song sheet courtesy of Sheila Sadler)

Bakewell

She was such a young woman, so completely enveloped in her work, almost too slight to be operating that large tractor. She stood out for the Bank Street student who was visiting Bakewell's farm, not solely for her age and size but for how well she managed that "big machine," her straight bearing and deliberate movements, and mostly for a sense of pride, of *self* she exuded. She wasn't there to impress anyone; she was just working and seemed unaware that she was being watched. For the student, just seeing this young woman at work gave her the feeling of hope for the future.

The residents of Bakewell, all African Americans, owned their own land and machinery in common and had regular community meetings during which they followed parliamentary procedure. Their farm was one of the first to make full use of TVA services by doing test demonstration farming. They competed for and won cash awards offered by the TVA for exemplary farming. In her diary entry dated March 31, 1948, a student described their visit to Bakewell as "a thrilling, inspiring experience."[47]

Many remembered how welcomed the community made them feel, how gracious the people were. Some of the students visited the school and met with the children's teachers, who also were African American, and others visited the farm. Afterward, the community residents and the students all came together for a community meeting.

Being at Bakewell was different for most, if not all, of the students. Wilbur Rippy had grown up with the belief that "all human creatures are God's children." As a musician he had played at Fisk University and had mixed with all kinds of people in the navy. Yet he had never had close relationships with African Americans. His very brief visit to the home of a Bakewell craftsman remained striking and important. When he saw the man's silverwork, he was taken with its clean, simple beauty and the skill with which it was created. Rippy, a craftsman himself, felt an intimacy he had not expected. It was the kind of person-to-person exchange that Mitchell had hoped for, the kind students experienced when they spoke with the miners and the steelworkers. That visit at Bakewell, more than any other experience, offered Rippy the possibility that the future would be different from the past. It was the realization "that after all that has happened you could be accepted by a black person, that somehow it was possible still to meet as human beings."[48]

That was the first time he had been invited into a black person's home.

Reverend De Jarnette, community leaders, and Eleanor Hogan had arranged the community meeting. The Bakewell farmers spoke about how they were learning how to treat the land properly after years of misuse. They also spoke of the discrimination they had experienced. One man told the story of how he had risked his life to save a white child from drowning, only to be given half a keg of liquor from the child's parents. In her diary entry, a student wrote how humiliating it must be to be treated in this way "from persons less capable and worthy because he is Negro and they are white."[49]

The leaders also spoke of how conditions were getting better, but there was so far to go. Eleanor Hogan spoke for her students by telling the community what it meant to the students to meet with them. The meeting offered hope, just as the visit to the craftsman's home did for Rippy: it ended with the children singing "Gonna Lay Down My Burdens." The beauty of their voices overwhelmed the students. Because they felt so honored by the singing, the students decided to sing back to them. They sang a rousing Israeli song they learned on the bus from the Israeli student and had sung together on the bus. Sadler described that experience as the most emotional meeting of different cultures that you could imagine.

Like the students who went to Highlander and Bakewell, students from across the span of long trips remember their long trip as a defining moment in their lives. The trip built on previous experience in the teacher education program, extended their understanding in ways they had never anticipated, and ultimately influenced the contours of their future experience.

Chapter 7

Participants in a World More Vast, Yet Less Remote

"Every experience is a moving force," wrote John Dewey. "Its value can be judged only on the ground of what it moves toward."[1] To be "educative," an experience would propel the learner into a fuller arc of experiencing, connecting past, present, and future.[2] Many, speaking from the perspective of forty-five to sixty years later, described such an experience. A student who participated in the first long trip (1935) said that the trip left "a fluid understanding of people and the earth that could be dipped into,"[3] and a student on the last of the original trips (1951) said the trip "acted as a kind of gathering source for future experience."[4] Many thought the trips cast their teacher education program in relief, sharpening, clarifying, and extending its social and educational aims. Just as Mitchell and Hogan had hoped, students from across the full span of trips felt the experience made the world out there more vast, yet less remote.

Land, labor, and race were no longer abstractions. Land became the changing surface of the earth that they had marveled at through the bus windows; the farmers who struggled to produce crops from eroded and overworked land; the farmers who benefited from the TVA educational services and flood control; the utter destruction at Ducktown; and the lushness of TVA. Their eyes were opened to the interactions among the earth's surface, the current social issues, and how government could respond on behalf of its people.[5] One student said that they "learned that you could use up land and you could use up people." And for the first time in her life, she saw the two as inextricably connected. She said that suddenly they were "made aware of what Lucy Sprague Mitchell was saying with the rocks, what the farmers at Bakewell showed [them], and the meaning of Ducktown—that land is the core of life, something to run your fingers through to see what the nature of it is, that *land is earth*," a universal human inheritance.[6]

Labor became the miners who, at great risk, dug their own mines so that their families would have food; the vitality and humor of the miners as they welcomed and engaged with the students; the slag heaps that dominated the company towns and filled the air with coal grit; the miners' wives and children; the steelworkers, their skill and bravery as they endured the searing heat and danger of the mill; the camaraderie at their union meeting; the danger they felt for themselves at the picket line of striking steelworkers; and Zilphia Horton teaching labor songs to striking workers across the South. Labor became raw materials vividly transformed before their eyes into essential aspects of the material world through the time and energy of the workers, all taken for granted and rarely seen.

Race became Allen Ohta standing before the "colored" drinking fountain; the signs of Jim Crow everywhere; the integrated staff at Highlander living and working together in the South during the 1930s, '40s, and '50s; Highlander's idealism and conviction matched with the knowledge and courage to realize their ideals; Highlander's work training community groups in nonviolent resistance, its literacy drives, its voter registration, its joy in its work; Zilphia Horton singing "We Shall Overcome," and their singing it over and over all the way back to New York. Race was the man from Bakewell given a half a keg of liquor for saving a white child's life, the capable young woman operating that huge tractor; the beauty of the children's voices as they sang for the students, and the students' excitement of singing in return; the craftsman showing the fine silver he created; the teachers who with so little were offering a rich education; the Reverend De Jarnette, who, like the people at Highlander, had the knowledge, skill, and courage to take on difficult issues and not get thrown in jail; and the people at Bakewell who shared their successes, struggles, and hopes at the community "civil rights" meeting.

Land, labor, and race were now people and places the students were connected to *personally*. Like Karen Kriesberg at the Shinnecock Reservation, Ronnie Igel at the Hunts Point market, and the first and second graders at Mr. Albok's tailor shop, the long-trip students forged a connection they had not expected. The students had been moved and inspired by the workers and others that they met. They respected the skill, bravery, and pride in their work, and they felt concern for their health and safety and for the well-being of their families. As never before, the students perceived themselves as participants in a larger world, and in doing so expanded their circle of empathy, caring, and commitment as Mitchell had hoped. Of course, ways of living and working are never simply cause and effect. Their actions as teachers and citizens drew from a life of experience before and after attending Bank Street College; however, as one student expressed, "it was the intensity with which we learned during that one week, that then played off the rest of the time."[7] One student described the feelings of many when she said that the trip "was a kind of completion and yet an opening to how many more things there are in the world, and how much could be done, and how much should be done, and how [they] in some small way would have a part in this."[8]

The Contours of Future Experience

And indeed many of the students did "have a part" as citizens and throughout long careers in education and related fields. Many became labor advocates and some union organizers; many participated in the civil rights movement and some worked to integrate schools in the most segregated areas of the country. Some became members of Highlander and supported its work. Based on their experience shadowing a visiting nurse in a mining community, two students actively supported the work of visiting nurses, one as a board member, the other as an administrator. Some became writers for children, illuminating the diverse worlds in which children live and grow by consciously portraying a racially integrated world. Another student, whose imagination was sparked by the ways in which human life and the natural environment were so inextricably connected, became a city planner. She said that the human-geographic relationships illuminated on the trip and in all her work in Mitchell's environment class led her to view city planning as a means to social justice.

They became more active as citizens and brought this consciousness to their teaching of children. Elizabeth Helfman, after teaching children for years, became a writer for children. So much of her work focused on the interdependence of humans and the physical world.[9] Her last book, *On Being Sarah*, which she wrote in her eighties, was about how a severely paralyzed child learns to communicate using technology.[10] She said that her teaching and her books reflected "a way of feeling into another's life," which she developed through meeting the miners and steelworkers. Florence Krahn also taught children until her retirement. She said that in whatever she did with children, it "had to be real" and vital, part of the living world around them. She talked about how in the early 1970s her fifth graders studied the problems of using the major energy sources, such as oil and coal. They interviewed experts, visited power plants, searched newspapers and periodicals, discussed and debated the issue, and proposed alternatives, such as geothermal, nuclear, wind, and solar energies. It is ironic how in thirty years since the children's recommendations, relatively little has been done even though we sit at the brink of environmental disaster.

Willie Kraber, after teaching young children, became an elementary school principal who, even after so many years, remains legendary. From school administration, she moved to teaching teachers. She said that to each of these jobs she brought the understanding acquired on the long trip, that there are many kinds of people in the world. Wilbur Rippy, who originally pursued a career in teaching because he thought it would be easier than truck driving, taught children for years, then, like Willie Kraber, moved to teaching teachers. Among his many accomplishments, he headed a program designed to help teachers work in difficult urban schools. Each of these people and so many of their peers brought their classrooms to life for me. As though it were yesterday, they spoke about class trips they had taken, children they especially remembered, poignant and difficult situations, and the kinds of funny situations to which any teacher of young children could relate. Like these four people, so many graduates of the long-trip years became committed educators. They worked as teachers, school administrators, researchers, and writers in public and experimental independent schools, Head Start, day care, colleges, museums, social service agencies, and hospitals.

The long trips influenced the students as teachers in two special ways: students felt the trips enabled them to think that they could teach in diverse settings and stimulated the desire to do so; and the trips offered the "final proof" that learning from experience was central to a vital education, which, throughout their careers as educators, they worked to incorporate into their teaching.

Teaching in Diverse Settings: "Why Did I Expect Them Not to Be Happy?"

The whole time Esther Smith visited the miner's wife during the 1939 trip, the three boys played. The house was two rooms—a small bedroom for the parents, one large living space where they cooked and ate and where the children slept—and a large porch out front. Out back was a vegetable garden, laid out in clean straight lines, and next to it a brood of fluffy chickens. The house walls were wooden planks, with rolls of newspaper filling the crevices to keep out drafts. Esther noticed the quilts that covered the children's beds. It was as though every shade of blue, all pieces of old jeans, were crafted into the striking, intricate patterns.

As Esther and the miner's wife spoke, sipped coffee, and enjoyed the warmth of the coal stove, the boys rolled under the table laughing, bumping into their feet. Their mother asked them to play somewhere else, and they moved their play to the porch. As Esther heard their laughing from inside, she wondered, "Why did I expect them not to be happy? Why did I expect them to be so different from other children, children I know and teach?" In our conversation on the phone, Esther said, "That was 1939, in a Pennsylvania mining town, and is as though it were yesterday." She said that in all of her years of teaching, every time she taught a child of a different background from her own, she saw those three boys. And she said, "I can see them now and always will." [11]

Many, like Esther, who came to know the "other children" she would teach through that brief visit, entered teaching with the feeling that the focus of their future professional work had been enlarged. Some sought work with children of similar backgrounds to those visited on the trip.

Seeing the miner's children happily engaged in their play was jarring to Esther Smith (1939 long trip). She realized that she had expected them not to be happy. She wondered why she had expected them to be so different from other children. The scene on the miner's porch may have looked like the one captured in this photo by Marion Post Wolcott, which is from the same time and place. (Library of Congress, Prints and Photographs Division, FS-OWI Collection, LC-USF33-030160-M5. Untitled. Location: Pursglove, WV. Items from series dated 1938.)

One taught in a country school in West Virginia, with no running water. Later she served on the school board and worked to desegregate the community.[12] Another student taught in a settlement house in Richmond, Virginia, whose population was children of families relocated from Appalachia.[13] Later she worked as a hospital teacher in a state hospital that served primarily inner-city families. And another student spent the seven years following the trip working at Highlander, five as the nursery school teacher-director, and the next two as executive secretary. The Reverend De Jarnette performed her marriage to the Highlander photographer, and their two children were born there.[14]

When asked about professional impact, one student, like others, said that she had always sought "the most challenging kind of teaching," that she has spent her life working with children with emotional and learning disabilities and "people in difficulty."[15] When considering the impact of the trip, another described teaching as "a matter of commitment and excitement and keeping relevant and dynamic"—all of which he said had been modeled on the trip. And he has tried to bring these qualities to his work as an administrator of residential treatment centers for emotionally disturbed children and for court-committed delinquents. He set up a facility in New Hampshire "to demonstrate that there is a way to work the field into regular schools." He said that he tried to incorporate in his preparation of staff members what he saw demonstrated on the trip: that teachers need to care enough to be "involved *together* with their students, as active participants."[16]

Courtney Cazden, who participated in the first postwar trip in 1948, became a prominent researcher in education. Her work has focused on the uses of language in classrooms. She has researched how the patterns of language children acquire can affect the educational opportunities offered to them. Cazden said that "the trip was profoundly important for [her] work, making connections to this day, putting substance under professed politics, under an intellectual, verbal veneer." She said the trip had offered her "the first chance to get out of circles she lived in, which were not working class, and see issues, conflicts, struggles that she was verbally committed to."[17]

In her later work as a museum educator at a colonial manor restoration, another student tried especially to help children for whom the experience of the manor was different from anything they had known, many of whom were inner-city children. She viewed the museum visit "as a distinct teaching situation." She said she believed that the children's teachers and the museum had to trust the students to learn from what they themselves experience, just as Hogan had done with them. She said, "Let the child alone, let him look." She worked to create a sense of safety for the children, to free them to have an experience. She wanted the trip to be embedded in what the children were learning at the school; she wanted their teachers to prepare them for the museum visit and to follow it up—"the way Eleanor was teaching us on that trip."

Learning from Experience: "It Has a Certain Elegance"

Years after participating in the 1951 long trip, when Wilbur Rippy was teaching five-year-olds, a parent of a child in his class was asked to write about the school for its new brochure. She photographed a chart Rippy had made with the children that synopsized a trip he had taken with his class. The chart showed their bus route from the school building, across the Triborough Bridge, along the highway, to their destination, La Guardia Airport. The parent wrote that many of the children were interested in transportation and had even built airports with blocks. She described the animated class discussion before the trip; how they made popcorn right before the trip; the conversation, laughing, and popcorn eating en route; the wonder at seeing the entire airport from up high when they went up in the observation tower; how engaged they were when a traffic controller spoke with them and answered their questions; their excitement at seeing the takeoffs and landings from such a dramatic angle; how eating lunch at the airport was such an event for them; then finally how quietly they traveled home together—they were all tired, including the teachers. The parent wrote that on the next day during morning discussion, the children gave detailed descriptions of what they found especially interesting. She described and photographed children intently examining books on planes and airports and the wave of airport drawings, writing, paintings, and block buildings. When Rippy examined his work reflected through someone else's eyes, he saw it as though for the first time and thought, "It had a certain elegance." Then he asked himself, "Where does a teacher get such notions and the conviction that they make a difference?" [18]

Most felt that from the many local trips taken with Mitchell and Hogan, their experiences student teaching, and the program in general, they were already convinced that firsthand experience and taking trips was "the way you taught." But many felt the long trip, like no other experience, "elaborated everything their faculty wanted for [them] as teachers"[19] and gave "the final proof that learning things firsthand was the way to go."[20] And from across the span of trips, students said their experience translated into how and what they taught children. Most said they used trips very deliberately—even in the most "hide-bound schools." They said that they offered to children just what the trip offered them, the opportunity "to become more aware of what's around them, to see people, to learn other ways, how others are making their way, to open horizons."[21]

For some students the relationship between their experience of the trip and their teaching became clearer over time. It was over the course of years that they came to see how much of their teaching was drawn from the careful preparation for the trip, all the planning that enabled them to venture into worlds they had only read about, the questions Mitchell and Hogan asked, the discussions they had with their peers on the bus, and, most important, the abiding focus on the people whose work sustained their own lives. Some said they "grew into understanding." Mitchell had anticipated this when she said that it would take years see the results of the trip—that "growth is slow and growth is individual."[22] It's important to note how these understandings didn't follow a rigid schedule of narrowly defined outcomes. In fact, the "outcomes" were too complex to be narrowly defined and were shaded differently because each student was a different person. This current preoccupation with rigidly defined time frames to acquire skills and information interferes with the learning process, which is different for each individual, and requires time, continued experience, and reflection.

Most said they felt that the connection to their teaching was clear but required an adaptation to young children and their environment. Florence Krahn expressed the opinion of many when she said that "no matter what group of children or what strata of society you happen to be teaching," it was a teacher's job to move the children outward—"You want them to start with their own close environment and move outward from there, just as Lucy Sprague Mitchell had done with [them]."[23] And in the interview and questionnaire accounts, many moved directly from talking about an experience on the long trip to the ways they ventured beyond the school building with their own students.

Teachers of three-, four-, and five-year-olds said they took the children on trips in their immediate neighborhood—to see how the world worked, "little trips," "all simple beginnings" to be built on. Many described their children's excitement as they "looked behind the scenes" and discovered some of the sources of their everyday world. One student remembered taking children on walks down the street from the school, observing the worker delivering coal to a house, listening to the sound of the coal as it rushed down the chute; doing the same at their school and then watching the custodian shovel coal into the huge school furnace; then going to the river to observe coal arriving on barges. And because she had been to coal mines herself, the student talked with the children about where the coal came from. She said, "We couldn't take them to a coal-mining area but, after we had gone to local grocery stores and produce markets, we could go to a farm to find out where vegetables came from." [24]

Another student remembered taking the children to watch construction down the block from the school and then visiting it again and again as the workers began new phases of the construction. She described how the children marveled at the drama of the great machines and spoke with the impressive workers who operated them. They wanted to know what the workers were doing and why, and later in their dramatic play they became the machines and the workers. She remembered how in winter, they'd dress warmly to watch the worker shoveling piles of snow into trucks and taking it away. Her class then went to the river to see all the snow dumped into it. [25] Perhaps many shared Florence Krahn's belief that "you never really know anything until you get to its source."

One student, like many of her peers, emphasized how it made a "tremendous difference" for her children that their introduction to academic learning was through going out into the neighborhood. She described how, throughout her twenty-five years teaching in New York City public schools in Harlem, she took her children on trips and brought the outside into the classroom. She remembered how fascinated they were watching workers on their school block drill into the street to lay gas pipes that would supply gas to the stoves in their homes; and that while watching the workers, their attention was diverted by the sound of fire engine sirens. The piercing sound grew increasingly louder until a series of red engines sped by. They waved to the firefighters, who waved to them in return. Their obvious interest led them eventually to the fire station and to speaking with the firefighters. She remembered how serious—and tiny—they looked while trying on the "impossibly heavy and large" coat, hat, and boots. Like Laura Gerrity and Trish Lent, she believed that there was "this connection" to the people and places in the world around them that was "tremendously important" to the children as learners and members of their community.

Students described how the trips led to the children reliving their experience through animated class discussions, painting, music and movement, writing, and especially dramatic play using blocks. This was Mitchell's "outgo," the ways in which an experience is reflected on and transformed, bringing it to another level of understanding. The children became doers and thinkers as they spoke and worked together to build houses and trucks and then deliver the coal, which they fashioned out of small bits of clay, to the houses they had built. They constructed coal barges and had tugboats push them down the river they created with a strip of blue oilcloth laid out on the floor and built busy construction sites that evolved into towering skyscrapers. They made signs for their buildings and learned the words. And from their writing about their experiences, which was often assembled into books, many of the children learned to read.

Teachers of older children described leading children further outward into their world. As one student said, the long trips had been a "learning experience in *all different areas*," which she believed was "exactly what you wanted for children—not to just go see one phase of anything." Helen Quick, who attended the first long trip in 1935, described this type of experience from her years teaching second and third graders in San Francisco. She said that at her school, teachers would work with each group of children for two years. The class was studying how they got their food. In the spring of the children's second-grade year, she contacted a rice growers' cooperative that was prominent in their area. A member of the association came to the school to speak with the children about its work. He invited them to one of the member farms to see the rice planting by plane. The children showed their interest immediately, and when their teacher accepted the invitation they cheered. At the farm, they stood in rapt attention, completely focused on the planes as they zoomed overhead, dropping rice seed like rain over fields of water. Later they got to speak with one of the pilots. A child's grandfather, who came from China, visited the class to describe how rice is planted by hand, which he had seen in China when he was a boy. During the fall of the children's third-grade year, they went to the same large farm and observed the enormous threshing machine, and heard its relentless rapid-fire beating, as it separated the grain from the husks and shells. Then they went to a mill in Sacramento. The trips led to discussion, research and reports, artwork, and eventually to an assembly program for the younger grades.

Similar to Quick, a student who eventually taught in a high school said that he learned on the trip how "real life experience" stimulates the desire to learn more and deepens the meaning of subsequent reading and research. He said that though the high school he worked in "wasn't amenable to progressive methods," he "knew what good education was" and tried to apply what he had learned on the trip and in the program. He gave an example of how he did this for older children, within the constraints of his school:

> I was teaching "standard of living" and I wanted to make the concept real to the kids. I asked them to look through magazines to find and cut out all the things they thought a family would need over the course of a year. I had them price them out and then compute the income that would be needed. The kids were all surprised at just how much money they would need to sustain the material existence they had put together. It had an impact.[26]

One final example captures the full range of possibilities envisioned by Mitchell. Olga Smyth, who had participated in the 1935 trip as a student, founded a small independent elementary school for students with learning disabilities. Each winter, Smyth, the teachers, and the entire student body of the school traveled from upstate New York to spend a week in a small village south of San Juan, Puerto Rico—a truly enormous undertaking. There they learned firsthand how the people of that village met their basic needs, which meant they studied the work being done and spoke with and got to know the workers. They grew familiar with the noisy markets filled with the scents of spices and herbs and enjoyed how almost everywhere they went in town there was music. And during their visits to the local schools, they became friends with the town children. In their explorations, they learned how the geography of this sea town affected the people's lives. They learned some of the language, how to cook the foods people ate, and, best of all, how to fish. Smyth said that over time "they knew everyone and everyone knew [them] and expected [them] back each year." A new class identity was formed as the children shared the excitement, seriousness, and satisfaction of learning: their sense of community had grown beyond the school and the nation. "I always felt that what we experienced on those trips was such an important part of the children's education," she said. Many of the children had struggled with basic reading and writing skills. The trip stimulated a desire to communicate with the people of the town, each other, and their families when they returned. They also returned with a new energy to confront their struggles, because they had so much to share, which they expressed in discussion, writing, and artwork.[27]

A Complex Synthesis

Lucy Sprague Mitchell and her colleagues evolved a complex, and I believe unique, process of educating children and teachers. Mitchell's synthesis blended ways of thinking about education, teaching, and children that many had considered and continue to consider separate. Because so many strands are woven together, the synthesis is hard to capture clearly. Yet many of the strands came together in the use of trips.

Building a Concept of the World

For both children and adults, trips become a way to help build a concept of the world and their place in it. Achieving this is not simple and asks a lot of learners. They are asked to be fully present, to interact as thinkers and learners with each other, the world around them, and the people they meet. And they are asked to reflect deeply on their experience and express their reflections through discussion, writing, and the arts. Most important, they are placed in a position to interact as people, person-to-person, with those they meet, each other, and their teachers. In the process of building a concept of the world and their place in it, they learn how their lives are sustained by the work done by the people they meet, and how earth resources are critical to their own lives, such as coal and oil for heating and land, water, and sunlight for their food. They form emotional connections to the people and places they engage with and become participants in that world in new and often unexpected ways, very much the way Laura Gerrity's children did when the parent and teacher visitors spoke with them and the people they met in the neighborhood were so giving with them.

Because Mitchell's way of educating is so grounded in a sense of place and in the specific individuals being taught, it offers no blueprint. Yet she does set a framework for thinking about teaching. She believed that being familiar with one's everyday world is not the same as *knowing* it, that the children's venturing into the world around them satisfies a need to understand and be competent in their world and nourishes their interest in how things work. The encounters spark their imaginations and stimulate questioning and the desire to know more, and give them the impetus to use reading, writing, mathematics, and science to delve deeper into the subject, just as the trips to bridges did for Trish Lent's children. Children are freed to learn through their bodies, their muscles, their senses, which is in keeping with how they learn most intensely.

The ventures outward enable children to build a concept of the world based on their own unfiltered experience—not someone else's—and offer the basis for forming opinions, sharing their opinions, modifying and enlarging their thinking based on the ideas and opinions of others. Through the emotional connections to the people and places children encounter that are formed through person-to-person exchanges, the children become participants in an ever-enlarging world and develop a sense of responsibility toward that world.

It was the job of teachers to learn about the children's everyday world and how children engage with that world; to research it so that they discover its uniqueness, the connections among its particulars; and to discover how that world is connected to networks of work that sustain people's lives in that area. In the process of research, teachers come to realize the power of discovery and the dynamism of learning from experience; they form connections to the environment themselves, just as Karen Kriesberg did when she explored the Nissequogue River and visited the Shinnecock Reservation. Ultimately, teachers' discoveries enable them to place children in a position to make their own discoveries.

Teach as We Teach

To understand the depth of meaning in this type of teaching and learning, to know it in their muscles and hearts so that they grow committed to it, Mitchell believed teachers also should have a "curriculum of experience." On an adult level, student teachers would have experiences analogous to what they might offer children. The students from the original long-trip years (1935–51) believed that the dual curriculum—teach as we teach—had a profound and lasting impact on their teaching and on their lives. Too often we hear teachers say that education courses are something "to get through" so that you can really learn to teach by being on the job—which usually becomes replicating the ways in which they were taught. This negative attitude toward their preparation to teach stands in dramatic contrast to the comments of the people I interviewed.

Essentially, through the curriculum of experience the adult students, like the children they student taught, would be building a concept of the world and their place in it—geographically as well as socially. Mitchell saw the progression outward as a developmental continuum of exploration, which continues throughout a person's life. As children grow older and consolidate a sense of time, their world enlarges to include its past and how that past influences their lives in the present. And with maturation and experience, their world grows beyond their own society and includes other societies and cultures.

Hence, the student teachers traveling to other areas of the country would be a part of a progression within a continuum of experience that was growing in time, place, and also complexity. While this is happening, the learners are becoming ever more aware of how humans rely on the earth and its resources for their existence and eventually realize that even if they live in Detroit, St. Petersburg, or Java, the 4 million gallons of oil spilled into the Gulf of Mexico, the melting of a glacier in Iceland, the breaking off of a part of Greenland, or the decimation of the Appalachian Mountains will ultimately affect everyone regardless of where they live.

What would start as connections to those in the learners' immediate world would grow to include people in other parts of the country and world, people whose lives and struggles may be dramatically different from their own. In the search to understand, students would enter people's world and learn from them and that world itself. For Mitchell, this was not enough. She wanted students to marshal all they learn from their encounters and try to entertain the point of view of the people they are visiting, to see the world through their eyes. This is by no means easy or always achieved, but in the attempt lives would touch and an emotional connection would be formed—one that *counteracts separateness*. I experienced this type of connection when I witnessed how the devastation of mountaintop removal affected people's lives and the environment, and also when I saw the ways in which these people joined together, formed organizations, and forged partnerships across organizations, all to stop mountaintop removal.

Mitchell's ultimate purpose, in Wilbur Rippy's words, "wasn't solely to understand the world but to change it."[28] The process that would begin with student teachers observing and listening to the traffic on the street corner would progressively move outward in human connections, cultivating teachers who were social individuals who actively participate in the world to make it more just, not solely for themselves but also for people whose lives are dramatically different from their own— because they had learned that the barriers between self and other are so often based on lack of experience, on ignorance. Because teachers had enlarged their own circles of knowing, caring, and commitment, they would be in a stronger position to do the same for the children they teach. Mitchell saw the movement outward as a way to create and sustain a more democratic society for all of its citizens. Not unrelated, the movement outward would also cultivate citizens who, ever mindful of the human reliance on the earth's resources for their very existence, work to prevent abuse.

The resulting education of children and teachers would be highly intellectual: rich in content, alive with exchanges with others, furthered by the learners' questioning and finding out, sustained by discussion, and kept vital by using the arts as a way to express and deepen understandings. This type of learning and teaching demands academic rigor, not to score high on tests but as a way of engaging the world, thinking critically, and living one's life. To teach in this way is certainly not easy, but it is tremendously stimulating and energizing. The teachers, like the children they teach, would be developing a concept of the world in which they would have an important role and be active participants. It is little wonder the lives of the people I interviewed were so transformed by their teacher education.

PART THREE

Staying Vulnerable

After reflecting on the retrospective accounts of the graduate students' experiences, I began to think about learning and teaching in more complex and nuanced ways. My descriptions of the work of Laura Gerrity, Trish Lent, and Karen Kriesberg reflect this deepened perspective. I also saw the roots of what led me to bring the first and second graders to Mr. Albok's tailor shop and saw what led me to take adult students into the college boiler room.

When I asked myself what all this would mean for me as a teacher educator, I thought of the questions Wilbur Rippy asked himself when he read what a child's parent wrote about his curriculum. The parent had accompanied his class on a trip to an airport and wrote an article that conveyed in detail how the experience stimulated the children's imaginations, sparked their thinking, fueled questions, and led to writing and reading. After seeing his work reflected through the parent's eyes, he asked himself: "How does a teacher learn to use trips in this way?" and "What gives a teacher the conviction that it is important?" The obvious answer to Wilbur's questions seemed to answer my own— *experience*. Adult students today, no less than in the past, need to experience a way of learning and teaching that uses the children's world as raw material.

Part 3 examines how I experimented with offering adult students opportunities to experience the world around them as an important part of their becoming teachers, the trip I incorporated into the curriculum class I teach, and the environment course a colleague and I created and taught that was inspired by Lucy Sprague Mitchell's original course.

Chapter 8

A Modest Experiment

For ten years, I had taught a curriculum course in which taking trips was an important topic, yet I had never taken the adult students on a trip. After learning about all the trips Mitchell and Hogan led, I wondered why I hadn't done this. Time was an issue, yet I usually make time for what I consider important. I think I feared the vulnerability that went with being a model for what I was asking of the students. Inspired by Mitchell and Hogan, I tolerated the vulnerability and ventured outward with the students, and those modest first steps changed all my subsequent teaching of adults.

I wanted to plan a *short* trip that incorporated some of what I believed had made the long trips so powerful. Because of the constraints on students' time, I had only the two hours of the class session. I wanted to lead the students away from their everyday world; to engage with people and the physical environment and experience how both are intimately connected; to shake up preconceived notions; to spark their imaginations; to bring the students closer together as a group so that they could gain some insight into the power of a shared experience; to address social issues when they are part of the situation; to convey to students that they can make a difference; and to demonstrate on an adult level a way of teaching children.

It was impossible—so I thought. But I didn't let go of finding the perfect place, and somehow, I did, *right in the neighborhood*. Just a mile and a half from the college existed a community unlike any other in New York City, which many students didn't know existed at all, the 79th Street Boat Basin. It's a community of houseboats in the Hudson River, a community mostly of families. A former student, Leslie Day, who lived

there, was willing to be our guide. Leslie and I met at the basin to discuss what I was attempting, and together we planned the trip by going
through it ourselves. Leslie would add an important dimension to the
trip. As a science teacher of children and adults, she had helped teachers
throughout New York City integrate the study of the natural environment into their curriculum. She knew the potential of this trip.

The wind blasted through the city that day, and at the basin the wind
was so fierce I thought that any minute I'd be blown into the water.
Walking up the floating dock was an experience. I wanted to crawl but
saw Leslie maintaining her balance, so I tried to do the same, though
not nearly as well as she. I pictured a class of adult students blown into
the Hudson River and wondered if it was such a good idea after all. Leslie
said the wind was unusual and there wasn't anything to be concerned
about. Once we were on the stationary dock, I could stand straight and
think about the trip. I was struck by all the signs of a small-town community: dogs and cats sleeping on the boat decks, oblivious to the wind;
neighbors standing and talking across their boats; and carefully tended
plants decorating the decks of these river houses. Leslie introduced me
to her neighbors and explained the trip to them, and two said they'd
welcome students into their homes and would talk with them about
their lives at the basin—one was a ninety-one-year-old resident and
the other was a young mother of a seven-year-old. We discussed many
of the details: why we would be visiting the basin, questions students
might ask, how long we would stay, alternate dates in case of rain, and
anything special the residents wanted the students to see.

In the curriculum class, we had been discussing ways of studying the
neighborhood with children, and as an example I introduced the trip. I
also prayed that the day of the trip would not be as windy as when Leslie and I planned it.

The class met on the street corner closest to the entrance to the basin,
which is also an entrance to Riverside Park. It was a clear, crisp fall day;
the sun was shining and the trees of Riverside Park were golden—fortunately the wind was mild. Leslie greeted us there and escorted us
through Riverside Park, down a series of granite steps, through a large
stone rotunda, right to the entrance of the boat basin. We all noticed
that homeless people were living in the rotunda. Leslie told us that residents of the basin had asked if they could be of any help to them. They
said they preferred living there to city shelters but did need clothing,
blankets, and food. Residents collected some of the things they needed

and agreed that when they shopped for food they would also buy something for the people living in the rotunda.

Upon entering the basin, Leslie informed us that it was built in the
1930s as part of the New Deal Works Progress Administration. We met
the captain in charge of the facility, who explained his job, and then
we walked together through the community. Students were surprised
to see paintings done by young children hanging in boat windows,
children's bicycles, dogs on leashes sleeping on the deck of a boat, cats
peering out from a boat window, and a family walking past us with a
baby in a stroller. They were surprised to learn that the resident who
was windsurfing a few yards from us was an anesthesiologist.

Leslie pointed out the icebreakers and explained how critical they
were during winter when storms blow chunks of river ice toward the
basin. She spoke of how clean the Hudson was, how through massive
environmental effort the river was now teeming with sea life, and also
how the unpolluted river freezes over more readily than it did in the
past—making the basin more vulnerable. We watched as a worker re-
stored one of the floating docks. Then, as planned, we divided into three
groups of nine to visit in the homes of the ninety-one-year-old resident,
the family with a seven-year-old child, and Leslie herself, who with her
husband had raised their seventeen-year-old son at the basin.[1]

I went with the group to the older resident. As evening descended,
it grew colder, and students who hadn't brought sweaters were sorry.
When we entered the houseboat, students were surprised at the physical warmth of his home and felt immediate relief from the cold. The
intimacy and excitement I felt evoked trips I had taken with children.
We learned that he had moved there after retiring at the age of seventy
and started a business servicing the boats, the work from which he had
just retired. The group that visited the family was toured through the
boat by the seven-year-old, who, the visitors said, did a thorough job.
Leslie showed her group that the river was teeming with life; she showed
an aquarium of river water with some vegetation at the bottom, which
she had made using a regular fish tank. Although it looked as though
there was nothing but plants, when she dropped some food in the water
scores of tiny eel-like pipefish, as though from nowhere, swam to the
top. She talked about how she had studied the life cycles of ducks and
other aquatic birds, and showed photographs that documented the life
cycles. (Students said they had been so used to thinking of the river as
polluted that the experience was jarring.) They asked Leslie about living

in such confined space. She asked them to look out the windows that surrounded them. They saw a vast expanse of river enveloped by the sky.

As planned, we reassembled at a certain time and walked the narrow pathway to the north pier to sketch the view. As it was growing dark, we looked north and saw the lights of the George Washington Bridge turn on. It seemed magical. Students gasped at the beauty of the light reflected in the water. It was like living the moment of a haiku. There was complete silence as students sketched the bridge. We thanked Leslie, and before we departed I asked the students to represent their experience in some way and bring that to the next class.

I was unprepared for what they brought and how they spoke about our trip. Discussion emerged spontaneously as soon as they entered the class. Their excitement was palpable as they unpacked paintings, rich portrayals of the sunset, the bridge, houseboats; detailed models of boats; maps of the basin showing the relationship to the adjoining Riverside Park, Manhattan, and New Jersey. I asked them to discuss in small groups of six their experience and how they portrayed it. The discussion was alive, rich—and everyone had something important to share. Students had also written reflections that expressed their own excitement and pleasure, their enlarged concept of community, their physical sense of being there, their awareness of the planning and organization of the trip—essentially what I had hoped for and more:

> I felt like I was in grammar school again, anxiously awaiting the day of the trip. Back then my mom had to sign the permission slip three to four weeks prior. It was always the longest wait. The excitement brought back memories of field trips that I went on as a child. I carefully prepared my warmest clothes because I knew it was going to be cold down by the water.[2]

> After I had visited the Boat Basin on 79th Street and the river, my eyes had been completely opened to a different way of life in New York City. I was intrigued by the sense of community.[3]

> When I first began thinking about the trip after I got home, I thought more generally about the community as a whole, and the fact that I might never have realized that this particular community existed. I thought that I had added an entirely new component to my conception of what a neighborhood can be—a neighborhood can include a

group of people (and their surroundings) living near each other on land or on water. And then after I thought about it a little more, I realized that instead of expanding it, I had actually honed down my personal definition of what a neighborhood is: it is a group of people (and their surroundings) living near each other. Period. The only thing you need to have as a community is people to share with. Whether you live in a house in suburbia, an apartment on the Upper West Side, a boat in the 79th Street Boat Basin, or on the floor of the rotunda near the marina, everything that lives around you—the people, the stores, the ice breakers, the buildings, the restaurants—makes up your neighborhood, and in a way, defines the realities and perhaps, the priorities in your life.[4]

As I reflected on the experience I can easily say it was the most worthwhile educational experience that I have had outside the classroom in quite a while. The most exciting part of the trip was going into the family's home. They greeted us warmly at the door. Their seven-year-old child gave us a tour of the boat. We saw how they utilized every possible inch of space. After the tour, we sat down in their back room, drank coffee, and talked about what life is like living in a houseboat, the good and the bad. We heard a little bit more about the political side. . . . Everyone had such interesting questions. I could have sat there for hours listening and talking.[5]

This summer I had been to the Boat Basin area with friends. We assumed that people docked there temporarily, so I was excited when I learned we would visit the community. I quickly learned how wrong my assumptions were. By visiting the community in person, it became so much more alive and real. This holds true for children as well, as long as the trip is as well planned and organized as this one was for us. When I went home I couldn't stop talking about the trip. I hope that my students will emerge from trips with such knowledge and pleasure.[6]

After the trip, I had gone to babysit my two-year-old niece. As she was being put to bed, I read her the story, *On Mother's Lap*. Many aspects of this story reminded me of the Boat Basin. It was the repetitive phrase, "Back and forth, back and forth we rocked." In the story the child is soothed and comforted by the rocking motion. The boat and the rocking chair provide an atmosphere of warmth, comfort, and a sense of home.[7]

Muted,
slight sounds
float down
Distant from above.
Taxi horns and
Giant despair
far away.

Sleep
floats down
With the clear, soft dark.
Rocking gently
as the river
Walks on.[8]

The students' representations enabled them and their peers to deepen their understanding of the experience, which gave me fresh insight into the importance of reflecting on and representing a learning experience. They were also excited by each other's work and felt they knew one another differently. Their imaginations were sparked and many wanted to know more.

We learned that each group asked the residents similar questions, all spontaneous: Why did they choose to move there? How do they get their food, their heat, their electricity; how is waste handled; what do they do in bad weather—all questions that focus on how basic human needs are met, all central to any social studies curriculum. We also learned that the basin was twelve stories below Riverside Drive—quite a surprise to most of us—giving us a sense of the island's contour.

Many incorporated what they experienced on the trip to the boat basin into the social studies curricula they developed for the final assignment. The trips they planned were thoughtfully conceived, well integrated—and, most obvious, they were alive and vital.

This was only one instance in which *teachers* venturing out into the world was considered an important part of their education, and the results were striking. In the years that followed, when I'd run into students from that trip, they'd tell me how meaningful it had been or how they had gone there with their class. This is not to say that a two-hour trip can serve the same purpose or match the intensity and power of a full curriculum of trips or of the long trip. However, it does show that the principles can be applied, even on a modest scale, and have an impact.

Chapter 9

A Less Modest Experiment

Following the trip to the boat basin, a colleague, Karen Weiss, and I wondered about creating a current-day environment course modeled on Lucy Sprague Mitchell's. But Mitchell and her students ventured out together onto the streets of New York over sixty years ago. What would a "curriculum of experience" be today? We wondered what we would focus on, where we might go with the students, what such a course would demand of us, how we would come to know the content, how we would model observing with a new eye, how we'd help our students venture out on their own—and whether we could pull it off.

This chapter moves the focus of the book back to the present, to the process of teacher educators and their students today. Essentially, this chapter examines how a modest four-week current-day "environment" course was crafted and lived, and the impact it had on the students. It follows the process of:

- researching the content and evolving course aims
- coping with the ever-present constraints of time as we design a syllabus that fulfills our course aims
- modeling teaching in the classroom as well as on trips
- experiencing the trips and reflecting experience through the arts
- students creating curricula based on their own ventures into the world.

As an introduction to the process of the course, the chapter begins with a teacher of second graders leading our adult curriculum class students on a simple and powerful trip, the same trip she had taken with her second graders: a silent walk around the school block. The chapter ends with students' perceptions of how the course influenced their teaching from the perspective of seven years later.

Karen and I knew that the thrust of the course would be going against the tide, against the pervasive, narrow focus on skills disembodied from the contexts that make them vital. We knew that curriculum based on children's experiences was becoming increasingly rare—and as part of a teacher's education close to nonexistent. This chapter that traces a four-week summer course is a statement on the enduring power of a pedagogy spearheaded by the progressive movement, of a vision of education that contributes to our understanding of relevance, personal engagement, and community. Ultimately, it is plea to teacher educators to think differently and take a risk.

On a "Silent" Walk Around the School Block

No one said a word. We followed her gaze, which was fixed on an old redbrick school building that must have been constructed in the 1920s. Attached to it was a newer version of the old structure, a recent extension. It had the same dark-and-light-striped brick pattern across the facade, and some playful brick patterning toward the top. The addition was the same height and approximately the same length and width as the old building. We saw through the windows of the new structure, in which on each floor workers were finishing walls, installing light fixtures, and painting.

Then we followed her across the street as she led us slowly to the east corner of the block. Some of the adult students began to talk with each other. She calmly looked at them, placed a finger on her lips, and pointed to the school yard. Our task was to observe, hear, and touch but not speak. We saw that one of the building walls that adjoined the school yard was covered with a long, brightly painted student mural of the Hudson River and the surrounding areas. I imagined children of different ages standing on ladders and chairs with paintbrushes in hand working alongside one another. The tall wrought-iron fences that enclosed the yard on two sides had two entranceways. Over one, in intricate ironwork, was the word "BOYS," and over the other, "GIRLS"—an indication of what school was like when the building was constructed. Then we followed her around the block and saw many redbrick town houses, some of which must have been constructed in the 1800s and some new; like the addition to the school, the new houses seemed to be constructed to blend with the old. We passed huge garage doors, and I wondered what was behind them. We passed a busy luncheonette, a church rectory, a missionary residence, and then we arrived at the side of the newly constructed school addition.

As we made our way clear around the block to the front of the new building, we had to walk around looming stacks of boxes of materials that were needed to complete the structure. We followed her into the school entrance, up the steps of that old building, into her classroom. As we climbed the steps, I realized how intensely I had concentrated, how I was more aware of what was in front of me physically—the colors, shapes, and sounds of the world around me. I heard a plane overhead, looked up, saw it slowly traveling through the clear blue sky, and I wondered where it was going. I also heard traffic in the distance, but I was most aware of all the birds, whose songs seemed to fill the street with music. I wondered, if I hadn't been on this "silent" walk would I have heard them? Mitchell's trip to the street corner came to mind—how she so wanted her adult students to perceive the world as a child does, through the senses; how she wanted to fine tune their sensory awareness; and how she wanted them to see the potential for curriculum in the world around them.

Our guide on that silent walk was Pat Arpino, a second-grade teacher who had spent the year studying the construction of the new school building. She wanted the curriculum class students who were visiting her classroom to experience exactly how she began the study with her second graders, but when her class went on the walk, the new structure wasn't even a skeleton. When I taught the same age, I had seen how the entire process of construction fascinated children: the workers bravely balancing themselves on steel beams, the skill and concentration of operators managing impossibly high cranes, the drama of the great machines, the different raw materials arriving to bustling sites for each new phase of the process. I had also seen how the study of construction offered the opportunity to study a complex process over time, research the planning of a building, meet architects, examine blueprints, learn about the science of what makes a building stand, explore the geography upon which a building would be constructed, observe the work of individual machines, and meet the construction workers and learn about their work. Each aspect can offer the fertile opportunity for children to reflect on and extend their experiences—through discussion; building with blocks, wood, cardboard; through music and movement, artwork, and scientific experiments, similar to what Trish Lent did when studying the engineering of bridges.

As we entered Pat Arpino's classroom, everyone gravitated to the large wooden model the children constructed of the new building. Pat explained how the children's construction of their structure followed the process of the building, and virtually spanned the year. Papier-mâché figures of workers were perched on the exterior and within the model, each in active working positions. Pat described how the entire model was the product of intense observation of the building site, interviews with the workers, and of an ongoing process of problem solving. The full class, small groups, and individuals struggled with the problems of constructing the sources of heat, water, electricity; of building a foundation; of adding new levels, and especially of installing staircases that would work. She described how the study integrated math, science, geography, reading, writing, and artwork. She said that on one Monday morning a startled child who was looking at the model shouted that everyone had to come and look—a family of mice had made a nest and set up home on the basement level of the model, "just like in a real building!" We imagined the excitement of those children jostling each other to see this mother mouse with her family of babies. Then we spent time examining the display of photos that documented the construction process of the school building and the classroom model, and how they paralleled each other.

Inspired by the yearlong construction of their new school building, the second graders replicated the building process in this class model using wood, screws, glue, and blocks. Notice the workers, fashioned from papier-mâché, perched outside and inside the building. The detail shows a worker operating a drill. (Photographs by and courtesy of Pat Arpino)

When Pat had mentioned to colleagues that her class would be constructing a large wooden model in the classroom, they said it was too hard a project and the children were too young, but Pat knew about building with wood—her father had been a carpenter. She also knew how primary-aged children have a drive to be industrious, to use real tools and do real work. Though she had never tackled anything so ambitious, or that demanded so much from her or her children, she felt it would work, and it turned out to be a high point in her teaching. She believed the children would never forget what they had created.

The summer curriculum course did not begin with the trip to Pat Arpino's classroom; it began months before the first day of class, when Karen and I discussed general aims for the course. We wanted to cultivate sensitivity to potential learning opportunities in the students' environment and, in the process, sharpen their sensory awareness. We wanted students to experience the potential for integrating literacy into a rich curriculum in which we used the world around us as a stimulus for discussion, writing, and reading. We wanted to spark insight into the meaning such activities might hold for children, and we hoped these insights would be reflected in the social studies curricula the students would develop for children. Most important, Karen and I wanted the adult students' prior experiences, interests, knowledge, and skills to factor into the curriculum. We wanted the course to evolve as an interaction among the individual students, the people and places they engaged with, and us, their teachers.

Researching the Course and Evolving Course Aims: Venturing into the Neighborhood

We began by getting to know our familiar environment in a new way. We literally walked *up* and *down* the streets of the Upper West Side of Manhattan. Though many think of Manhattan as completely flat, we felt the contours in our leg muscles as we walked the dramatic incline on 113th Street between Broadway and Riverside Drive—just around the block from Bank Street. On 114th Street, just two blocks from the college, we spent some time examining a huge outcropping of rock oddly situated between two buildings, wondered whether it was bedrock or a glacial deposit, and wondered why it was still there. We knew we might return to this rock. We were trying to get a rudimentary sense of the neighborhood in which Bank Street College is situated, of what it had in common with other neighborhoods and of the features that made it unique. Though I had lived in the area for ten years, it was as though I were seeing it for the first time—there was so much I hadn't seen or expected to see. On each walk, Karen and I were trying to see the area through our students' eyes and through the eyes of children.

After combing the area, our aims grew more specific. We decided that we wanted the students to come away with a sense of how the area was tied to the rest of the city, geographically, through transportation, and through services. We wanted them to have exchanges with people whose work sustained them and residents of the neighborhood, with people who modeled skill and competence, and with recent immigrants to the neighborhood to get their perspective on the area as well as to learn about their experience of coming to this country and settling in New York City. We wanted the students to learn about the area in the past and see how the neighborhood had grown and changed. And we wanted the students to see how the neighborhood assisted people who needed help—getting food, services, and housing. These aims led us to a Caribbean luncheon-ette, a construction site, a lumberyard, Pat Arpino's classroom, a major bus depot, a recycling plant, a soup kitchen, a neighborhood development or-ganization, a pottery studio, and, of course, the boat basin. With each new place we visited, we experienced the discomfort of approaching strangers. We tolerated the anxiety, forged ahead, and experienced the resulting rewards. Each time, those magic words, "We are teachers and . . . ," really did work, just as we had been telling our students for years.

While exploring the neighborhood for the July course, Karen Weiss and I came upon this unusual outcropping of rock just two blocks from the college. We knew we needed to find out about it and why it was there. (Photograph by author)

When we entered the Caribbean luncheonette, a young woman greeted us with a bright smile. She had recently emigrated from the Dominican Republic and established the luncheonette on her own— and spoke with such pride in what she had accomplished. We learned why she moved to New York, and how she felt about living here. We asked who frequents her restaurant, what she served and why, how she learned to cook and run a restaurant, and how she gets her foods—much of which, we found out, was imported. We noticed that she had two menus, one for adults and one for children. She explained that local elementary and middle school children, many of whom are of Caribbean background, are able to leave the school at lunchtime and noisily crowd into her restaurant for lunch and for after-school snacks. For them she developed a special menu that she thought their parents would approve of. Not only were the menu items healthful, tasty, and familiar, they were also inexpensive. She said parents have come in to check the place out and were pleased with what they saw. She smiled when we asked if she'd be willing to welcome a group of adult students or a group of school children into her store to learn about her work and her experience in the neighborhood. She said she'd demonstrate making a simple dessert.

Afterward, Karen and I discussed how taking this trip with primary-aged children might grow out of a study of ethnic groups in the area, of immigration, or of how we get our food in the neighborhood. We also brainstormed the various ways the trip could be followed up with adult students as well as with children, through cooking, writing, artwork. For each place we visited, we thought about a chain of possibilities embedded in the trip. Even with the limited amount of time we had for the course, we wanted students to build a concept of the neighborhood in relation to the larger world to which it is intimately connected—and we wanted to do this by forging human connections.

The visit to a massive Columbia University construction site just a few blocks from Bank Street led us to a lumberyard and eventually to Pat Arpino's classroom. (We knew of Pat's work through having student teachers in her classroom.) When we entered the lumberyard, we felt enveloped in the loud whirring of electric saws and the scent of freshly cut wood. We saw customers wearing carpenters' aprons with hammers and screwdrivers hanging from the many pockets. The owner said he would show adult and child students a display of different planks of wood next to pictures of the types of trees from which they were cut. He would also show a map of the Western Hemisphere that pinpointed the origins of the different woods and would talk about how they get the wood to the lumberyard. Karen asked if he would demonstrate some aspect of his work, and he said he'd show how to measure a board accurately and cut it, and would take students into the workshop to see cabinets being made. Karen and I thought about how well this trip would fit into a study of construction, how it could lead to examining all the aspects of our world made from wood, to students doing woodworking in the classroom, to learning about trees and conservation.

At the ceramics studio, the potter said she'd demonstrate making a pot on a wheel and would give students the opportunity to create simple hand-built pots. Karen and I thought this trip illustrated one way in which people in the neighborhood satisfied the need to create, to create something beautiful—which we came to think of as another basic human need. We thought about how this trip could be embedded in a study that integrated art, geography, science, reading, and writing. Like construction, clay offered the opportunity to engage with a process, but this process the children could perform themselves at school. The class could meet in Staten Island, which is rich in clay deposits (about an hour's travel from the college), dig raw clay, process it at the college, model with it, and even build a homemade kiln with bricks or a metal garbage can, and then fire their work.[1] We thought about how much of the physical world, most prominently all the brick buildings around us, is made from clay. We also thought about how satisfying it is to work with clay, and that clay had been used from the beginnings of human society by peoples throughout the world, that 60 percent of the earth's surface is covered with clay.

Not all of our ventures were fruitful: the managers of the local recycling plant would not accept groups of visitors. If we were crafting the syllabus today, we wouldn't stop at that; we'd find a way to travel outside the neighborhood to a larger recycling plant. Not only is the topic critical, it also has the potential for children to make a difference—now.[2] After interviewing workers at the neighborhood development organization and soup kitchen, we thought each place would help create a fuller portrait of how the neighborhood functioned.

Even before Karen and I began researching the course, I knew that, if possible, we would include a trip to a major city bus depot. I had taken a group of first and second graders to a NYC Transit Authority bus depot in the mid-1970s. That trip grew from a child's father's visit to the classroom to discuss his work as a bus driver. The children had watched and listened intently as he showed us his route on a street map of Manhattan. They were excited when he invited us to ride on his bus. I thought such a trip would add an important dimension to our study. We would be seeing how the work of one child's parent was integral to our lives. On a cold winter day, we traveled downtown by subway to get to the origin of his bus route. I remember how excited the children were when we saw him waving to us as he pulled into the bus stop. The children stretched their legs as they climbed the steep steps onto the bus, and as they passed him he shook their hands. His daughter hugged him and then proudly shook his hand. We traveled uptown, and as we got close to the school, to every passenger's consternation he departed from the regular route and dropped us off right in front of the school building!

In the block area and at the woodworking bench, children built all kinds of buses and drove them through the roads they had constructed. When I said we would be visiting a bus depot, they were thrilled. Those bus trips became a highlight of the school year. Little wonder the children were so excited when we consider the passion many children have with anything that "goes"—cars, trucks, buses, airplanes, helicopters, and boats. Those trips led to animated discussion, to mapping the bus routes, measurement work when crafting buses out of wood, writing, drawing, and music and movement. It was because the bus trips sparked such interest and led to such rich follow-up work with the children that I wanted the adult students in our July course to have a similar experience.

The depot for our neighborhood was approximately one mile north of the college. The managers and drivers spent a lot of time with Karen and me helping us plan for a July trip to the depot. They took us through a day in the life of a bus driver and introduced us to many of the workers we'd be meeting on the trip. We made one special request: Could we go through a bus wash? The bus wash had been a high point when the first and second graders and I visited the depot. We knew that this trip would be important—it held the seeds of so much we wanted students to come away with.

The Eastern Woodland Indians room of the Museum of Natural History showed how people in the past, who lived in the same geographic area we were studying, fulfilled basic human needs. We saw the trip, coming toward the very end of the course, as one way of synthesizing what we had learned; as an opportunity to cast all that we had done in the course in relief by examining what was unique to each period and what surfaced as salient across time; and as an impressionistic way to begin a study of a culture in the past. The trip would also add the important aspect of using a museum as a resource. We did use this trip, and, in retrospect, felt that while our aims for the trip sounded good on paper, if we were to repeat it in the future we would devote a great deal more time to embedding the trip into the fabric of the course and doing the follow-up work. It was as though we were giving short shrift to an important topic, which was just what we didn't want to do. Perhaps a trip to Inwood Park, which is located on the northern tip of Manhattan, might have suited the course better. It was the site of a major Native American settlement and still has original Indian caves, and the geographic features of the area have changed little from the time the Native Americans lived there. Right up to the 1940s, people were digging up arrowheads. Like Karen Kriesberg, when she discovered the site of a major Native American settlement where the Nissequogue River opens to the bay, the students would have been in the actual physical context of people's lives and have had the opportunity to explore how the people who lived there might have fulfilled their basic human needs of food, shelter, and travel.

Time, Our Greatest Constraint

When Karen and I began to decide which trips we'd include in the course, we found time to be our greatest constraint. Though our research was by no means exhaustive, we had enough material to last for two years. Unlike Mitchell, who had a full year to develop her curriculum of experiences, we had the duration of a July course—four weeks, one hour and fifty minutes four times a week. It wasn't nearly enough time, so as an experiment we added three three-hour Friday morning classes for trips. During registration, students were informed of the additional days and time.

Still, time was our greatest constraint. Rather than crowd the time we had with as many trips as possible, we wanted each trip to be embedded in a chain of experiences that progressively built on one another, that enabled students to evolve an increasingly complex concept of the world and their place in it. We needed time to develop the context in which each trip would be integral, time to plan with the students for the trip, and time to reflect and build on the experience. We wanted students to see what was possible when there was time—*unrushed* time. We didn't want to *cover* a subject, we wanted students to have the time to engage with and develop it. We wanted students to realize that time was a fundamental aspect of the learning process. Also, we wanted the students to meet a classroom teacher who made the time to do the kind of work we would be discussing in class.

We planned a course sequence that mirrored children's evolving and growing sense of their environment: the study of family, the neighborhood, the city, and the city in the past. The four trips we selected to include seemed to most readily fulfill our aims (stated earlier in this chapter), were most accessible to full class groups, were places we thought the adult students would want to return to with their own students, and would offer the greatest opportunity for follow-up. We chose the bus depot, Pat Arpino's classroom, the boat basin, and the Museum of Natural History Eastern Woodland Indians room. Somehow we knew that all the exploring that didn't find its way into the course would make the course richer for our having done it. We could be more responsive to the students' questions, ask more thoughtful questions, and be more flexible. Also it was through all the venturing out that we grew more excited and more committed to what would evolve. For me, and I know for Karen, the course remains a high point in our teaching careers.

Modeling Classroom Life

Each day and throughout the course, Karen and I attempted to simulate on an adult level what and how one might teach children—in the organization of the classroom, the ways we allocated time, the discussions we had, the classroom charts we created and used, and the activities we worked on. We organized the room like a classroom, with students sitting in table groupings that would accommodate small-group discussions and the project work we would be doing. We developed an attendance chart on which individual photos of each student would be attached with Velcro, just as you might do with children. Karen had photographed each student's face and the backs of their heads. She printed them so that the face was visible on one side of the card and back of the head on the other. Each morning as they entered, they'd turn the card face forward and when they left, turned it around. In our meetings we examined the chart as you might do with children and made note of who wasn't there. They realized that their presence was important and got to know each other quickly, and, because of all the work they did together, got to know each other deeply. After trips, we'd display digital images that reflected aspects of their experiences of the trips. These images became another way of reliving our experiences together, and students referred to them during discussion and in their writing and artwork. We displayed an agenda of what we would be doing, as you might do with children so that they feel in control of the day. Early on, Karen and I noticed how the students entered the class with expectation, with excitement at what would be happening.

We'd begin each class formally with a message written on chart paper that invited discussion, such as: "What did you find most interesting about our trip yesterday? Did you find anything surprising?" Or we might write, "Spend ten minutes writing what stands out for you from our trip, then discuss at your table ways you might extend the experience with children?" Or, "How might we thank Leslie for escorting us through the boat basin?" Or, "Let's think about how we might plan transportation-related trips for children of different ages for the locations in which you will be teaching." Or, "Let's discuss how the creation of bike lanes on city streets might affect getting around in the city." Or, "What questions surfaced for you from our trip to Pat Arpino's classroom and how might we find answers to them?"

We posted a street map of New York City on which students located where they lived, the route they traveled to the college, and the places we visited together. We discussed the many ways such a map might be used with children and demonstrated how the information could be used for math activities, for example: Who lives furthest from the college? What three students live three blocks from the college? How many blocks more does Anne travel than Ron? Graph the distances traveled. Graph the different ways students travel to school, and so forth. I remember examining a similar map when I visited a second-grade class. I was surprised when a child walked up to me and said, "I love this map." She pointed directly to a pin placed over a lower Manhattan street and showed me where she lived. Then she pointed to a Brooklyn street and said, "This is where my father lives." I saw how grounding that map was for her, how it enabled her to unite what was important to her. I thought about the many children who might find it satisfying to be able to locate and in a sense define their world so concretely. I thought of how important it might be for immigrant children to do a similar activity on a world map. The map might show where they came from and how they traveled to their current home, so that their two worlds can exist together and be acknowledged in school.

A critical part of the classroom life in that July course was all the time Karen and I spent working on the course together. It was stimulating, energizing, and also fun—and we brought all of our excitement to our work with the students. We had been partners in exploring the neighborhood; together we got to know the people we would visit, planned the trips, worked out all the logistical considerations, planned follow-up activities, and designed the syllabus. After each class, we discussed the day, the students' comments, their work, what seemed to work well and what needed refining, and then we planned the next day. It would be impossible for me to catalog all that I learned from our working together. I experienced what I had been telling new teachers— that it is critical to discuss their work with colleagues. I remember how, when I taught children, I would meet over lunch with a friend who taught the same grade at a different school. At one meeting I worked out how I would integrate into our immigration curriculum a study of land formations, continents, mapping continents, relief maps, and the making of globes. I had struggled unsuccessfully for days to come up with a feasible plan, yet I left that relaxed hour-and-a-half lunch meeting with clear direction—and it worked. After one such meeting my friend said that our schools should pick up the lunch tab.

The Bus Depot

The bus depot trip became a high point in the course. We arrived at the depot on 135th Street between Broadway and Riverside Drive. Before entering the depot, we asked the students to look down 135th Street toward the Hudson River. The steep incline downward was striking. Like the outcropping of rock a few blocks from the college, the incline illustrated that the city existed upon and within the natural world; we would talk about this throughout the course. A bus driver and the supervisor who had helped Karen and me plan the trip met us at the door. During our visit we met with managers, drivers, mechanics, and a customer-service representative. They described the rigorous process of becoming a bus driver, how routes and shifts are determined, how drivers occupy their time between shifts, the role of seniority and their union, how buses are maintained, how passenger complaints are handled, about the new hybrid models that use electricity as well as gasoline, and the different ways buses are being made wheelchair and handicap accessible.

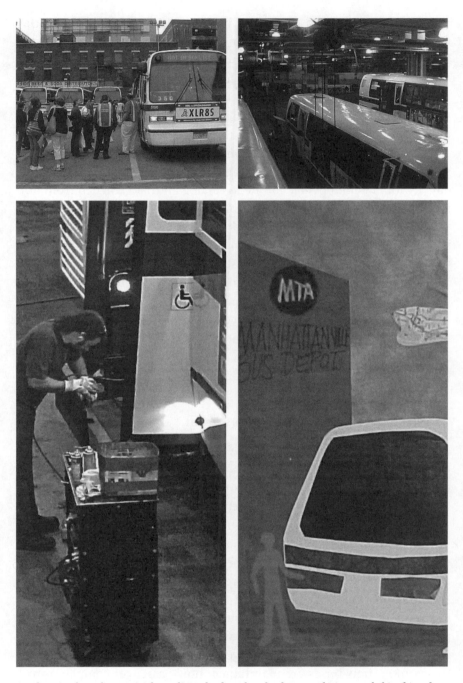

At the city bus depot: (a) boarding the bus for the bus wash (upper left); (b) refurbished, freshly painted, and spanking clean buses (upper right); (c) mechanic repairing a wheelchair-access device (lower left); (d) student-made class thank-you card for the bus workers (lower right). (Photographs by and courtesy of Karen Weiss)

Both Karen and I saw how seriously and thoughtfully the students engaged with the workers. I think the workers felt honored that these adult students were so genuinely interested in *their* work. At one point a manager and driver led us to a large room to answer any additional questions. The workers who were sitting at tables nearby eating lunch joined in the discussion. We saw the camaraderie among the workers and for the brief duration of the trip we became a part of that camaraderie. They had always been an important part of our world, but now we knew them and a connection was forged. Before we left the depot to board a bus and go through the bus wash, a manager showed us a bulletin board with a photo of himself, some of the drivers we met, and a class of smiling school children. Next to the photo, in young children's distinctive handwriting, were thank-you letters and drawings. He said that too few groups of children come to the depot, and that they treat them well when they visit—which had been my experience in the 1970s. Going through the bus wash was the perfect end to the trip. It was as though we relived the wonder and fun of being children as water and soap and brushes and long hanging flaps of cloth assaulted our senses.

The "Outgo"

As soon as students entered the classroom on the following Monday morning, they began discussing the trip with each other. The full group discussion that formally began the day was just as animated. Roberta Altman, a colleague who accompanied us on the trip, was an active member of that discussion. When Roberta had heard about the planned visit to the depot, she asked to come along and offered to do movement work with the students as a follow-up. As a teacher of children, though I knew how readily children expressed themselves through movement, I never felt comfortable about doing movement with them. Consequently, I didn't take those first shaky steps that are so critical to learning. I was glad Roberta would be addressing this in the course. She was a seasoned movement teacher of children and adults.

Following the discussion, Roberta led the class through a series of activities they might do with three- through eight-year-old children, the ages covered in the course. For the youngest children—three-, four-, and five-year-olds—the class sang bus songs, many of which incorporated movement, then did a number of simple movement activities. For primary children—six-, seven-, and eight-year-olds—she asked students to work together in small groups to express one aspect of the trip through movement. I remember how one group simulated the vacuuming of coins from the coin box. A student's body, held up horizontally by peers, became the hose. When they turned on the machine, her body began to wiggle to the musical accompaniment of coins being shaken in a metal can. As they held up the wiggling "hose" and shook the coins, their voices joined to form the loud sound of air suctioned into a tube.

Roberta also incorporated an activity for children older than eight. She wanted students to think about a possible developmental continuum of how children might be asked to reflect on the experience. Because the bus drivers spoke repeatedly about the importance of their union, Roberta brought in some of the evocative songs that grew from the labor movement. Students sang a number of these and created new stanzas. Finally, the full class worked together to orchestrate and perform the bus wash. Riding a NYC bus would never be the same. It was a grand and joyous finale to an eye-opening morning.

When I had tried that first modest experiment of going to the boat basin with the curriculum class I was then teaching, that trip was inserted into a fully formed syllabus, which left no class time for follow-up. I simply asked the students to reflect on their experience and represent it in some tangible way and bring these to the next class. What they brought showed how seriously they engaged with the assignment. I know this type of individual expression is important. That Monday morning following the bus depot trip and repeatedly throughout the July course, I saw how important it is for adult students, just as it is for children, to experience the stimulation of simply seeing what others are doing; to experience the benefits and challenges of working with others; and to be offered a variety of ways to reflect on and express experience.

During that Monday morning with Roberta, I had witnessed the depth with which the students relived the experience through movement, their attention to detail, their inventiveness, and the fun of it all. When speaking with Roberta afterward, she said that by doing this type of movement, students "activated a deep and primal form of communication, a way of knowing and expressing that goes beyond words." She said that representing experience through movement is at once cognitively, socially, and physically demanding. Learners had to share their thoughts and opinions to arrive at the one aspect they'd depict. They had to discuss and review the particulars of that aspect, and as a result everyone's understanding of the experience was extended. They had to

Students engaged readily with the variety of materials with which they expressed their experiences of the trips. (Photographs *a*, *b*, and *c* by and courtesy of Karen Weiss; photograph *d* by and courtesy of Sinming Law and Anthony Bradfield)

sequence the events and work together on an imaginative retelling—
any way they wanted to. In reexperiencing, they fleshed out aspects of
the original experience, adding layers of meaning, bringing it to a new
level of consciousness. Essentially, Roberta had illustrated Mitchell's
concept of "outgo," how an experience was not complete until a learner
reflects on the experience and crystallizes that reflection through discussion, writing, dramatic play, or, most powerfully, the arts.[3]

Besides using movement, Karen and I extended ourselves in ways we
never anticipated. We brought in materials for collage, tempera paints
for individual paintings and murals, and a sand table for modeling
maps. We also brought in children's building blocks as another means
of representing experience. From a student-generated list of words that
evoked the boat basin experience, we introduced poetry. We offered students a choice on how they wanted to express their experience. Some
students right away had a clear idea of what they wanted to do and
worked alone. Some spent time observing their peers busily working at
their tables or on the floor, gluing bits of collage materials that would
become the George Washington Bridge, setting up paints, sketching
the broad outlines of a mural, consulting books on bridges or boats, or
sitting in a quiet corner writing, then got an idea and went to work. I
remember how one student spent a long time just staring at the list of
words that evoked the boat basin trip. Then she walked to the back of
the room, sat down, stared at the list from a distance, walked right up to
the list again, and stared at it intensely. At a certain point she sat in an
isolated corner and wrote three poems, one right after the other.

The class noise level seemed to epitomize what some teachers describe as a level that reflects productivity. As they worked they got to
know each other differently—and Karen and I got to know them differently. There was camaraderie and energy I hadn't seen in an adult
classroom. It was obvious how proud so many students were of what
they had created, and Karen and I displayed their work for all to ad-
mire. When given the option, most students chose to discuss their work
or read their poetry with the full class.

After class, when Karen and I examined the students' work, we tried
to define what fostered the high quality of their work. We knew that it
was *not simply going on a trip* that supported this quality of investment.
Rather, it was the *kind* of trip they went on. It was the richness and expansiveness of their experience of the bus depot or the boat basin. It was
that the trips were tightly woven into the course curriculum. It was the

The students' work brought their experiences to life. (Photographs by and courtesy of Karen Weiss)

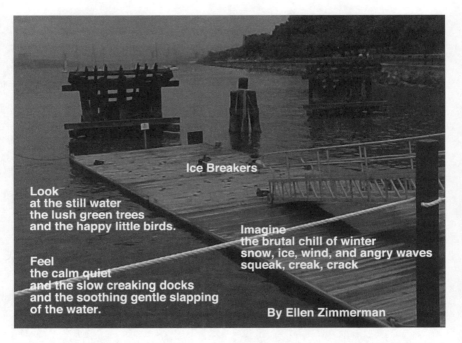

Ice Breakers

Look
at the still water
the lush green trees
and the happy little birds.

Imagine
the brutal chill of winter
snow, ice, wind, and angry waves
squeak, creak, crack

Feel
the calm quiet
and the slow creaking docks
and the soothing gentle slapping
of the water.

By Ellen Zimmerman

"Ice Breakers" by Ellen Zimmerman. (Photograph by and courtesy of Karen Weiss)

person-to-person interactions, the experiencing of the physical world in a new way; it was all the situations the learners had found interesting, exciting, fun, surprising, and engaging. It was the stimulation and energy they received from each other. On the trips, they had the time to explore, question, and discover; back in the classroom, they had the time, space, and materials with which to express, share, and extend their experience. It was that the students were directing their own education. It was the quality of *their* experiences that led to the deep investment in their work.

Curricula the Students Designed

Their final papers reflected this investment. Students were asked to develop in detail a series of related social studies opportunities for a specific age or grade that would lead to and grow out of a specific trip. We wanted the activities to be part of a larger study. For example, a trip to a bus depot for five- and six-year-olds might be embedded in a study of how people travel in the neighborhood or the city. Students submitted much more than what was asked of them; they submitted fully developed studies that incorporated a number of trips and interviews. Many students who were practicing teachers crafted studies of the neighborhood in which their schools were situated or of their specific schools. The school studies focused on the people and work that sustained a child's experience in the school. Other studies were of how Central Park is maintained, which focused on the people who did the work and the machines they used. A student who lived in a suburban community planned a study of recycling in which children would investigate the town dump, which was essentially a recycling center. They'd interview the workers, and follow the process of recycling. In each study, children would uncover a network of relationships among the people and places in the world around them, and as a result form a network of human relationships.

As we read their studies, it was striking to both Karen and me that their work, in contrast to the final studies in the regular curriculum class, showed a clearer sense of how to use the world around them. The papers incorporated much of what we did in the class: discussion was central; trips were carefully planned, introduced, and followed up; digital photos were used as a way to document the trips; mapping was threaded throughout many studies; reading, writing, mathematics, and science were used to extend their students' understandings; the arts were thoughtfully used to reflect on, express, and share experience, and most included movement, collage, poetry, painting, and mural making.

When I think about those papers, the students' process of creating them stands out—how vulnerable they felt venturing outward and making connections with people, how these connections fueled their investment in the topic, and how their explorations were filled with surprises that sparked their imaginations and propelled them forward— which was very much what Karen and I experienced when we designed the course. A student who taught in Washington Heights comes to mind because of how her visits to her school neighborhood to plan a community study profoundly influenced her thinking and teaching. She had been hesitant about doing a neighborhood study. She thought store owners and people on the street would view her as an outsider and show it. During the school year, in the mornings she would walk quickly from her train to the school and after work directly back to the train. However, when she explored the area on the weekend, she kept running into children she had taught and their families who invariably were excited to see her. When store owners learned that she was a teacher in the neighborhood, they were especially friendly and giving and said they'd be happy to receive groups of her children. She felt that through the study she became much less of an outsider; she began to become a part of that neighborhood and more of a teacher of her children.

Like Laura Gerrity, Trish Lent, and Karen Kriesberg, the students tolerated vulnerability and ventured into new terrain to plan their curricula. Students said that through their interactions with the world around them, they came to know a topic more deeply and thus became committed to it—and to a way of learning about it. Many said they realized in a new way that knowledge was found not solely in books or curriculum manuals, that they and their children could be sources of knowledge. Some thought that even if they were required to use a prescribed curriculum, they would have the means to analyze it, adapt it, and make it vital. And many hoped they'd have the opportunity to bring their planning to life in their classrooms through the dynamic interactions among the children, the content, and themselves. The students expressed these thoughts and hopes at the end of the course. Neither Karen nor I had kept close contact with the students and had no idea how or whether what they experienced that July influenced their work as educators.

Seven Years Later

As teachers, we usually don't get to see or learn about the impact of our teaching. We work with faith and hope that our efforts will make a difference. So it was with fear that the course wouldn't have meant as much to them as Karen and I hoped that I began to call the students—out of the blue, seven years later. Using alumni office records and searches, I was able to contact twenty of the twenty-five students. I was greatly relieved that the students remembered me. I asked them essentially what I had asked the long-trip participants: "What stands out, if anything, from the course?" and "What impact, if any, did it have on you professionally and personally?" Most have been teachers for the last seven years; some had become administrators, literacy coaches, museum educators, and curriculum developers. To say that I was surprised by the students' responses is an understatement. Of the twenty students, almost all of them recounted particulars of the class in detail. Many described the course as a formative experience that they continue to draw from in their daily work. They spoke of how they experienced the trips and the follow-up activities as a child might and as a teacher—giving them valuable insight into how a child might perceive the world. Virtually all of them use trips as an integral part of their curriculum, and many spoke of how they plan the trips so that children have meaningful experiences with the people they visit. Over and over students described how they had developed studies that trace chains of interdependence. The trip to the bus depot was especially important to most of them because of how deeply they connected with the workers and the insight they gained into a system they had just taken for granted as they led their lives. I asked students, if they had time, to e-mail me a paragraph or two that recounted what they had said to me on the phone.

What follows are parts of just some of their responses:

Inherent in every meeting of the class was our collaboration and support of each other, which translated into community building in the classes we ourselves would teach. Integrating all subject areas into an overarching social studies curriculum makes learning so much more meaningful for both children and adults. Through this course at Bank Street, I learned how to create a yearlong unit of study that would enhance and tie together reading, writing, math, and art. I also gained great insight into researching and planning field trips, pre- and post-trip activities to help process understanding, and class visits from community members related to the topic of study.

The course turned the world into an exciting laboratory to explore with an open mind and a sense of responsibility. It encouraged us teachers to help children develop curiosity, creativity, and the courage to work unafraid. It put us on a quest to inspire in students a love of learning that will last a lifetime, just as ours will.[4]

—Tracy Wiessbrod

The curriculum class had a big influence on me. When I started here at my school, I changed the kindergarten curriculum to a social studies based curriculum. We study family the first half of the year and we have been studying our town, Napa, for the second half. When we explored the Napa River, Jerry, our local grocer who has a passion for the river accompanied us. The class was very interested in the signs on our storm drains that read, "Drains to the Bay." When Jerry heard about the children's interest in the storm drains, he contacted the water district and had a worker open a hydrant so that we could see the water go down the storm drain and then out the pipe on the other side of the street and into the river.[5]

—Elizabeth Cholas

The course was an invaluable experience. Field trips elevate learning and understanding to a whole new level and stimulate children's desire to learn more. However, moving out into the world, into a place of business that we ourselves may not be familiar with, can be daunting. We ask ourselves: How will we be received? How will we make the experience meaningful for the children and ourselves? Will what we see, hear, and touch, offer the needed context for a greater understanding of the world around them? The visits to the Bus Station and the 79th Street Boat Basin showed me how easy and rewarding trips can be. It was also an affirmation that teachers are often very well received. Our hosts were so appreciative and proud to share their expertise and personal experience with us; it made me feel connected to them. It made me want to learn more.[6]

—Rebecca Elvin

It was extraordinary to live these trips not only as a graduate student and teacher but also through the eyes of a child. For a child to understand the interdependence of all New Yorkers, from making sure buses run to get us from place to place to how our food gets to our table is a powerful lesson about how communities, cities, and countries thrive. We all help each other through our work, and in addition we all have homes, families, friends, and personal histories. The class was a formative experience for my teaching practice.

I now teach in a French dual language kindergarten classroom in a public school in Brooklyn. Half of my students are native French speakers, and half are native English speakers. Each year, trips provide the basis for our social studies curriculum. As we explore the neighborhood, where most of the children live, we get to know the people who do the work to make our community flourish. The trips are especially beneficial for stimulating language acquisition in both French and English. The kids are so absorbed in their work and exploration that vocabulary development becomes automatic.[7]

—Olivia Ramsey

Over the years, I have explored many aspects of the curriculum and have been determined to tie them into their application to the "real world," in the school's neighborhood and beyond it. I believe that, overwhelmingly, my students benefited from these explorations, and I have grown as an educator through these experiences. Yet, without the fundamental growth experienced during this particular summer course, I might have not known how rewarding such interactions could be for all involved in a school's community.

I never let go of that class.[8]

—Ron Azoulay

Before the course I felt New Yorkers seemed to be living on the surface, and I didn't want to raise a child in New York. I think that hope like fear can be infectious. This class in curriculum was something of a wake-up call. I learned that field trips can take place every day in even the most minute but profound ways if you view your world as a place to reach out to people. One can begin to feel a sense of belonging and ownership even to a place like New York—the kind of belonging that begets responsibility and even affection. After all, New Yorkers just as much as anyone else and perhaps even more so can be humane and hopeful and yearning for the kind of connections that make a city into a community.[9]

—Annie Dycus

I was able to design curricula that stemmed from the children's lives. I decided to schedule at least two field trips per month. I made this a particular priority because I felt that it was so important both to expose my students to the wealth of resources that their neighborhood had to offer and enhance their understanding of their own home. We even returned to the bus depot that we had visited as teachers in the course—this was one of my favorite trips to take, because it allowed us to gain further knowledge of a transportation system that affected their everyday lives.[10]

—Laura Gutmann

I began to question what I'd taken for granted, such as bus service or lifestyle choices in the city. I also began to wonder what else was there behind the facade of the everyday assumptions we make. As a teacher I try to employ direct experiences. I feel that for any of us, seeing the world through a fresh lens is essential. Social studies enables us to become a more thoughtful and aware part of the world around us, be it a small community or a larger more global community; to touch it, question it, explore it, and begin to understand its complexities. For me, it is an awakening of the senses to all that is around me.[11]

—Barbara Shindler

The experiences were what remained memorable: (a) seeing a different way of life in New York City (upper left); (b) learning in ways they might replicate with children (upper right); (c) feeling the ground move under them as they walked (lower left); (d) seeing the fledgling oyster beds raised from their home in the Hudson River. (Photographs by and courtesy of Karen Weiss)

Like the long-trip participants of the 1930s, '40s, and early '50s, the experiences were what remained memorable and influenced the students' teaching: hearing the bus workers speak "of their profession with great pride and camaraderie and with a sense of responsibility"; "surprise at seeing such a different way of life in [their] own neighborhood (the boat basin) and especially how *unstable* their lives could be, *literally rocking*"; seeing and hearing with "a new eye" as Pat Arpino led us silently around the newly constructed school building; becoming brushes rapidly spinning around, their "arms and legs pumping up and down,"[12] as they "became the bus wash"; and venturing out on their own to research their curriculum assignment topics, feeling the vulnerability of being a learner and the thrill of discovery. Their comments affirmed the enduring power and vitality of this form of learning and teaching, of going out into the world and learning from experience.

The stories of children and teachers from the past and the present form the substance of this book. Over and over again, they have confirmed for me that venturing outward is essential to being a learner. In the next and concluding chapter, I examine where these stories of venturing out take us—what we as teachers, students, and citizens can incorporate into our work and into our lives.

Conclusion

"This Going Off Together, There's Something to It"

As we were ending our interview, I asked Allen Ohta if he had anything else to say about the 1948 long trip to TVA areas. (For most of his classmates, the photo of him standing before the Norris Dam colored drinking fountain symbolized the intensity of their experience.) He thought for a minute and said seriously, "You know, this going off together, there's something to it." The stories of children and teachers venturing outward—into the social world of a neighborhood barbershop, into the wet darkness of a coal mine, to the majesty of Norris Dam, down into the heat of the school boiler room, to a bustling wholesale market, to a tailor shop to learn how to sew a button—all attempt to penetrate what Ohta's "something" is, what it can be. I conclude these stories of children, teachers, and the people and places they came to know by focusing on what *we* might take away from their experiences and use as educators and citizens, specific principles that can guide our thinking as we plan for and teach students, whether they be children or adults.

The following statements are not neatly separate. To be realized and lived in classrooms, they function together and rely on one another. All but one apply to the education of both children and teachers. Across all of them is the force of learning from experience, the power of learning with and from others, and a vision of a more just society and the individual's role in creating that society:

- The major focus of the education of children and teachers should be on the full development of the person.

- Deciding how children and teachers "live" the process of schooling and deciding what is most important for them to learn should be influenced by a vision of a more democratic society.
- For learning to become a force in their lives and work, children and teachers should learn from firsthand experience.
- The process of educating teachers should be a model for and parallel to—on an adult level—a way of educating children.
- The education of children and teachers should move the learner outward physically and socially as well as intellectually.
- In the education of children and teachers, there must be a relationship between aims, curriculum content, and methods.
- The education of children and teachers should be a social process.
- The education of children and teachers should integrate many ways of knowing the world.
- Children and teachers should be offered opportunities to give form to their experience of the curriculum through the arts.
- Time must be allocated for these principles to be realized.

I briefly discuss each statement in light of what has become clear to me through my own long trip into the work of educators featured throughout this book. Each is a statement of what I have come to believe educators *should* consider as they decide what is most important to offer their students. Consequently, each statement is value laden. Each asks teachers of children and adults to take a stand, to embrace their work as a stake in the future of individuals and society, as a hopeful declaration of self.

The Major Focus of the Education of Children and Teachers Should Be on the Full Development of the Person

In curriculum guides it is common to see statements of what children *will* do and *will* learn and rubrics that delineate the particulars of what teachers must look for in children's work. In recent years these "will learns" and so-called objective rubrics have been increasingly applied to the education of teachers as well. These declarations of what will be learned and how teachers should evaluate students' work have been developed independent of who the learners are, their life experience, what they already know, and what teachers know about the individuals they teach. It is as though the mandate of holding teachers or learners accountable for where a learner "should be" will make it so. It implies that learners can bypass where they are at the moment. In the process of fulfilling the "will learns," behavioral objectives, and rubrics, the learner is bypassed. And once educators narrowly focus on specific objectives for the individuals they teach—objectives they had no role in creating—they can be blinded to what the learners are offering, what the learners know, and what they care about, essentially blinded to the person.

In many cases, the objectives for teachers translate into their ability to perform specific teaching techniques, essentially, "how-tos." Yet what about the individual teachers—what they bring to the role of teaching that is important and special? When people think about a teacher who profoundly influenced them, usually they recall a unique individual, someone who was responsive to them, who took the time to get to know them, who sparked their imagination, and placed them in a position to experience their strength as learners. An education that focuses narrowly on teaching technique may help teachers get through a Monday morning, but what of the rest of their career? What about their ability to understand children and the world in which children live? What about their ability to design curricula that incorporate the lives and worlds of the children? What about their questions, their concerns, their professional struggles, and their hopes for themselves and the children they will teach? Where do *they* fit into the role of teacher?

It's much easier and requires so much less time to focus exclusively on what has to be covered than to reflect on and be responsive to individuals. Yet whether we acknowledge it or not, the person—child or adult—responds to the world as an integrated entity, a "whole person," a thinking, feeling, physical individual. And this person brings into school each day a personal history—with knowledge, interests, aptitudes, fears, hopes, and a constellation of personal relationships that gives meaning to his or her life. Unfortunately, the term "whole person" has become a cliché. It's one of those nice-sounding statements that finds its way into mission statements, curriculum guides, and methods texts for teachers—but seldom is used as a guiding principle. A learner becomes an active agent in his or her education when educators engage the person, when they value their students' experiences, thoughts, and feelings; when they seriously consider students' questions and do not rob them of opportunities to find out; when they enable students to bring their world into the classroom.

Instead of sapping students' energy and dulling them to possibility, the process of education can generate energy and stimulate imagination, curiosity, questions, and the desire to learn more. Unfortunately, in schools it is all too familiar to see students looking tired, appearing uninterested, finding it difficult to attend as they sit through what many experience as a lifeless regime that has little to do with them or what interests them.

Deciding How Children and Teachers "Live" the Process of Schooling and Deciding What Is Most Important for Them to Learn Should Be Influenced by a Vision of a More Democratic Society

How and what we teach is not neutral or objective and never was—be it reading, science, or mathematics. It is driven by values, someone's values. Mitchell and Hogan asked their students to accept responsibility for the kind of society they and the children would be a part of, to accept that the process and content of what they offer children would play a major role in shaping that society. Their convictions drove the curriculum they offered adults, which Mitchell called "Social studies for teachers."[1] They placed their adult students in situations that demanded their thinking; shook up preconceived notions; caused them to question and challenge themselves; caused them to enlarge their circle of knowing, caring, and commitment—all essential to democratic living. Of course what they selected for their students to encounter revealed their own values; however, they exposed them to many vantage points on a position. They never accepted pat solutions to complex problems. Their adult students learned about mining from mine owners, management, miners, miners' families, and from going into a mine—and ultimately formed their own opinions.

Each time children go out into the world with their class and are free to experience it from their own perspective, they are offered an opportunity to form their own opinions about what they see and hear and feel, not simply to accept the second- or third- or fourth-hand opinions of someone else. Encountering the complexity of that world and meeting the people who make it function, when carefully planned, can forge new connections that enlarge that child's community. It is not solely the child's concept of the world that is enlarged, but also the child's participation in that world. Engaging the world out there—whether it be the people living in Grand Central Station, construction workers skillfully operating cranes that seem to go up to the sky, sanitation workers showing what happens to massive amounts of garbage—provokes questions, *real* questions; the *need* to find out; the *need* to share their impressions with others; and in some cases the *need to act*.

Democratic living is not achieved simply by having a Constitution. Rather, it's a rigorous and continuous process of communicating with others and of assuming responsibility for active participation. The children who ran a bakery to earn money for the soup kitchen were participating on their own level. We give children such a meager portion of life in schools. Learning lessons to pass or score high on tests just doesn't make it. American education has lost its mooring. If we value democratic living, then we must make the time and space in our classrooms to live democratically—time to question and find answers, discuss, think, solve problems with others, collaborate on common endeavors, go beyond narrow self-interest, be an active participant, and ultimately make time to engage with people and places in new ways.

For Learning to Become a Force in Their Lives and Work, Children and Teachers Should Learn From Firsthand Experience

When Mitchell and Hogan led students into mining, steel, and TVA areas, there was no television, no Internet, people didn't travel nearly as much as they do today, and regional differences were more pronounced. Hence, a case might be made that there was greater need to experience situations firsthand. Yet when we traveled in 2008 on a long trip to New Orleans it opened all of our eyes. There had been endless news broadcasts, powerful documentary films, and endless feature articles in newspapers throughout the country. My colleagues who went on that trip and I had consulted Internet sites, read about the aftermath of Katrina, and seen the documentaries. Yet it was only by being there that we began to understand the magnitude of what had happened, the disgrace of government inaction, and, perhaps most significant, how people took their fate in their own hands to rebuild New Orleans—"in spite of the government." Like my experience on Kayford Mountain in West Virginia, nothing even approached the intensity of meeting those people who were so passionately tied to New Orleans, not as a concept but to the specific block they lived on, their neighbors, their histories in that area—all of which gave meaning to their lives.

Because of all the exposure and travel, we think we know. And with virtual reality at children's and adults' fingertips, the concept of experiencing grows more complex. This was illustrated for me while waiting on a movie theater line. I was listening to a boy approximately nine years old as he excitedly gave a blow-by-blow account of the baseball game to his parents. The game had just ended and he was brimming with excitement. He demonstrated how he leaped in the air and caught that fly ball, how he hit a ball way into the outfield, how three guys on the team made it to home plate and he ran frantically and slid safely into home just in time, how his teammates cheered as they lifted him on their shoulders. It felt good just to hear the pride in his voice. Then he thanked them for buying him the video ball game. I was stunned, not so much at the fun he had with the game but by how he spoke, as though he were in a real ball game. It's clear that he had an experience. And I'm sure some would argue that it is just as valid as being in an actual ball game. The significance of children experiencing the world virtually is a large, complex topic—too large to be addressed here. However, given the pervasiveness of virtual experiencing, educators, parents, and researchers must give serious thought and attention to it.

Consider what the boy did *not* get from the video game: he did not feel the force of that high fly ball as it hit his glove nor use his hand muscles to secure that ball in the glove. He didn't feel the power of his legs as he ran the bases nor get the vital benefits of the oxygen filling his lungs as he ran. He didn't have to skillfully balance his body so that he could slide into home plate nor feel the force of the ball slamming the wood of the bat. He didn't sweat from the sun's heat or from running as fast as he could. No friends lifted his body off the ground so that he could feel the exhilaration of being on top of the world, and he didn't have the fun of recounting the game, play by play, as he walked home with a friend.

We have to ask ourselves, What does knowing mean? What does it mean to truly experience? Mitchell distinguished between "knowing about" and "knowing." A similar distinction can be made between physical experiencing and virtual experiencing. We must ask ourselves whether we want education to be a vital force in children's and teachers' lives. If we do, the process of education itself must be vital, and nothing is as alive as to be *fully present*, to have *all* of one's senses engaged—to hear the din of cars speeding over the great bridge, to feel its vibrations spread up through your body from your feet, to try to wrap one's arms around the impossibly grand cables, to observe a worker standing in relief against the sky at the very top of the bridge tower, to sit in the warmth of a special room in a neighborhood restaurant and eat a slice of the pumpkin pie that has made the restaurant famous, to smell the hair tonic and hear the buzz of the electric razor as a classmate's hair is expertly fashioned into the coolest cut.

It was through the carefully planned excursions into Brownsville that Laura Gerrity's children—and Laura—overcame the stereotypic ways they viewed their neighborhood. Mitchell struggled throughout her life with how to get people to see beyond what they have been conditioned to see. She thought that she came closest to the "how" through experience, experience that would shake up preconceived notions and beliefs. It is even more important today to learn from firsthand experience because of the increased superficial exposure to the world. We must accept that this form of learning takes time—time for the teacher to explore the community, get to know the neighborhood people, plan, prepare the children, venture out with them, follow up the experience in the curriculum, and then plan the next logical steps. In contrast to instant access to information, learning from experience requires a carefully thought through process, which demands more from teachers and children. *Anything worth learning takes time!* We make time for what we value: do we make the time for education to be a vital force in children's and teachers' lives?

The Process of Educating Teachers Should Be a Model for and Parallel to—on an Adult Level—a Way of Educating Children

Recently, at a dinner party, a young woman was describing how disgusted she was with her degree. She told everyone there how she had gone from a full day of teaching, rode the subway to class, rushed into class a bit late, took a seat in the darkened room, and looked up at a list of bulleted items projected onto a screen. She said that after the reading and explaining of the list, the instructor projected another—just as he had done each evening, from the very first class. She said she had to fight off sleep as she sat there trying to listen. She had arrived too late to pick up the photocopied list given out at the beginning of class so that they could take notes on it. She said that that evening the professor covered "Needs of the Learner," which, like every other topic, was reduced to a series of bulleted items. She laughed as she said, "What about me? Don't I have needs? Or don't teachers have the needs of learners?"

Unfortunately, this young woman's experience is not unusual. It was as though what was being said has nothing to do with the circumstances of how it is being conveyed. Too often, we hear teachers describe how they just had to get through education courses so that they could really learn to teach by teaching. Yet when new teachers finally do make it through the courses and confront the difficulties of teaching, they tend to go back to what has been ingrained through years of schooling. Undoubtedly, some are replicating the methods that excited them to learn, but many, out of expediency, tend to replicate a form of bureaucratic education that they felt was inadequate at best. Mitchell and Hogan wanted to break the replication cycle by having students grow committed to a process of educating that they came to know in their hearts and bodies as well as their minds.

Reading and explaining the bulleted items in a PowerPoint presentation require less time and effort from teacher educators. Ultimately, the question of how we teach teachers comes down to what we value most, what we envision as the role of teachers and of schools in the lives of children and in society: Is replicating what currently happens in classrooms good enough? Are we willing to devote the time and energy to cultivate teachers who question, who think for themselves, who are committed to making a difference for children, society, and the environment?

The Education of Children and Teachers Should Move the Learner Outward Physically and Socially as Well as Intellectually

Underlying every story in this book is the belief that education is an outward-moving process. The sensorial vividness of experience, the emotion evoked from person-to-person exchange, and the *newness* of it all are powerful. When going "behind the scenes," defamiliarizing the familiar, and going beyond the dailiness of one's life, adult students as well as children experience the intensity of "firsts"—first impressions, first experiences. What teacher doesn't recall teaching her first class or parent recall the first time his child rode a bike all by herself?

As the child and adult students from the past and present ventured outward, their world was broadened. Even more important, their participation in that world was broadened through the connections they forged with each other and the world:

- Laura and the children created a community in the classroom that extended into the school itself, the neighborhood, and the worlds of their parents and ancestors;
- Trish and the children moved beyond their school building to the great bridge, to the workers who service the bridge and people who use it, to the workers of the 1800s who risked their lives every day to build it, to the Roeblings whose dream made the bridge a reality;
- Mitchell, Hogan, and their students went beyond their familiar worlds and realized that behind the news articles about mining, unions, civil rights, and natural resources were stories of people, people like themselves; as a result, the boundaries of their caring and commitment were pushed outward;
- My colleagues and I, on a recent long trip to West Virginia, were led by Larry Gibson beyond our comfortable worlds to the other side of Kayford Mountain and witnessed the devastation, the irreparable damage being done to the earth. I knew by the look of disbelief and horror on everyone's face that we were all affected. For myself, I am forever connected to Larry's struggle. I cannot hide behind ignorance.

A student in the 2003 July curriculum class expressed the feelings of so many of the adult students across time and place when she said that she felt like a stranger as she took her first steps outward, and in the process of going beyond those first steps felt "connected to people who previously had simply represented to [her] the 'machinery' of the world," people whom she "had never before bothered to get to know." She said she "woke up," felt a sense of belonging she hadn't expected, "the kind of belonging that begets responsibility" and hope.[2]

In the Education of Children and Teachers, There Must Be a Relationship Between Aims, Curriculum Content, and Methods

Aligning aims, content, and methods is a difficult process to describe or summarize without using examples. One striking example comes to mind. Michelle Shemin, a young teacher who participated in a 2008 curriculum class I taught, struggled with how she and her first graders could work toward social justice, while at the same time attending to academic skills. For many of her students, school was completely separate from their regular lives. They had struggled through the academics now required in kindergarten, and many entered first grade feeling like failures. She wanted to change that. She wanted them to have an impact on their environment, experience the vibrancy of learning from their own experiences in the world, know the satisfaction of working productively with others, and feel the satisfaction that comes from working hard on something *they* think is important. Also, through the study Michelle wanted to break the stereotypic ways in which some of the children viewed themselves and were viewed by others—as hard to teach, uninterested, unable to attend, and not capable. She wanted their schoolwork to spark their curiosity, to "grab them," to "captivate" them. Essentially she wanted their interest to drive their learning. She knew that given her aims, they couldn't simply study "the facts." Michelle struggled to find the content that would offer the means to achieve these aims.[3]

She suddenly realized that the children had repeatedly presented the content she was looking for: the trash on the streets. The children had complained about it for weeks. Here was her opportunity. She focused on a study of recycling and pollution. She knew that first graders have a "drive to find out how things work" and are natural investigators. She wanted to build on this. She thought recycling would be concrete and "real" enough for them to experience, and also that it would have the "hint of abstraction that would push their thinking," fuel their desire to "figure out." And a social studies curriculum on recycling could integrate science, math, reading, writing, and the arts. There would be much that the children could bring to the study from their lives outside of school.

Since the topic was recycling, Michelle departed from teaching methods that simply required children to acquire information; she wanted them *to experience* recycling in school, at home, in the neighborhood, and in the city. She knew the teaching methods had to engage them actively from the very first lesson. So for that first lesson she gathered her children in a circle, laid out a sheet of plastic, and put on plastic gloves. Their interest was sparked. They kept asking, "Miss Shemin, what are we doing?" She then unraveled the knot around a plastic bag that was placed next to her and dumped its contents right onto the plastic sheet. The children were startled. They shouted, "Miss Shemin, that's garbage, home garbage! That's disgusting."

Then they started noticing familiar items and with obvious interest and excitement began to name items they have in their homes. Michelle began to ask them about the particulars: What do we call this? What is it made of? What can we do with it? They then diligently itemized each object by writing what it was on a Post-it. They created a chart that showed the categories of garbage they had seen, such as food, glass, paper, aluminum, plastic, and cardboard and one by one each child placed Post-its under a category. As they discussed and debated which item went where, Michelle noticed how earnest they were, how they supported each other, and how every child was engaged, including children considered behavior problems. She felt that for the first time, the class had "just the right noise level." She ended that first lesson by asking them to think about what would happen if she just left the garbage right there on the floor. They laughed at the idea.

This was just the beginning of an adventure that led them outward into the city and enabled them to change recycling practices in the classroom and at home. Throughout, they eagerly did their work, recorded and discussed their findings, and were proud of the recycling changes they spearheaded. They saw themselves as capable, and became participants because, through the study, they grew to know and care about their environment.

The power and coherence of the curriculum grew from the clear relationship between the teacher's aims, content, and methods selected to achieve those aims. Mitchell and Hogan wanted their students to care about society and the environment, so that they—in turn—would educate their students to care. To achieve this aim, they and their students studied the social and physical worlds, which led them outward to confront social and environmental issues. If we want social justice, if we want a more democratic society, if we want children and adults to think critically, if we want children to work together harmoniously, if we want less pollution, if we want children to see the richness in their neighborhood, to understand how a bridge works, then the *what* and *how* of schooling must be aligned with these aims. American public school systems claim to prepare children for a democratic society but invest practically all of their resources and effort into passing standardized tests.

The Education of Children and Teachers
Should Be a Social Process

When the tired students exited the bus at 69 Bank Street after their long trip into mining, steel, and TVA areas, they were in a sense different people from just one week before, when they boarded that bus and felt the excitement of an adventure about to happen. Like all of the students and their teachers and the people they encountered, the process of "going off together" into the world out there moved them beyond simple group membership. Together they had participated in a larger world that commanded their attention, and in the process their group became a community that extended beyond the walls of their classroom.

The linking of individuals to each other and to the group evolved through the time they spent together: listening to street noise as they stood on the corner with their eyes closed, talking to each other while walking around the block to visit a tailor shop, hearing rice seeds pelt a wet field as a plane zoomed overhead, talking and laughing with coal miners, seeing Allen Ohta standing in front of the "colored" drinking fountain, having city bus drivers seriously consider their questions, hearing how river ice can destroy people's homes, talking about being made fun of, jumping backward in surprise when the school janitor pulled open the furnace door and fire blazed from the opening, using all their strength as they became the Brooklyn Bridge with their bodies, building a bus depot with blocks, hearing a teacher talk about seeing the "Doorway of No Return" through which their ancestors passed before they boarded the slave ships, baking breads for days and running a bakery to earn money for a soup kitchen, and changing the recycling practices in their homes and at school.

It is through the human exchanges in the classroom and beyond described throughout the book that children and adults grew into responsible social beings. A sense of "we" emerged that included their peers and the people in the world around them. Like Laura Gerrity when her colleagues encouraged her to discuss issues of race with her children, the adult and child students become more of themselves through the exchange. Through the "we," students' ideas and opinions were formed, expressed, challenged, and enlarged. Through the stimulation and the energy generated from being an important part of a caring, interactive group, the students achieved beyond their own expectations. When teachers from the past and present experienced this type of learning community, they came to know its value and worked hard to create a similar learning environment for their students.

I am not implying that all learning must or should take place in full-class groups. Whether children are taught in full groups or in small groups or as individuals depends on what the teacher is trying to accomplish, the specific content being taught, and the needs of the learners. However, when the subject is *social* studies, and the content is people's relations to people, and an ultimate aim is cultivating a social individual, then the *how* must be social. This means that physical space in the classroom and time in the schedule must be given for children to think together; problem solve together; go out into the world together; interview class visitors together; share their experiences, ideas, and opinions with each other; work together; and create together. Laura Gerrity, Trish Lent, and so many of the teachers featured throughout the book made the space and time for their students to learn about their community by going out into it and bringing it into their classroom and, in the process, became community participants, in the classroom and beyond.

The Education of Children and Teachers Should Integrate Many Ways of Knowing the World

The power of the three studies that form part 1 of this book grew from the thoughtful integration of many ways of coming to know a topic. Trish's students could not have created the poetry bridge had the study not integrated science, mathematics, history, geography, and the arts. Some students are fortunate to learn in these expansive ways, but it is uncommon for education students to experience the power of integrated learning. When they do, as Mitchell and Hogan's students did, they tend to understand its importance and work hard to incorporate this way of learning into their own teaching. Similarly, students who participated in the 2003 four-week curriculum class felt they came away from the class with a dynamic form of learning that mirrors the ways in which people experience the world, as a totality.

The stories of children and adults learning together on the street corner and in the classroom illustrate how teachers integrated into their curricula many ways of coming to understand a topic. When on trips and in the classroom, science offered child and adult students a way of perceiving the world—through observing, wondering, questioning, and testing one's thinking as an ongoing process. Mathematics offered a way to perceive patterns of relationships, such as among location, weather, and ways of life; the diameter of a bridge cable and its function; the combined weight of a month's worth of classroom garbage and the issue of too much trash being produced.

Fiction, poetry, folklore, and nonfiction offered other means to understand a topic—through evocative language and compelling situations. Literature enabled readers to bring their whole selves—their thoughts, their life experience, their emotions—to their experience of Native American stories in which humans and animals share common origins, to a poem in which a subway is like a fire-breathing dragon, to the story of a family driven by a dream to create the world's greatest bridge. History illuminated how people, based on evidence, have made sense of the past: how the present grew from the past; how ideas and values have origins in the past; how human accomplishments (such as building a bridge or creating a boat basin in New York City) or human disgrace (such as slavery) are grounded in time; and how individuals have made a difference, individuals like the Roeblings who overcame huge obstacles to build their bridge, and Myles Horton, who founded and led the Highlander Folk School that helped unionize the South and educated leaders of the civil rights movement. For Laura Gerrity's children, it was a tremendously important realization that they were not marked by fate, that the disgraceful practice of legally sanctioning the "owning" of human beings happened to many different peoples throughout history, and that the slavery of Africans in the 1600s was a cold-blooded business venture.

Students learned that it is impossible to separate the human story from people's dependence on the earth, from the physical settings that sustain human life. Awareness of the intimate relationship between humans and the natural world grew from the many experiences students had as they ventured into the world: peering down from the bridge walkway at the river flowing beneath them, descending into a coal mine, being shocked at the vastness of a landfill site, witnessing the devastation of mountaintop removal, watching as Metro North trains emerged from and sped into a tunnel, and hearing how bus routes tie New York City together.

As teachers integrate subject areas meaningfully, they and their children come to know the topic in depth. They became "experts." However, integrating subjects is less straightforward than a compartmentalized curriculum and requires time to research, plan, and teach—and therefore forces a teacher to confront the very real issue of *when*, in an already packed schedule, time can be made. Though the problem may on the surface seem insurmountable, it need not be. The various academic subjects that make up a child's day in school—reading, writing, mathematics, and science—can be used to further a children's immersion into a topic. Michelle Shemin (whose first graders studied recycling), Laura Gerrity, and Trish Lent used time flexibly as their classes graphed and analyzed temperatures in different parts of the world; measured bridge roadways and cables; weighed bags of garbage; performed dehydration and decomposition experiments; wrote reports, stories, poems, letters; and read folklore, poetry, fiction, nonfiction, maps, and cooking recipes. These teachers and many who teach in this way say their students do their finest writing because they have so much to say, they read with greater comprehension, and they come to see science and mathematics as ways of understanding the world.

Children and Teachers Should be Offered Opportunities to Give Form to Their Experience of the Curriculum Through the Arts

For Mitchell, the various ways of coming to know the world (discussed in the previous section) offer the first phase of a learning experience, what she called the "intake." It would remain incomplete until a learner transformed the raw materials of experience—information, feelings, impressions, imagination—into a new entity, what Mitchell called the "outgo," a crystallized form of remembrance: a model of a suspension bridge in which the roadway is supported by its other bridge members, a paper focusing on the final portal newly enslaved Africans passed through before they were forced onto the slave ships, a story for children of a miner's son wanting nothing more than to go into the mine and work alongside his father, a mural showing Long Island Native American life in winter, a dance drama enacting the speed-up of a factory assembly line, a discussion in which ideas are bound and rebound and new relationships are drawn. As learners transform the raw materials of information, they come to "have" and "own" that information in new ways; they transform information into *knowledge*, which they "bring with them" to future learning. The creator then "owns" that information or experience in a new way. Also, through the externalizing of one's experience, it is made public, shared with others, and enlarges everyone's concept of the experience conveyed.

The concept of "outgo" is similar to the current formulation that writers "make meaning" through the process of writing, that writers transform the raw materials of experience, knowledge, feelings, and imagination into written language. Unfortunately, the current discussion in education of making meaning seems to be limited to writing. Mitchell found, and my interviews with her students confirmed, that the most intense, memorable forms of outgo were through the arts. And during the summer curriculum class, Karen Weiss and I saw that intensity in students' artistic expressions of their experience of the bus depot and boat basin.

Through artistic expression of experience, creators use language evocatively; use the sensuousness of color as the full sweep of their arms directs the brush to paper; use form, composition, and the sensorial qualities of textures in collage; use words, actions, facial expression, voice to bring life to plot line and characterization in drama; use their hands to give form to experience through the sensorial medium of modeling materials as they form relief maps, models, and figures in clay; use the intimacy of the human voice in song, storytelling, and poetry reading; and use their bodies as the medium to re-create the rhythmic patterns of movement as they become aspects of their experience, like the bus wash or the factory speed-up.

Using the arts in this way is analogous to the ways young children use dramatic play to "play out" and "play with" the significant events, people, and places of their lives. Like dramatic play, the artistic expressions are the product of mind and body and offer a powerful outlet for the emotional aspect of experience. There is a deep connection to the self because it is through one's physical and emotional being that experience is expressed. As a result, creators come to know themselves, their peers, and the experience differently. The "wholeness" of the individual is honored as aspects of experience are relived and re-created in heightened form—but not quite relived or re-created because there is a purposeful transformation of events in the process.

One can view artistic expression of experience as utilitarian, a way to integrate and consolidate learning, which are both tremendously important; however, it is much more. The need to create, to create beauty, is integral to the human experience, a basic human need, which is as intense for adults as it is for children. Mr. Albok, the tailor, seemed to know this when he observed the children drawing and said, "It is very important what you are doing. Too many people stop drawing as they grow up."

Time Must Be Allocated for These Principles to Be Realized

We continue to educate children as though to feed the burgeoning industries of the late nineteenth and early twentieth centuries. We measure how much productivity we can squeeze out of learners within the shortest amount of time and call our findings "scientific." We act as though each six-, ten-, or fourteen-year-old can and should "master" certain information and acquire certain academic capabilities by a certain point in the academic year—the point by which they are tested. But people are not machines that can function along rigid, predictable schedules. The human brain is more complex. And individual human brains function differently. Every teacher knows that children learn at different rates. Therefore, whether we acknowledge it or not in the ways we think about and plan for our students, time is an essential factor in the learning process for each individual. The guiding principles that are the focus of this chapter cannot be put on a rigid time schedule. Mitchell recognized this when she said that "growth is slow and growth is individual."[4] Not one of these principles can be realized within forty-minute segments once or twice a week. Each must be *lived* within the rich fabric of classroom life, which means that we must continually ask ourselves not what is the shortest route to knowing but what is the richest. It takes time, unrushed time to attend to the full development of the student; to cultivate democratic living; to experience firsthand; to model a way of learning and teaching; to move beyond our comfortable worlds and expand our perspective; to learn with and from others; to explore a topic through different academic disciplines; and to express, synthesize, transform experience into art.

Each story throughout this book is an attempt to illustrate what can be done when teachers give time to a way of learning and teaching they believe important; to what they most want for their students, themselves, and society; to what they value as educators. Part 1 follows the evolution of three current studies (Brownsville, Brooklyn; the Brooklyn Bridge; and Long Island Native Americans). It penetrates each teacher's thought process as she moves beyond her own comfortable world of experience and tolerates the vulnerability of becoming a learner. Ultimately, as their own venturing outward—exploring, discovering, experimenting, and reflecting—is transformed into the fabric of classroom life, we see that all their efforts were worth it. In a sense they and their students wake up and realize that what happens in school has to do with them, their families, and the world around them. And we see what children and their teachers are capable of when they "wake up" and are inspired.

Part 2 reflects my own long trip into the work of Lucy Sprague Mitchell, Eleanor Hogan, and their students. I saw how Mitchell and Hogan's work was inspired by the early progressive drive to make the democratic process work for all Americans and by a belief that education was pivotal in achieving that end. I saw how the stark backdrop of the Depression created a sense of urgency for them and how their experiments in teacher education grew from that urgency.

Because they wanted their students to have an impact in the world as teachers and citizens, they ventured outward together into that world—as a way to explore, discover, provoke questions, forge connections with others, and ultimately foster caring and commitment to that world. When I interviewed Mitchell and Hogan's students—forty-five to sixty years after they ventured outward together—I found that their education experiences had a lifelong impact on how they taught, what they taught, where they taught, and on what they valued as teachers and citizens. The passion with which they described the details of their teacher education experience speaks to the enduring power of this form of learning and teaching.

Part 3 shows how even in modest ways—a trip to a boat basin and a four-week summer course—this form of learning and teaching can have a formative impact. Karen Weiss and I walked the streets of our neighborhood, overcame our apprehension about approaching strangers, and entered many places of business. Although I lived in the neighborhood and Karen worked in the neighborhood, it was as though we were seeing it for the first time. We had done this type of curriculum planning years before when we taught children and approached neighborhood exploration as one of the major tasks we had to complete. However, once we met the young Caribbean woman, smelled the rich aroma wafting from her kitchen, and heard the pride she felt in what she had achieved, Karen and I were no longer merely completing a task. Together we rediscovered the vibrancy, the validity of learning from the world itself.

We realized once again what we had been saying to our students for years: that there is a living, breathing world beyond the school building with a standing invitation to go out into that world and make it an essential part of our classrooms. There is so much to explore, to discover, to wonder about, and to enjoy. We realized that education, if it is worthy of the name, awakens possibilities for the self as it invites us into a larger world of experience, thought, and action; we realized that education is a life-changing force. Yes, Mr. Albok, as we grow up we should not forget that we can draw, that we can create. And, yes, we should all know how to sew a button.

APPENDIX:
ITINERARIES OF OLD AND NEW LONG TRIPS

TVA Trip Itinerary

April 7–16, 1950

Friday, April 7

8:00 AM	Leave Bank Street
1:00 PM	Arrive Lancaster, PA (140 mi.)
	Lunch at Village Restaurant
	Short visit to Farmers' Arcade Market (Queen and Chestnut Sts.)
3:00 PM	Leave Lancaster. PA
6:00 PM	Arrive Frederick, MD (100 mi.)
	Dinner at Eberts
7:15 PM	Leave Frederick, MD
8:15 PM	Arrive Harpers Ferry, WV (22 mi.)
	Night at Cliffside Cabins
	(US 340—2 miles south of Harpers Ferry)
	(262 mi.)

Saturday, April 8

8:00 AM	Breakfast
9:00 AM	Leave Clifton Cabins
1:00 PM	Arrive Staunton, VA (122 mi.)
	Lunch at Triangle Tea Room
2:30 PM	Leave Staunton, VA
8:00 PM	Arrive Wytheville, VA (174 mi.)
	Dinner and night at Spring Court Motel (Udells)
	(296 mi.)

Sunday, April 9

8:00 AM	Leave Wytheville, VA
11:00 AM	Arrive Kingsport, TN (95 mi.)
	Dinner at Kingsport Inn
1:00 PM	Leave Kingsport, TN
3:30 PM	Arrive Knoxville, TN (93 mi.)
4:00 PM	Leave Knoxville, TN
6:30 PM	Arrive Fontana, NC (68 mi.)
	Mr. O. A. Fetch, Government Service, Inc., in charge of living arrangements
	(256 mi.)

Monday, April 10

The day at Fontana is being arranged by Mr. William Shafer of the TVA. It will include a visit to Fontana Dam and discussions with TVA officials.

Tuesday, April 11

8:00 AM	Arrangements are being made for small groups to go by car to visit the Indian community, Robinsville, and to homes of people in the area.
12:00 Noon	Luncheon at Phillips Hotel, Robinsville
2:00 PM	Leave Robinsville, TN
4:30 PM	Arrive Ducktown, TN (106 mi.)
5:30 PM	Leave Ducktown, TN
6:30 PM	Arrive Chattanooga, TN (64 mi.)
	Dinner at S&W Cafeteria
	Night at Hotel Patten
	(170 mi.)

Wednesday, April 12

8:00 AM	Breakfast at S&W Cafeteria
9:00 AM	Discussion of employee health, work, safety program—representative of Health and Safety Department. Meeting in Old Post Office Building in Chattanooga.
10:30 AM	TVA and low-cost electric power—representative of Power Divisions. Power building auditorium.
12:00 Noon	Lunch at S&W Cafeteria
1:30 PM	Visit Chickamauga Dam and proceed to Monteagle, TN
6:00 PM	Arrive Highlander Folk School (55 mi.). Dinner and evening with Myles and Zilphia Horton and Highlander staff.
	(55 mi.)

Thursday, April 13   *Highlander Folk School*

AM	Plans for the day will be arranged by the Highlander Folk School Staff, and will include time in the nursery school, walks around the area, visits to nearby mining towns, etc.
3:30 PM	Leave Monteagle, TN
6:30 PM	Arrive Chattanooga, TN
	Dinner at S&W Cafeteria
	Night at Hotel Patten

Friday, April 14

7:00 AM	Breakfast at S&W Cafeteria
8:00 AM	Leave Chattanooga, TN
9:00 AM	Arrive Bakewell, TN (25 mi.)
	Visit Bakewell Community School, talks with parents and teachers at lunch, visit surrounding test demonstration farms, etc.
12:30 PM	Leave Bakewell for Knoxville, TN
3:00 PM	Arrive Knoxville, TN (95 mi.)
	(Take Jean and Doris to the airport?)
4:30 PM	Leave Knoxville via Hot Springs
7:30 PM	Arrive Asheville, NC (116 mi.)
	Dinner at S&W Cafeteria
	Night at George Vanderbilt Hotel
	(296 mi.)

Saturday, April 15

7:00 AM	Breakfast at S&W Cafeteria
8:00 AM	Leave Asheville, NC
12:30 PM	Arrive Winston-Salem, NC
	Lunch
2:00 PM	Leave Winston-Salem, NC (157 mi.)
7:30 PM	Arrive Orange, VA (234 mi.)
	Dinner and night at James Madison Hotel
	(391 mi.)

Sunday, April 16

8:00 AM	Breakfast
9:00 AM	Leave Orange, VA
2:30 PM	Dinner at Delaware Room (Rt. 40 just before Pennsylvania Ferry)
10:00 PM	New York City
	(320 mi.)

(Total miles traveled: approximately 2,000).
(Reprinted courtesy of Ellen Hausknecht who attended the 1950 trip)

New Orleans Itinerary

April 13–17, 2009

Monday, April 13

6:50 AM	Leave Newark on Continental flight #716
9:00 AM	Arrive in New Orleans, 9:02 AM
11:30 AM	Lunch at Cafe Reconcile (1631 Oretha Haley Blvd and Rafia-Castle) Speak with staff
1:00 PM	Meet with Juvenile Justice Project of Louisiana, Bridget Butler, Community Youth Organizer
2:30 PM	Leave for Bienville House Hotel, 320 Decatur Street, 504-529-2345
6:00 PM	Dinner at Iris Restaurant in hotel
7:30 PM	Meeting at Vieux Carre Room at the Bienville House with Mary Williams, Deep South Center for Environmental Justice and Darryl Wiley of the Sierra Club

Tuesday, April 14

7:00 AM	Breakfast at the hotel
8:00 AM	Depart for tour, Deep South Center for Environmental Justice, 3334 Annette St., with Darryl Wiley and Mary Williams
9:00 AM	Wetlands Tour, 5145 Fleming Park Road, Lafitte, Louisiana
12:00 Noon	Toxic Tour, Old Diamond Plantation. Meet with community activist Margie Richard
1:00 PM	Box lunch
1:45 PM	Toxic Tour, Agriculture Street Landfill, New Orleans
2:45 PM	Lower Ninth Ward Center for Sustainable Engagement, 5130 Charters and Lizardi
4:00 PM	Return to the Deep South Center for Environmental Justice
6:00 PM	Dinner at the Gumbo Shop, 630 St. Peter's Street, 504-525-1486
7:15 PM	Preservation Hall (performance at 8:15)

Wednesday, April 15

7:30 AM	Breakfast at the hotel
8:45 AM	Leave hotel for Dillard University
9:00 AM	Panel discussion—Dr. Amy Lessen, Dr. Lowell Agwaramgbo—Dillard faculty
11:00 AM	Leave Dillard for Vietnamese community (New Orleans East)
12:00 Noon	Lunch in Vietnamese restaurant Meet people from community, visit center, charter school, etc.

| 6:00 PM | Dinner at Mr. B's, 201 Royal Street, 504-523-2078 |
| 7:30 PM | Preview rough cut of film by JoLu Productions on rebuilding New Orleans, with Evan Casper-Futterman |

Thursday, April 16

7:30 AM	Breakfast at hotel
9:00 AM	Leave hotel for full day bayou trip to Houma Native American Community (hotel to Raceland, down bayou to Dulak)
12:00 Noon	Lunch on the road
5:00 PM	Leave for hotel
6:00 PM	Dinner at Liuzza's, 3636 Bienville Avenue, 504-482-9120

Friday, April 17

8:00 AM	Group breakfast and reflection wrap-up meeting in private room at Bienville House
11:00 AM	Leave hotel for airport
1:40 PM	Leave New Orleans on Continental flight #217 to Newark, New Jersey
6:00 PM	Arrival time, Newark Airport

NOTES

Introduction

1. Larry Cuban, *How Teachers Taught: Constancy and Change in American Class-rooms 1890–1990*, 2d ed. (New York: Teachers College, 1993).

2. Joyce Antler, *Lucy Sprague Mitchell: The Making of a Modern Woman* (New Haven: Yale University Press, 1987).

3. Lucy Sprague Mitchell, *Two Lives: The Story of Wesley Clair Mitchell and Myself* (New York: Simon and Schuster, 1953).

4. Ibid., 472.

Part One: Teachers "Experimenting with the World"

1. Harriet K. Cuffaro, *Experimenting with the World: John Dewey and the Early Childhood Classroom* (New York: Teachers College, 1995). Quoted from Cuffaro's book title, which Cuffaro adapted from a quote by John Dewey in *Democracy and Education* (New York: Macmillan, 1916), 140.

Chapter 1: "Slavery Was a Business!"

1 Material for this section on Laura Gerrity's curriculum is drawn from Laura E. Gerrity, "Reflections on a Third Grade Social Studies Curriculum" (MS thesis, Bank Street College of Education, 1997). The thesis documents the study.

2. Ibid., 13.

3. All the names of teacher and parent visitors have been changed.

4. Gerrity, "Reflections on a Third Grade Social Studies Curriculum," 19.

5. Ibid., 24.

6. Ibid., 30.

7. Ibid., 31.

8. Ibid.

9. Ibid., 59.

10. Ibid., 44.

Chapter 2: "Could We Build a Poem Like a Bridge?"

1. Material for this section is drawn from two sources: Trish Lent, interview by author, audiotape recording, New York, NY, 29 October 2009; and my own observations of the classroom, which are cited in the text.

2. This chapter is longer than its two companion chapters because it required more explanation to convey the detail of the teacher and the children's learning process.

3. Elizabeth Mann, *The Brooklyn Bridge* (New York: Mikaya Press, 1996).

4. David McCullough, *The Great Bridge: The Epic Story of the Building of the Brooklyn Bridge* (New York: Simon and Schuster, 1972).

5. Mann, *The Brooklyn Bridge*, 16.

6. Ibid., 17. See also McCullough, *The Great Bridge*, 195–214.

7. Trish and her husband cut out a simple drawing of a caisson and the stone tower that would sit on top of it, which they cut into individual rows of stone. They attached magnets to the backs of each of these parts, because in school it would be demonstrated on a magnetic board. On a sheet of paper they drew layers of bedrock, mud and rocks, and water, which they attached to the magnetic board. They positioned the caisson right on top of the layer of mud and rocks on this background drawing. As each row of stone was placed on the caisson, they moved the caisson farther down until it hit the bedrock. When she demonstrated the process with her class, Trish repeated what they had already read, that while the stone was driving it down, workers were digging out layers of mud and rocks, which were scooped out by large clamshell scoops through shafts leading from the caisson to above the water level. For a description of this process, see Mann, *The Brooklyn Bridge*, 16–23, and McCullough, *The Great Bridge*, 168–247.

8. Mann, *The Brooklyn Bridge*, 31–36. See also McCullough, *The Great Bridge*, 397–416, and the illustrations on 417–22.

9. Florence Krahn, interview by author, New York, NY, 28 July 1997. Krahn emphasized that Lucy Sprague Mitchell considered this an important idea, which Krahn said influenced her work throughout her own long teaching career. Krahn participated in the 1939 long trip to the Pittsburgh coal mines.

10. The bridge experiments were adapted from experiments described in Nicola Baxter, *Bridges* (New York: Franklin Watts, 2000); and from Carol A. Johmann and Elizabeth J. Rieth, *Bridges! Amazing Structures to Design, Build and Test* (Charlotte, VT: Williamson Publishing, 1999).

11. For many of the trips, Trish had prepared trip sheets to help the children focus. At a certain point in the trip, Trish would hand out pencils and the trip sheets, which were attached to clipboards. The challenge with these worksheets is to offer just enough structure to support focusing, while still being open-ended enough for children to make their own discoveries. Trish believed that asking children to do a lot of writing on a trip sheet tends to take the focus away from the experience, whereas sketching helps children to observe with focus, to "train their eyes to see." Writing and reflection can be done in the classroom.

12. Mann, *The Brooklyn Bridge*, 30.

13. Mitchell, *Two Lives*, 280. Mitchell describes how children's verbal recall of experience reveals how they perceive experience—through "their five senses and their muscles."

14. Elizabeth Mann, who was inspired by Mitchell's writings, would describe the forces that led to building the Brooklyn Bridge as an intersection of culture and geography in which the values, knowledge, and thrust of that culture are revealed in a dramatic way through a major construction project, such as the pyramids of Egypt, the Great Wall of China, Machu Picchu of Peru, and the Taj Mahal of India—which are all topics of other books by Mann.

15. Bobbi Katz, "Things to Do If You Are a Subway," in *Upside Down and Inside Out: Poems for All Your Pockets* (New York: Franklin Watts, 1973; Honesdale, PA: Wordsong/Boyds Mills Press, 1993).

Chapter 3: "I Didn't Even Know There Was a River"

1. Material for this section is mainly drawn from two sources: Karen Kriesberg, interview by author, audiotape recording by telephone, 22 October 2009; and Karen Mims [Kriesberg], "The Long Island Native Americans" (MS thesis, Bank Street College of Education, 1990). Information taken from the thesis is cited.

2. Lucy Sprague Mitchell, *Young Geographers: How They Explore the World and How They Map the World* (New York: Bank Street College, 1991); Mitchell, *Two Lives*, 406–7, 416–30.

3. Mitchell, *Young Geographers*, 19.

4. John Dewey, *Experience and Education* (New York: Collier, 1969), 39–46.

5. Mims [Kriesberg], "The Long Island Native Americans," 111–12.

6. Ibid., 112.

7. Ibid., 113.

Chapter 4: Three Teachers Honoring Children's Environment

1. Gerrity, "Reflections on a Third Grade Social Studies Curriculum," 1, quoting John Dewey, *Experience and Education*, 26.

2. Dewey, *Experience and Education*, 33–39.

3. When thinking about integrating crafts into a study of a culture, I am reminded of how Gandhi asked *Life* magazine reporter Margaret Bourke-White to learn to weave on an Indian loom before she interview him. At the time, to make Indians self-sufficient, Gandhi led a boycott of British cotton. He wanted the reporter to have insight into the time, patience, and skill required; essentially, Gandhi wanted the reporter to gain insight into the experience of Indians across the country who followed his lead and spun their own cotton. The craft became a route into the understanding of people at a specific time and place.

4. Elizabeth Helfman, interview by author, audiotape recording, at her home in Medford, NJ, 28 June 1997. Helfman participated in the 1939 long trip.

5. Dewey, *Democracy and Education*, 87.

6. Mims [Kriesberg], "The Long Island Native Americans," 5.

Part Two: "An Education in What America Is, What It Could Be"

1. Norma Simon, telephone interview by author, audiotape recording, 31 January 1997. Simon was a student during the 1949–50 academic year and participated in the 1948 long trip to TVA areas.

2. Henry Steele Commager, *The American Mind: An Interpretation of American Thought and Character Since the 1880s* (New Haven: Yale University Press, 1950), 342.

3. Miriam Ludwig's March 26, 1948, journal entry. With the questionnaire response, Miriam Ludwig included a copy of her journal entries that recorded the events of the 1948 long trip.

4. Simon, interview, 1948 long trip.

5. Vecelia McGee, interview by author, audiotape recording, at Bank Street College, NYC, 7 June 1995. McGee was a student during the 1947–48 academic year and participated in the 1948 long trip to TVA areas.

6. Allen Ohta, telephone interview by author, audiotape recording, 11 April 1997. Ohta was a student during the 1949–50 academic year and participated in the 1948 long trip to TVA areas.

7. Lucy Sprague Mitchell, "Social Studies for Future Teachers," *The Social Studies* 24, no. 5 (May 1935): 297.

Chapter 5: "We Went on Trips Morning, Noon, and Night"

1. Sally Kerlin, interview by author, audiotape recording, at Bank Street College, NY, NY, 25 October 1994. Kerlin was a student during the 1935–36 academic year and participated in the 1936 long trip to West Virginia mining areas.

2. Marguerite Hurrey Wolf, telephone interview by author, audiotape recording, 30 June 1997. Wolf was a student during the 1936–37 academic year and participated in the 1937 long trip to Pennsylvania mining areas.

3. Leonard Marcus, *Margaret Wise Brown: Awakened by the Moon* (Boston: Beacon Press, 1992), 60.

4. Ruth Bigel, interview by author, audiotape recording, at her home, NYC, 23 May 1995. She was a student during the 1937–38 academic year and participated in the 1938 long trip to Pennsylvania mining areas.

5. Ellen Hausknecht, interview by author, audiotape recording, Bank Street College, NY, NY, 14 November 1994. Hausknecht was a student during the 1949–50 academic year and participated in the 1950 long trip to TVA areas.

6. Lucy Sprague Mitchell, "The Environment, Work Processes, and Community Patterns" [annotated course outline], December 4, 1944, Bank Street Archives, Office of the President, Bank Street College. See also in the same collection Mitchell's 1934–35 outline for "Environment," and Mitchell's 1937–38 outline for "School Use of the Environment in the Teaching of Geography, History, and Social Studies." Although Mitchell's course ran with a variety of formats from the 1930s through the early '50s, when Mitchell retired, the purpose, trips, and assignments remained essentially similar.

7. These assignments are described in the annotated course outlines and also in Mitchell, "Social Studies for Future Teachers," 294–95. In Mitchell's "first geography book for young children," *North America: The Land They Live In for the Children Who Live There* (New York: Macmillan, 1931), roads, houses, and work patterns form the organizing structure of the book. Each topic is developed through a series of fictional stories, which she hoped would spark understandings of human-geographic relationships and also place the child in a position to view the topic from a number of vantage points; for example, in stories a "river

road" is presented from the perspective of a fish, a bear floating on an ice raft, and the river itself.

8. Mitchell, *Young Geographers*, 6.

9. Krahn, interview, 1939 long trip.

10. Ibid.

11. Ibid.

12. Herb Barnes, interview by author, audiotape recording, at Olga Smyth's home, Clinton Corners, NY, 30 September 1995. Barnes was a student during the 1949–50 academic year and participated in the 1950 long trip to TVA areas.

13. Isodora Sahl, "A New Side to People," paper for Curriculum in Early Childhood class, 21 November 1999.

14. Krahn, interview, 1939 long trip.

15. Ronnie Igel, "How the Neighborhood Gets Its Food," final paper for Curriculum in Early Childhood class, Bank Street College, 19 December 1995.

16. Willie Kraber interview by author, audiotape recording, at her home, Brooklyn, NY, 30 September 1994. Kraber was a student during the 1940–41 academic year and participated in the 1941 long trip to Pennsylvania mining areas.

17. See Mendel E. Branom and Fred K. Branom, *The Teaching of Geography Emphasizing the Project, or Active, Method* (Boston: Ginn, 1921), 1, 3–19, 51–55; Claude C. Crawford and Lois P. McDonald, *Modern Methods in Teaching Geography* (Boston: Houghton Mifflin, 1929), 9–13; and Ellwood P. Cubberly, introduction to Crawford and McDonald, v–vii.

18. Harold Rugg's comprehensive social studies series develops this idea. *Man and His Changing Society* (Boston: Ginn, 1929–1931), a series of six volumes, co-authored with Louise Krueger, was intended for third through sixth graders. (Rugg also authored and edited two series that follow, for junior high and high school students.) The totality is a massive effort to integrate the social sciences and humanities in service of understanding the major social issues of the time, with the ultimate aim of cultivating citizens who would act intelligently on behalf of a more humane and more democratic society. Mitchell's social studies series, *Our Growing World* (New York: Heath, 1944–45), also shows how the cumulative study of work patterns leads to an understanding of major social issues. The series includes three volumes intended for first through third graders. The first two volumes, *Farm and City* and *Animals, Plants, and Machines* (1944), were co-authored by the celebrated children's author Margaret Wise Brown, and the third volume, *Our Country* (1945), was co-authored with Dorothy Stall. Through fictional stories told from the vantage point of children and animals, the series progressed with increasingly complex chains of interdependence, focusing on patterns of human work across regional areas and across the nation. The people who did the work were central throughout.

19. Olga Smyth, interview by author, audiotape recording, at her home in Clinton Corners, NY, 24 June 1995. Smyth was a student during the 1934–35 academic year and participated in the 1935 long trip to West Virginia mining areas.

20. Mitchell, *Two Lives*, 239.

21. Lucy Sprague Mitchell, "School Use of the Environment in the Teaching of Geography, History, and Social Studies" [annotated course outline], 1937–38, Bank Street Archives, Office of the President, Bank Street College.

22. Jean Ewing, interview by author, audiotape recording, at her home,

Medford, NJ, 22 February 1997. Ewing was a student during the 1939–40 academic year and participated in the 1940 long trip to Pennsylvania mining areas.

23. Dewey, *Experience and Education,* 38.

24. Mitchell, "The Environment, Work Processes, and Community Patterns," describes what Mitchell believed students learned from the course.

25. Mitchell, *Young Geographers,* 9–12; Mitchell, *Two Lives,* 406–7, 416–30.

26. Mitchell, *Young Geographers,* 9.

27. Ibid., 9–15.

28. Mitchell, "Social Studies for Future Teachers," 291–93; Lucy Sprague Mitchell, "Social Studies and Geography," *Progressive Education* 11 (January 1934): 103.

29. "Cooperative School for Student Teachers Annual Report, 1934–1935," Bank Street Archives, Bank Street College.

30. Ruth Bigel, interview, 1938 long trip.

31. The major published sources on Lucy Sprague Mitchell's life are her autobiography and Joyce Antler's biography. Mitchell's *Two Lives* is both an autobiography and a biography of Wesley Mitchell, her husband, showing the intersection of their lives at home and in his work as an economist and hers as an educator. Antler's *Lucy Sprague Mitchell* meticulously documents Mitchell's life. For Antler, Mitchell's intense personal and professional struggle to unify the spheres of home and family with demanding, fully engaging work makes her a significant figure in women's history.

32. Jane Addams, *Twenty Years at Hull-House* (New York: Signet, 1981), 69.

33. Lucy Sprague Mitchell, unpublished autobiography, 60, Lucy Sprague Mitchell Papers, Rare Books and Manuscripts, Columbia University, quoted in Antler, *Lucy Sprague Mitchell,* 33.

34. Information on Eleanor Hogan's life is drawn primarily from Mary Ellen Gilder, Hogan's daughter, interview by author, audiotape recording, at her home, Scarsdale, NY, 8 September 1994; from the long trip interviews and questionnaires; and from the "Eleanor Hogan Memory Book," which was lent to me by Mary Ellen Gilder. It includes student and faculty letters—and a letter from Mitchell—sent to Hogan at the time of her retirement. Many of the photos featured in the book are from long trips, and many of the student letters allude to the content and personal significance of the trip.

35. Gilder, interview.

36. Ibid.

37. Elizabeth Helfman, who was a student during the 1938–39 academic year, sent me a copy of this and other diary entries that related to her experience at Bank Street.

38. Elizabeth Helfman, interview; Janet Greenwell, questionnaire response to author, 15 March 1997. Greenwell, like Helfman, was a student during the 1938–39 academic year and participated in the 1939 long trip.

39. "Tentative Plan as of November 28, 1934" [annotated course outline for "Environment II: Current Social Issues"], Bank Street Archives, Office of the President, Bank Street College; "Environment II: Current Social Issues" [course outline 1934–35], Lucy Sprague Mitchell Papers, Rare Books and Manuscripts, Columbia University. This particular outline lists the trips they would take. See also Mitchell, "Social Studies for Future Teachers," 296–97, and Antler, *Lucy Sprague Mitchell,* 311.

40. Gilder, interview.

41. Mitchell, "Social Studies for Future Teachers," 296–97.

42. Had the teacher been teaching older children, she could have pushed their thinking further by raising questions that might have stimulated additional actions. She might have asked about the government's role in addressing the needs of the people living in the train station and on the streets, such as: Did the government offer services? If so, what were they? How did people get them? Were they adequate? How could they find out about the services? What could *they* (the children) do? These questions might lead to contacting a local assemblyperson, congressperson, or public official or developing and circulating a petition. These might be ways in which *they, at their age,* could make a difference.

43. William Stott, *Documentary Expression and Thirties American* (London: Oxford University Press, 1973), 123–28.

44. A section of Elizabeth Wentworth Seaver [Helfman], "The Speedup," was published in the May 1940 issue of *Direction* (p. 8), a left-wing magazine of the arts. The magazine did not continue long into the forties.

45. Lucy Sprague Mitchell, *Our Children and Our Schools* (New York: Simon and Schuster, 1951), 167.

46. Mitchell, *Two Lives,* 276.

47. Antler, *Lucy Sprague Mitchell,* 311; Mitchell, "Social Studies for Future Teachers," 297.

48. Vera Lerner, questionnaire response to author, 13 February 1997. Lerner was a student during the 1936–37 academic year and participated in the 1937 long trip to Pennsylvania mining areas.

49. Bigel, interview, 1938 long trip.

50. Doris Hiller, questionnaire response to author, 12 March 1997. Hiller was a student during the 1940–41 academic year and participated in the 1941 long trip.

51. Lucy Sprague Mitchell, "A Cooperative School for Student Teachers," *Progressive Education* 8 (March 1931): 251. "Cooperative" meant a "joint creation," "joint thinking and planning," examining issues from many vantage points, in essence working together collaboratively.

52. Mitchell, *Two Lives,* 469–71.

53. Ibid., 470.

54. Mitchell, "A Cooperative School for Student Teachers," 252–53.

55. The map contours were painted with watered-down tempera paint, which was easily washed off the floor.

56. Mitchell, "A Cooperative School for Student Teachers," 252.

57. Ibid., 253–54.

Chapter 6: "A Way of Feeling into Another's Life"

1. Kraber, interview, 1941 long trip.

2. Robert Butler, "The Life Review: An Interpretation of Reminiscence in the Aged," *Psychiatry* 26, no. 1 (1968): 65–76, corroborating many earlier studies in his influential work on the meanings of reminiscence for elderly people, maintains that while short-term memory grows weaker, long-term memory becomes stronger in later years. For many of the participants, the act of constructing

connections between an event from forty-five to sixty years ago and their subsequent lives was satisfying in ways they had never anticipated. Perhaps the act
of remembrance enabled participants to identify over the course of their lives a
chain of meaning and thereby affirm the directions they had taken.

3. Barbara Allen and Lynwood Montell, *From Memory to History: Using Oral
Sources in Local Historical Research* (Nashville: American Association for State
and Local History, 1981), 89. The authors emphasize that people think, act, and
react based on what they believe to be true. In his examination of "form and
meaning in oral history," Alessandro Portelli, *The Death of Luigi Trastulli and
Other Stories* (New York: State University of New York, 1991), 2, discerns the
personal significance of the death of an Italian worker through the points of
variation in the oral accounts of his death. Portelli found that "errors, inven-
tions, and myths" are strengths; they "lead us through and beyond facts to . . .
meanings."

4. Lucy Sprague Mitchell, "How Big Is Your Group" (presentation at the
Twenty-First Annual Session of the National Association of Supervisors of
Student Teachers, Atlantic City, NJ, 23–24 February 1941), p. 53, Bank Street
Archives, Bank Street College of Education.

5. Ibid., 297.

6. The long trip was characterized in these ways by many of the trip
participants.

7. Lucy Sprague Mitchell, "Before the Trip and After," *69 Bank Street* 1, no. 8
(May 1935): 2.

8. Ibid.

9. Sarah Underhill Nafe, questionnaire response to author, 22 February
1997. Nafe was a student during the 1939–40 academic year and participated in
the 1940 long trip to Philadelphia mining areas.

10. Courtney Cazden, telephone interview by author, tape recording, 18
September 1997. Cazden participated in the 1948 long trip to TVA areas.

11. Wolf, interview, 1937 long trip.

12. Barnes, interview, 1950 long trip.

13. Sheila Sadler, interview by author, tape recording, at Bank Street College, 4 November 1994.

14. This is reflected in the course notes of Marjorie Janis, 1941 long trip;
Miriam Ludwig, 1948 long trip; and Verna Rudd Kenvin, 1951. The course
notes were attached to their questionnaire responses.

15. Wolf, interview, 1937 long trip.

16. Sadler, interview, 1950 and 1951 long trips.

17. Barnes, interview, 1950 long trip.

18. Sadler, interview, 1950 and 1951 long trips.

19. Joy Watson, questionnaire response to author, 14 January 1997. Watson
was a student during the 1949–50 academic year and participated in the 1950
long trip.

20. Norma Simon, interview, 1948 long trip.

21. Dewey, *Democracy and Education*, 4–6.

22. Krahn, interview, 1939 long trip.

23. Joie Willimetz, interview by author, audiotape recording, NY, NY, 26
November 1995. Willimetz was a student during the 1947–48 academic year
and participated in the 1948 long trip to TVA areas.

24. Hausknecht, interview, 1950 long trip.

25. Martha Stott Oxenfeldt, questionnaire response to author, 23 January 1997. Oxenfeldt was a student during the 1950–51 academic year and participated in the 1951 long trip to TVA areas.

26. Wilbur Rippy, interview by author, audiotape recording, at Bank Street College, 5 November 1994. Rippy was a student during the 1950–51 academic year and participated in the 1951 long trip.

27. Since the 1930s we have learned that dams can cause environmental problems. In the interviews, many students said that no one seemed to know about how a dam could harm the ecology. That came later.

28. Cazden, interview, 1948 long trip.

29. Barnes, interview, 1950 long trip.

30. Cazden, interview, 1948 long trip.

31. Rippy, interview, 1951 long trip.

32. John G. Mitchell, "When Mountains Move," *National Geographic*, March 2006, 104–23.

33. Among the books on the effects on people and the environment of mountaintop removal is the account by Erik Reece of the destruction of one mountain over the course of a year: *Lost Mountain: A Year in the Vanishing Wilderness, Radical Strip Mining and the Devastation of Appalachia* (New York: Penguin, 2006).

34. "For 10s and Up," dated May 1939, was lent to me by Krahn, along with all of her course papers.

35. In April–June 1995, Carnegie Mellon University sponsored a series of public presentations and tours of the "Murals of Industrial Pittsburgh," including those that inspired Willie Kraber. In the article "Croatian Encounters with Christ," *Our Sunday Visitor* [a church publication], 25 June 1995, 10, Pat Bartos characterized the murals as "a blistering indictment of the exploitation [in Europe and in the United States] of these people," with "images of gas-masked figures, enraged soldiers, dead coal miners and a greedy, self-satisfied industrialist." David Demarest of Carnegie Mellon described these murals as "astonishing for a church."

36. Kraber, interview, 1941 long trip.

37. Mitchell, "Before the Trip and After," 2.

38. Cazden, interview, 1948 long trip.

39. Judith Mara Gutman, telephone questionnaire response to author, 19 March 1997. Gutman was a student during the 1949–50 academic year and participated in the 1950 long trip to TVA areas.

40. Claudia Lewis, interview by author, audiotape recording, at Bank Street College, NY, NY, 20 January 1995. Lewis, who later became one of Bank Street's most distinguished faculty members, was in the late 1930s a teacher in Bank Street's demonstration nursery school when she answered the ad for a summer job to assist in establishing Highlander's first nursery school. The teacher-director she was to assist never arrived, so she became the teacher-director. She was granted a leave from her job at Bank Street and stayed on at Highlander for the next two and a half years, before returning. In her book *Children of the Cumberland* (New York: Columbia University Press, 1946), Lewis recounts her experience as the Highlander nursery school teacher.

41. Emil Willimetz, interview by author, audiotape recording, NY, NY, 26

November, 1995. Willimetz was a nonstudent participant of the 1948 long trip to TVA areas. He was the Highlander Folk School photographer who had contacted Claudia Lewis to get her recommendations for a teacher for the Highlander nursery school. Lewis, a teacher at the Bank Street nursery school, had, a few years before, established and been the teacher for Highlander's nursery school. Lewis suggested he go on the trip and perhaps he would find the teacher from among the students. In our interview he said, "I found the perfect teacher, Joie Creighton, and I liked her so much I married her." They lived the next seven years of their lives at Highlander. While on the trip he documented the experience photographically. Among his striking photographs is the one of Allen Ohta in front of the drinking fountain.

42. Myles Horton, with Judith Kohl and Herbert Kohl, *The Long Haul: An Autobiography* (New York: Teachers College Press, 1998), chap. 9 *passim*; Frank Adams, with Myles Horton, *Unearthing Seeds of Fire: The Idea of Highlander* (Winston-Salem, NC: John F. Blair, 1975), 121–24. In the late 1940s Highlander moved its primary focus from labor to civil rights. Highlander had protested the expulsion from the CIO of communist unions and communist officials. The CIO had come to consider Highlander itself as a communist school and stopped using it to train labor leaders.

43. Highlander had defied Jim Crow as early as 1934 and had worked from its beginnings to include within the union movement African Americans and women. See Adams, *Unearthing Seeds of Fire*, 91–92.

44. Simon, interview, 1948 long trip.

45. Adams, *Unearthing Seeds of Fire*, 76; Horton, *The Long Haul*, 77.

46. Simon, interview, 1948 long trip.

47. Miriam Ludwig, diary entry, March 31, 1948.

48. Rippy, interview, 1951 long trip.

49. Miriam Ludwig, diary entry, March 31, 1948.

Chapter 7: Participants in a World More Vast, Yet Less Remote

1. Dewey, *Experience and Education*, 38.

2. Ibid., 37–39.

3. Helen Quick, questionnaire response to author, 20 January 1997. Quick was a student during the 1934–35 academic year and participated in the 1935 long trip.

4. Rippy, interview, 1951 long trip.

5. Wolf, interview, 1937 long trip.

6. Simon, interview, 1948 long trip.

7. Ibid.

8. Wilson, interview, 1948 long trip.

9. Among Helfman's books are: *Land, People, and History* (New York: David McKay, 1962); *Our Fragile Earth* (New York: Lothrop, Lee, and Shepard, 1972); *Rivers and Watersheds in America's Future* (New York: David McKay, 1965); *This Hungry World* (New York: Lothrop, Lee, and Shepard, 1970); and *Water for the World* (New York: David McKay, 1960).

10. *On Being Sarah* (Park Ridge, IL: Albert Whitman, 1992).

11. Esther Smith, telephone questionnaire with author, 28 February 1997.

12. Greenwell, questionnaire, 1939 long trip.

13. Silverstein, questionnaire response to author, 28 January 1997. Silverstein was a student during the 1947–48 academic year and participated in the 1948 long trip.

14. Joie Willimetz, interview, 1948 long trip.

15. Smyth, interview, 1935 long trip.

16. Barnes, interview, 1950 long trip.

17. Interview. Among Cazden's many publications are: *Child Language and Education* (New York: Holt, Rinehart and Winston, 1972); *Classroom Discourse: The Language of Teaching and Learning*, 2d ed. (Portsmouth, NH: Heinemann, 2001); and *Functions of Language in the Classroom*, co-edited with Vera P. John and Dell Hymes (New York: Teachers College Press, 1972).

18. Rippy, interview, 1951 long trip.

19. Joie Willimetz, interview, 1948 long trip.

20. Smyth, interview, 1935 long trip.

21. Gabriella Backinoff, questionnaire response to author, 3 March 1997. Backinoff was a student during the 1937–38 academic year and participated in the 1938 long trip.

22. Mitchell, "Before the Trip and After," 2.

23. Krahn, interview, 1939 long trip.

24. Jean Todd Welch, interview by author, audiotape recording, NY, NY, 15 October 1997. Welch was a student during the 1937–38 academic year and participated in the 1938 long trip.

25. Wolf, interview, 1937 long trip.

26. Robert Lepowsky, questionnaire response to author, 28 January 1997. Lepowsky was a student during the 1935–36 academic year and participated in the 1936 long trip.

27. Smyth, interview, 1935 long trip.

28. Rippy, interview, 1951 long trip.

Chapter 8: A Modest Experiment

1. The visits with the older resident and the family were arranged through Leslie Day.

2. Regina Gallo, "Trip to 79th Street Boat Basin: Reflection," 4 November 1997.

3. Heather Hazan, [Reflections on trip], November 1997.

4. Rachel Rosner, "Boat Basin Trip Reflection," 4 November 1997.

5. Gallo, "Trip to 79th Street Boat Basin."

6. Alexis Fortgang, "Response to 79th Street Boat Basin Field Trip," 30 October 1997.

7. Hazan, [Reflections on trip].

8. Chris Posluszny, "In Process at 79th Street," stanzas IV and V, 1 November 1997.

Chapter 9: A Less Modest Experiment

1. Karen and I were aware of the potential of digging, processing, modeling, and firing clay through the work of Lois Lord. As a Bank Street social studies consultant to two schools in Tuskegee, Alabama, she guided the children

and their teachers throughout the process from digging to firing. In groups, the children and their teachers explored the local area, found large amounts of clay, and shoveled it into buckets, which they lugged back to school. At school they learned that by immersing it in water, the twigs and rocks were separated from the clay; how to strain it, dry it of excess moisture, work it with their hands, and make it pliable; when it is just right for modeling. Then they fashioned pots, people, and animals. Using bricks and sawdust, they created an outdoor kiln, carefully laid their work into the kiln on layers of sawdust, lit the sawdust, and covered the kiln. The sawdust gives a slow, safe fire. The moment was intense when they opened the cover of the kiln to see that the sawdust was gone and all of their carefully crafted work was hard and black and lying piled up on the bottom. They had had an experience they would remember and build on throughout their lives. As a teacher of five- and six-year-olds, Karen Weiss worked with her class to create a homemade sawdust kiln out of a metal garbage can in which they fired clay objects they had created. She describes the process in her master's thesis that she co-authored with her student teacher: E. Bruce Barrett and Karen Weiss, "Children Firing Clay" (MS thesis, Bank Street College of Education, 1977).

2. Michelle Shemin, "Trash, Recycling, and Pollution: A Social Studies Curriculum for First and Second Graders" (MS thesis, Bank Street College of Education, 2009), shows how through an in-depth study of recycling children can make a tangible difference.

3. Roberta Altman, personal communication, July 15, 2003.

4. Tracy Wiessbrod, e-mail message to author, October 6, 2010.

5. Elizabeth Cholas, e-mail message to author, October 15, 2010.

6. Rebecca Elvin, e-mail message to author, October 8, 2010.

7. Olivia Ramsey, e-mail message to author, October 20, 2010.

8. Ron Azoulay, e-mail message to author, October 11, 2010.

9. Annie Dycus, e-mail message to author, October 11, 2010.

10. Laura Gutmann, e-mail message to author, October 10, 2010.

11. Barbara Shindler, e-mail message to author, October 24, 2010.

12. Ellen Cohn Maddrey, e-mail to author, October 31, 2010.

Conclusion: "This Going Off Together, There's Something to It"

1. Mitchell, "Social Studies for Future Teachers," 297.

2. Dycus, e-mail message to author.

3. Descriptions of Michelle Shemin's curriculum are drawn from interview by author, audiotape, 20 November 2009; and from Shemin, "Trash, Recycling, and Pollution."

4. Mitchell, "Before the Trip and After," 2.

SOURCES CONSULTED

Manuscript Collections

Bank Street College of Education, Archives, New York, NY
   Records of Bank Street College
   Lucy Sprague Mitchell Papers
   Edith Gordon Interviews
   Ellen Hausknecht Interviews
   Photograph Archive

City and Country School, Archives, New York, NY
   Bureau of Educational Experiments Papers
   Curriculum Studies
   Associated Experimental Schools Papers

Columbia University, Rare Book and Manuscript Collection, Butler Library, New York, NY
   Lucy Sprague Mitchell Papers

Published Sources

Adams, Frank, with Myles Horton. *Unearthing Seeds of Fire: The Idea of High-lander.* Winston-Salem, NC: John F. Blair, 1975.

Allen, Barbara, and Lynwood Montell. *From Memory to History: Using Oral Sources in Local Historical Research.* Nashville: American Association for State and Local History, 1981.

Allen, Frederick Lewis. *The Big Change: America Transforms Itself, 1900–1950.* New York: Harper, 1952.

Antler, Joyce. *Lucy Sprague Mitchell: The Making of a Modern Woman.* New Haven: Yale University Press, 1987.

Bailey, Jane. "An Exception to the Rule: Bank Street College of Education as an Independent Professional School (1916–1990)." Ed.D. diss., College of William and Mary, 1991.

Bartos, Pat. "Croatian Encounters with Christ." *Our Sunday Visitor* (25 June 1995): 10–11.

Bauman, John F., and Thomas H. Coode. *In the Eye of the Great Depression: New Deal Reporters and the Agony of the American People.* DeKalb: Northern Illinois University, 1988.

Baxter, Nicola. *Bridges.* New York: Franklin Watts, 2000.

Ben-Peretz, Miriam. *Learning from Experience: Memory and the Teacher's Account of Teaching.* Albany: State University of New York Press, 1995.

Bowers, C. A. *The Progressive Educator and the Depression: The Radical Years.* New York: Random House, 1969.

Branom, Mendel E., and Fred K. Branom. *The Teaching of Geography Emphasizing the Project, or Active, Method.* Boston: Ginn, 1921.

Butler, Robert N. "The Life Review: An Interpretation of Reminiscence in the Aged." *Psychiatry* 26, no. 1 (1968): 65–76.

Cenedella, Joan. "The Bureau of Educational Experiments: A Study in Progressive Education." Ed. D. diss., Teachers College Columbia, 1996.

Clapp, Elsie R. *Community Schools in Action.* New York: Viking, 1939.

Coles, Robert. *Doing Documentary Work.* New York: Oxford University Press, 1997.

Commager, Henry Steele. *The American Mind: An Interpretation of American Thought and Character Since the 1880s.* New Haven: Yale University Press, 1950.

Conklin, Paul K. *The New Deal.* 3d ed. Arlington Heights, IL: Harlan Davidson, 1992.

Cook, Blanche Wiesen. *Eleanor Roosevelt: The Defining Years, 1933–1938.* Vol. 2. New York: Penguin, 1999.

Cook, Lloyd Allen. "Intergroup Education." *Review of Educational Research* 17, no. 4 (1947): 266–78.

Cotkin, George. *Reluctant Modernism: American Thought and Culture, 1880–1900.* New York: Twayne, 1992.

Counts, George S. "Break the Teacher Training Lockstep." *The Social Frontier* 1 (June 1935): 6–7.

Crawford, Claude C., and Lois P. McDonald. *Modern Methods in Teaching Geography.* Boston: Houghton Mifflin, 1929.

Cremin, Lawrence A. *American Education: The Metropolitan Experience, 1876–1980.* New York: Harper and Row, 1988.

_____. *The Transformation of the School: Progressivism in American Education, 1876–1957.* New York: Vintage Books, 1964.

Crunden, Robert M. *Ministers of Reform: The Progressive Achievement in American Civilization, 1889–1920.* New York: Basic Books, 1982.

Cuban, Larry. *How Teachers Taught: Constancy and Change in American Classrooms 1890–1990.* 2d ed. New York: Teachers College Press, 1993.

Cuffaro, Harriet K. *Experimenting with the World: John Dewey and the Early Childhood Classroom.* New York: Teachers College, 1995.

Degler, Carl N. *Out of Our Past: The Forces that Shaped Modern America.* 3d ed. New York: Harper Colophon, 1984.

Dewey, John. *Democracy and Education: An Introduction to the Philosophy of Education.* New York: Macmillan, 1916; Free Press, 1966.

_____. "Education and our Present Social Problems" (1933). *John Dewey, the Later Works, 1925–1953*, ed. JoAnn Boydston, vol. 9. Carbondale: Southern Illinois University Press, 127–35.

_____. "Education and the Social Order" (1934). *John Dewey, the Later Works,*

1925–1953, ed. JoAnn Boydston, vol. 9. Carbondale: Southern Illinois University Press, 175–85.

_____. *Experience and Education*. New York: Macmillan, 1938; New York: Collier Books, 1972.

_____. *The School and Society*. Chicago: University of Chicago, 1900. Centennial ed. with *The Child and the Curriculum* and a new introduction. Chicago: University of Chicago Press, 1990.

Dewey, John, and Evelyn Dewey. *Schools of Tomorrow*. New York: Dutton, 1915.

Evenden, Edward S. *National Survey of the Education of Teachers*. US Office of Education, bulletin no. 10, vol. 6. Washington, DC: Government Printing Office, 1933.

Gerrity, Laura E. "Reflections on a Third Grade Social Studies Curriculum." MS thesis, Bank Street College of Education, 1997.

Ginsburg, Kenneth R., and the Committee on Communications and the Committee on Psychosocial Aspects of Child and Family Health, American Academy of Pediatrics. "The Importance of Play in Promoting Healthy Child Development and Maintaining Strong Parent-Child Bonds." *Pediatrics* 119, no. 1 (January 2007): 182–91.

Goodlad, John I. *A Place Called School: Prospects for the Future*. New York: McGraw-Hill, 1984.

Gordon, Edith. "Educating the Whole Child: Progressive Education and Bank Street College, 1916–1966." Ph.D. diss., State University of New York at Stony Brook, 1988.

Grinberg, Jaime G.A. "'Teaching Like That': Learning from the Education of Progressive Teachers at Bank Street during the 1930s." Ph.D. diss., Michigan State University, 1997.

Hausknecht, Ellen. "The Long Trip of 1950: A Reminiscence." *Pathways* (Spring 1991): 5.

Hertzberg, Hazel W. *Social Studies Reform, 1880–1980*. Boulder, CO: Social Studies Education Consortium, 1981.

Hofstadter, Richard. *The Age of Reform: From Bryan to F.D.R.* New York: Vintage, 1960.

_____. *Anti-Intellectualism in American Life*. New York: Vintage, 1962.

Holt, John. *How Children Fail*. New York: Pitman, 1964.

_____. *How Children Learn*. New York: Pitman, 1967.

Horton, Myles, with Judith Kohl and Herbert Kohl. *The Long Haul: An Autobiography*. New York: Teachers College Press, 1998.

Horton, Myles, and Claudia Lewis. "Highlander." In *Roots of Open Education: Reminiscences and Reflections*, ed. Ruth Dropkin and Arthur Tobier, 73–90. (Roots of Open Education Conference, City College of New York, 12 April 1975.) New York: City College Workshop Center for Open Education, 1976.

Johmann, Carol A., and Elizabeth J. Rieth. *Bridges! Amazing Structures to Design, Build and Test*. Charlotte, VT: Williamson Publishing, 1999.

Katz, Bobbi. *Once Around the Sun*. New York: Harcourt Books, 2006.

_____. *A Rumpus of Rhymes: A Book of Noisy Poems*. New York: Dutton, 2001.

_____. *Trailblazers: Poems of Exploration*. New York: Greenwillow/Harper Collins, 2007.

_____. *Upside Down and Inside Out: Poems for All Your Pockets*. New York: Franklin Watts, 1973; Honesdale, PA: Wordsong/Boyds Mills Press, 1993.

Kliebard, Herbert M. *The Struggle for the American Curriculum: 1893–1958*. New York: Routledge, 1987.

Knowles, J. Gary. "Models for Teacher's Biographies." In *Studying Teacher's Lives*, ed. Ivor F. Goodson, 99–152. New York: Teachers College Press, 1992.

[Kriesberg] Mims, Karen. "The Long Island Native Americans." MS thesis, Bank Street College of Education, 1990.

Lagemann, Ellen Condliffe. "The Plural Worlds of Educational Research." *History of Education Quarterly* 29, no. 2 (Summer 1989): 183–214.

Lash, Joseph P. *Eleanor and Franklin.* New York: W. W. Norton, 1971.

Lewis, Claudia. *Children of the Cumberland.* New York: Columbia University Press, 1946.

Lucke, Elmina R. "Travel Toward Economic Realities." *Progressive Education* 15 (March 1938): 617–28.

Lynd, Helen Merrell. *Field Work in College Education.* New York: Columbia University Press, Sarah Lawrence College Publications, 1945.

Mann, Elizabeth. *The Brooklyn Bridge.* New York: Mikaya Press, 1996.

Marcus, Leonard. *Margaret Wise Brown: Awakened by the Moon.* Boston: Beacon Press, 1992.

McCullough, David. *The Great Bridge: The Epic Story of the Building of the Brooklyn Bridge.* New York: Simon and Schuster, 1972.

Miller, Edward, and Joan Almon. *Crisis in the Kindergarten: Why Children Need to Play in School.* College Park, MD: Alliance for Childhood, 2009.

Mitchell, Lucy Sprague. *Animals, Plants, and Machines* (with Margaret Wise Brown). Boston: D.C. Heath, 1944.

_____. "Before the Trip and After." *69 Bank Street* 1, no. 8 (May 1935): 1–2.

_____. "A Cooperative School for Student Teachers." *Progressive Education* 8 (March 1931): 251–55.

_____. *Farm and City* (with Margaret Wise Brown). Boston: D.C. Heath, 1944.

_____. *Here and Now Story Book.* New York: Dutton, 1921; rev. ed., 1948.

_____. Interview by Irene Prescott. In "Lucy Sprague Mitchell: Pioneering in Education." Regional Cultural History Project. University of California, Berkeley, 1962.

_____. "John Dewey." *New Republic* (17 October 1949): 30.

_____. "Making Real Teachers." *Educational Outlook* 20, no. 2 (January 1946): 52–63.

_____. *My Country 'tis of Thee: The Use and Abuse of Natural Resources* (with Eleanor Bowman [Hogan] and Mary Phelps). New York: Macmillan, 1940.

_____. "Natural Regions of the United States: Their Work Patterns and Their Psychologies." *Progressive Education* 15 (March 1938): 187–209.

_____. *North America: The Land They Live In for the Children Who Live There.* New York: Macmillan, 1931.

_____. *Our Children and Our Schools.* New York: Simon and Schuster, 1951.

_____. *Our Country* (with Dorothy Stall). New York: D.C. Heath, 1945.

_____. *The People of the U.S.A.: Their Place in the School Curriculum.* New York: Carey Press, 1942.

_____. *Skyscraper* (with Elsa H. Naumburg and Clara Lambert). New York: John Day, 1933.

_____. "Social Studies and Geography." *Progressive Education* 11 (January 1934): 97–105.

_____. "Social Studies for Future Teachers." *The Social Studies* 24, no. 5 (May 1935): 289–98.

_____. *Two Lives: The Story of Wesley Clair Mitchell and Myself.* New York: Simon and Schuster, 1953.

_____. *Young Geographers: How They Explore the World and How They Map the World.* New York: John Day, 1934; Bank Street College of Education, 1991.

Moore, Clyde B., and Lillian A. Wilcox. *The Teaching of Geography.* New York: American Book, 1932.

Muessig, Raymond H. "An Analysis of Developments in Geography Education." *The Elementary School Journal* 87, no. 5 (1987): 519–30.

Myrdal, Gunnar. *An American Dilemma: The Negro Problem and Modern Democracy.* Twentieth Anniversary ed. New York: Harper and Row, 1962.

Pells, Richard H. *Radical Visions and American Dreams: Culture and Social Thought in the Depression Years.* Middletown, CT: Wesleyan University Press, 1973.

Portelli, Allessandro. *The Death of Luigi Trastulli and Other Stories: Form and Meaning in Oral History.* New York: State University of New York, 1991.

Pratt, Caroline. *I Learn from Children.* New York: Simon and Schuster, 1948.

Ravitch, Diane. *The Death and Life of the Great American School System: How Testing and Choice Are Undermining Education.* New York: Basic Books, 2010.

_____. *The Troubled Crusade: American Education, 1945–1980.* New York: Basic Books, 1983.

Reece, Erik. *Lost Mountain: A Year in the Vanishing Wilderness; Radical Strip Mining and the Devastation of Appalachia.* New York: Penguin, 2006.

Rugg, Harold, and Louise Krueger. *Man and His Changing Society.* 6 vols. Boston: Ginn, 1929–31.

Rury, John L. "Who Became Teachers? The Social Characteristics of American Teachers." In *American Teachers: History of a Profession at Work*, ed. Donald Warren, 9–48. New York: Macmillan, 1989.

Schlesinger, Arthur M., Jr. *The Age of Roosevelt: The Coming of the New Deal.* Boston: Houghton Mifflin, 1959.

Solomon, Barbara M. *In the Company of Educated Women.* New Haven: Yale University Press, 1985.

Stott, William. *Documentary Expression and Thirties America.* London: Oxford University Press, 1973.

Stull, DeForest. *Tentative Course of Study in Geography.* New York: Teachers College Press, 1927.

Vann Woodward, C. *The Strange Career of Jim Crow.* 2d ed. London: Oxford University Press, 1966.

Vickery, William E., and Stewart G. Cole. *Intercultural Education in American Schools*, vol. 1 of *The Problems of Race and Culture in American Education.* New York: Harper and Brothers, 1943.

Wallace, James M. *Liberal Journalism and American Education, 1914–1941.* New Brunswick: Rutgers University Press, 1991.

Walther, Elisabeth. "The Trip." *69 Bank Street* 1, no. 8 (May 1935): 3–10.

Wenner, Melinda. "The Serious Need for Play." *Scientific American Mind* (February 2009), 23–30.

Westbrook, Robert B. *John Dewey and American Democracy.* Ithaca: Cornell University Press, 1991.

Zacari, Elizabeth D. "Field Trip Experiences in the Intermediate Grades." *Journal of Geography* 33, no. 2 (February 1934): 49–60.

INDEX

Note: Page numbers in italics represent photographs and illustrations in the text.